HECKER STUDIES

HECKER STUDIES

Essays on the Thought of
Isaac Hecker

edited by
JOHN FARINA

 PAULIST PRESS • *New York/Ramsey*

Library of Congress
Catalog Card Number: 83-60654

ISBN: 0-8091-2555-2

Published by Paulist Press
545 Island Road, Ramsey, N.J. 07446

Printed and bound in the
United States of America

Contents

Acknowledgements

I wish to acknowledge my indebtedness to
Kevin A. Lynch, C.S.P.
for his suggestion for
the creation of this book.
To each of the contributors
I owe my thanks for
their first-rate scholarship and
their friendly cooperation.
Lastly, I wish to thank
my wife, Paula,
for her expert typing, copyediting,
and compilation of the index.

Introduction

by John Farina

THE FASCINATING FATHER HECKER

The nineteenth century was an age of optimism and comprehensiveness. Having been made confident in their abilities to order and utilize creation in the Age of Reason, the people of the last century were empowered in the Age of Steam and given license to dream idyllic dreams in the Age of Romance. They endeavored to build bigger buildings, faster ships, more powerful trains, more efficient manufactories, and a better society according to their sundry notions of the good life. The 1800s were a time of social reform movements that strove for amelioration through crusades for better working conditions, public education, prison reform, women's rights, temperance, and the abolition of slavery.

The nineteenth century was also a time of religious awakening in which men and women felt enabled not only to shape their external environments but also to mold their inner lives. It was an era in which people became convinced of the powers of their own nature to resist evil and participate with God in a more perfect life. Whether it was William Ellery Channing's eloquent defense of the "essential sameness" of God and man, Ralph Waldo Emerson's call to become newborn bards of the spirit, Nathaniel William Taylor's assertion of "a power to the contrary" in human nature to resist sin, the Methodists' call to go on to perfection, or Charles G. Finney's new techniques of revivalism that assumed that individuals at will could repent and receive the blessings of regeneration, the optimism of the day was evident.

This new-found confidence in human ability to shape the inner and outer environments bred an enthusiasm for compre-

1

hensiveness and efforts to encompass diversity in single harmonious systems. Hence Darwin sought to explain a topic as huge as the origin of the species in terms of his grand scheme of evolution. Millennialist William Miller proposed a system of interpretation that summed up all of biblical history and pinpointed the Second Coming. Political theorist Karl Marx devised a doctrine of socio-economics that claimed to encompass the sweep of history and all of modern humanity. And in philosophy, Hegel offered the grandiose picture of Universal Spirit moving all of history toward a synthesis.

Synthesis—what word better sums up the focus of this age? This desire for synthesis caused men and women to look for new interrelations among elements that in the past had been viewed as distinct. Thus they sought for new links between humanity and nature, God and man, science and faith, mind and body, the individual and society, and religion and politics. America, the new world created by a synthesis of the old world's peoples and cultures and founded on a faith in human power to govern and create a better society, was a land in which the nineteenth-century's optimism and desire for comprehensiveness found full expression. Nowhere was this American genius for optimism and comprehensiveness better displayed than in its men and women. One such man was Isaac Thomas Hecker.

Raised in a deeply religious Methodist environment, weaned on the practical realities of the economic and political issues that he encountered as part of his family's baking business, exposed as a young man to Orville Dewey's progressive Unitarianism and Parley P. Pratt's Mormonism, Hecker was in touch with basic themes in American social, political, and religious life in the 1830s. In the 1840s he opted to pursue the way of spiritual renewal and religion as the means to personal and corporate betterment. He became a Catholic in 1844 and carried his Methodist sensibilities and Romantic style into the church. As a Redemptorist missionary during the 1850s he fashioned a scheme for missions to non-Catholic Americans. With three other American Redemptorists, themselves converts, he founded the Missionary Society of St. Paul the Apostle in 1858. During the 1860s he was a leading figure in the American Catholic church, distinguishing himself as a missionary to his fellow Catholic and

Protestant countrymen, a public lecturer, an editor of a major journal, a pastor of a growing New York parish, and superior of the Paulist Fathers. In the 1870s he became an international figure, attending the Vatican Council and later touring Europe and the Middle East and formulating a plan for world-wide spiritual and societal renewal—a scheme that in its optimism and grandeur rivaled the visions of the century's greatest system-builders.

His theology reflected the influence of Wesley, Jacksonian Democracy, Orestes Brownson, German Romantics like Schilling and Richter, the Tübingen School of J.A. Moehler, the French eclectic philosopher Victor Cousin, and the Angelic Doctor, St. Thomas. Always he was motivated by a deep mystical experience of God, formed at his mother's side in the context of the heart strangely warmed, nurtured by the contemplative vision of Bronson Alcott and his many Transcendentalist friends, given definite shape by his study of the great Catholic teachers: John of the Cross, Teresa of Avila, and Catherine of Genoa. His spirituality was infused with an Ignatian sensibility to the whole of creation as the instrument for God's greater glory through the writings of Pierre Lallement and J.P. de Caussade. It was charged with an evangelical zeal, reminiscent of Methodists Nathan Bangs and Timothy Merritt, or Alphonsus Liguori, or his great patron, St. Paul, and it was devoted to the Holy Spirit's living in the soul, sanctifying the believer in a life of practical holiness, working in society to bring it to its highest destiny and in the Church to inspire, preserve, and insure her of ultimate triumph.

These and other influences Hecker held together in his life in a way that makes him a representative man of the nineteenth century—the Age of Synthesis. His life bridged forces that others saw as totally distinct: American Protestantism and Catholicism, liberal democracy and the Church, contemplation and action, and personal holiness and social reform. And he did it all with an openness to experimentation and innovation and a concern for the practical that were typically American.

He, then, is a fascinating figure who left his mark on a broad range of nineteenth-century life, and, not surprisingly, his ideas interest many today. He is looked to as a precursor of Vatican

II's *aggiornamento,* a forerunner of twentieth-century Catholic social action, an intriguing case study in the sociology of religious conversion, or the inspiration for an American spirituality to cite only a few of the uses to which his memory has been put.

Recently a new excitement over Hecker's ideas has emerged. Prior to 1981 only four scholarly book-length treatments of the Paulist founder had been done. Only one, Walter Elliott's *Life of Father Hecker,* dealt with Hecker's whole life. This relative ignorance of one who was by any standards one of the more important Catholics of the last century can be explained partially by the general neglect of American Catholic history that characterized the first third of this century. Indeed, the first book-length treatment of Hecker since 1900 was not done until 1939. Another reason for this neglect may have been the relative inaccessibility of Hecker sources that were until the seventies virtually restricted to Paulists. In addition, there are two factors that have played a role in creating an atmosphere that tended to discourage Hecker studies.

First and foremost were the effects of Leo XIII's encyclical *Testem Benevolentiae* that took as its subject ideas directly associated with Hecker. The freeze that the papal censure had on American theology as a whole is well known. That same freezing effect doubtless extended to the study of Hecker's life and thought. In this regard it is interesting to note that the book-length studies of Hecker that were done prior to 1981 focused on his life story and avoided any extended discussions of his religious ideas and reflected a hypersensitivity to the issues of the Americanist controversy.

The second reason is less well known and had less of an effect, though it was significant. Hecker suffered a long illness from late 1871 until his death in 1888. The malady, which exhibited all the symptoms of what today would be called chronic leukemia, sapped his strength, brought on an emotional crisis, and made a full return to his work impossible. The rumor, first intimated in the 1870s by the gadfly Julia Beers, was that his disease was more mental than physical. What that grew into was a disturbing uncertainty about the Paulist founder's emotional stability, never flatly stated but often intimated with all the damaging innuendo and vagueness characteristic of half-truths.

The historical record belies this insinuation. Despite the debilitating physical effects of the disease and the acute mental anguish it brought on, some of Hecker's most cogent writing and most optimistic thinking were done during his illness. The final seventeen years of his life were fruitful and purposeful—hardly the legacy of an unstable soul.

The new theological climate created by Vatican II lifted the chief barrier to Hecker studies, and when in the late 1970s the Hecker Papers, then under the care of Lawrence McDonnell, C.S.P., became more generally accessible, Hecker studies were off and running. Between 1977 and 1982, no fewer than six Ph.D. dissertations on Hecker were completed. Immediately there emerged an eagerness to regard his religious thought as serious theology as reflected by Joseph F. Gower's analysis of his apologetics and William L. Portier's study of his doctrine of providence.[1] To this were added two studies related to the other area implicated in *Testem Benevolentiae*—Hecker's ascetical theology. I studied his spirituality in the context of the American religious environment out of which it emerged and Martin Kirk studied his spirituality with an emphasis on his theories of spiritual formation. From a sociological perspective Susan Perschbacher studied the phenomena of religious conversion as seen in his life. Edward J. Langlois delineated the political theory of Hecker, addressing his analysis of the interface of religion and United States politics—certainly not a subject for a dissertation fifty years ago!

In 1981 the first book-length study of Hecker since the 1950s appeared with the publication of my *An American Experience of God: The Spirituality of Isaac Hecker*. It joined a reprint edition of Hecker's first book *Aspirations of Nature* and publication of the Hecker-Brownson correspondence edited by Joseph Gower and Richard M. Leliaret.

This present book is designed to make the benefits of this recent surge in Hecker studies available to a wider audience. It contains five essays: two written by historians, one by a political scientist, one by a theologian and one by a psychologist. Three are based on doctoral dissertations; two are the by-products of current writing projects on Hecker.

The first essay, "Isaac Hecker and *Testem Benevolentiae:* A

Study in Theological Pluralism," by William L. Portier deals squarely with a question that many readers will be asking: "Is the Americanism *Testem Benevolentiae* censures to be found in Hecker's own affirmation of American culture?" In an intellectually rigorous fashion, Portier deals with this question, reviewing the adequacy of the phantom heresy argument and the contrary claims of Margaret Reher. His answer is based on an analysis of Hecker's doctrine of providence, a doctrine which was, Portier claims, never directly addressed by the famous encyclical. His arguments will do much to further our understanding of Hecker's theology and the turn-of-the-century crisis.

Edward J. Langlois has contributed the second essay, entitled "Isaac Hecker's Political Thought." In it he carefully argues that the Paulist founder was the main source of "the apologetical bridge" between Catholicism and American nationalism. It was this bridge that enabled American Catholics to enter directly into the political life of the nation and assert their rightful place in the liberal democratic processes. The development of Hecker's political thought is traced, and the influences of Jacksonian democracy and Thomistic natural law theology on his theories are shown. The thesis is provocative and its implications for nineteenth-century American political history are manifest.

The third essay, "An Evangelical Imperative: Isaac Hecker, Catholicism, and Modern Society," is by social historian David J. O'Brien. In it he eloquently argues that Hecker cannot be understood by means of the traditional analyses based on the liberal-conservative, modernist-fundamentalist paradigms. Hecker probed the depths of both traditional Catholicism and modern American society and saw in them a compatibility that most of his contemporaries could not understand. He attempted an integration of American evangelical style and the substance of Roman Catholicism. He remains, O'Brien contends, "a witness to the most challenging possibilities of American Catholicism." The essay gives a convincing portrait of Hecker's views on the subject for which he is famous.

In responding to some of the recent literature on Hecker, certain critics have expressed the desire for an analysis of his personality from the standpoint of modern depth psychology.[2] Robert W. Baer has responded to this request in the third essay of this collection, "Individuation and the Collective: A Jungian Analysis of Isaac Hecker." In it, Father Baer probes the life of the Yankee Paul during the early 1840s at the time of the writing of his early diary, during his ensuing conversion to Catholicism, and during his final seventeen years. The revealing and often perplexing writings of ITH's early diary and later notes on his "interior states" are intriguingly analyzed by Father Baer with an eye toward the historical record.

Finally, I have contributed an essay entitled "Isaac Hecker's Vision of the Paulists: Hopes and Realities," in which I analyze Hecker's conception of the religious community he founded at three crucial junctures in his life: during his Redemptorist days in the 1850s; in 1858 at the issuance of the Programme of Rule; and in the 1870s and early 1880s. I argue that the Paulists were an amalgam of Hecker's hopes and the realities of nineteenth-century American Catholic life with which he had to compromise. It is the first comprehensive treatment of this topic and should be of particular interest on this the 125th anniversary of the founding of the Missionary Society of St. Paul the Apostle.

To these essays I have added an annotated bibliography and a dateline for Hecker's life that should aid in making this book a useful study guide in the thought of the fascinating Father Hecker—a man whose ideas have a relevance for our day that can now be heard and openly evaluated.

NOTES

1. Citations for all works discussed in the introduction may be found in the bibliography.

2. See for example, Richard M. Linth review of *An American Experience of God* in *The Journal of American History* (Dec. 1982): 697.

Highlights of the Life of Isaac Hecker

1819   December 18. Born in New York City.

1825   Caroline Hecker listed as an active member of Forsyth Street Church.

1832   ITH works for *The Christian Advocate and Journal and Zion's Herald.*

1833   The Hecker brothers begin their baking business.

1837   ITH becomes involved with Equal Rights Party.

1839   Attends Orville Dewey's Church of the Messiah.

c.1839   Meets Mormon evangelist Parley P. Pratt.

1841   July. Meets Orestes A. Brownson.

1842   December. Visits Brownson's home in Chelsea, MA.

1843   January to July. Resides at Brook Farm.

1843   July. Visits Bronson Alcott's Fruitlands.

1844   August 2. Received into the Roman Catholic Church.

1845   August. Joins Redemptorists. Departs for novitiate in St. Trond, Belgium.

1846   October 15. Takes Redemptorist vows.

1849   October 23. Ordained to priesthood in London.

1851   April 6. Begins mission work in U.S. with fellow Redemptorists Hafkenscheid, Walworth, Hewit, and Duffy.

1855   *Aspirations of Nature* published.

1857   August 5. Leaves for Rome to plead for English-speaking Redemptorist house.

1857   *Questions of the Soul* published.

1857   August 30. Expelled from Redemptorists.

1858   March 6. *Nuper Nonnulli* issued.

1858   July 7. "Programme of the Rule and Constitution of the Congregation of Missionary Priests of St. Paul the Apostle" issued.

1860   November. Construction of first church and convent at Fifty-Ninth Street completed.

1862   ITH engaged in Lyceum lectures to non-Catholics.

1865   April. Founds *Catholic World.*

1866   Establishes Catholic Publication Society.

1866   October 16. Addresses Second Plenary Council of Baltimore.

1867   Attends Congress of Malines, Belgium.

1869–70   Attends First Vatican Council.

1870   June. Returns to U.S.

1871   December–Spring, 1872. Gradual onslaught of illness.

1873   June. Journeys to Europe for recuperation.

1873   December to March, 1874. Travels in Egypt and the Holy Land.

1874   November. Writes "An Exposition on the Needs of the Church and the Age."

1875   October. Returns to New York.

1876   June 4. Cornerstone laid for St. Paul's Church and new convent.

1884   September. Reelected superior by General Chapter.

1887   *The Church and the Age* published.

1888   December 22. Dies in Paulist House at Fifty-Ninth Street.

ABBREVIATIONS USED IN NOTES

CW   *Catholic World*

ITH   Isaac Thomas Hecker

PFA   Paulist Fathers Archives

Isaac Hecker and *Testem Benevolentiae:* A Study in Theological Pluralism

by William L. Portier

Imagine for a moment that you are playing word association games with an American who has been trained in Catholic theology. Mention the name of Isaac Hecker. If there is any recognition at all, the most likely association will be "Americanism." This is because Isaac Hecker's fate at the hands of theologians and historians has been shaped until recently by events which happened a decade after his death in 1888. Shortly after Hecker's death, Walter Elliott, a Paulist who had been Hecker's constant companion during his last years, wrote an admiring account of his spiritual master's life. Elliott's *Life of Father Hecker* (1891) found its way to France by way of an adaptation and translation. In France Elliott's book became the center of the "Americanist" controversy.[1]

In 1899, Pope Leo XIII addressed an apostolic letter, *Testem Benevolentiae,* to Cardinal Gibbons.[2] The letter censured a set of doctrinal and ascetical aberrations subsumed under the heading of "Americanism." Although the letter mentions the publication of the French adaptation and translation of Elliott's *Life of Father Hecker* as the occasion for the French controversy, these doctrinal aberrations are not explicitly attributed to Hecker. Nevertheless, Hecker's name became associated with this suspect "Americanism." In France opponents often referred to such ideas as "Heckerism." The letter created a climate in which one detractor could refer to Hecker as "a dangerous innovator, and barely, anything less than a heresiarch."[3]

Testem Benevolentiae's brief mention of Hecker's name is, in my judgment, the single most decisive factor in accounting for

11

theology's near century of neglect of his ideas. Since 1899 the only mention of Hecker in standard theological reference works has been to note, either descriptively or by way of indictment, his association with the condemned Americanism. This should come as no surprise, since *Testem Benevolentiae*'s negative effect on the development of American Catholic theology in general has long been acknowledged.[4] Until recently, therefore, the question which logically accompanied any discussion of Hecker in Catholic circles was formulated with some degree of hyperbole by Robert Cross in 1974, "Was Hecker a heretic?"[5] A more tempered formulation of the question might be, "Is the Americanism *Testem Benevolentiae* censured to be found in Hecker's own affirmation of American culture?" Although this is not the kind of question with which contemporary theologians are accustomed to preoccupy themselves, it is the question to which this essay is addressed.

I can think of two reasons for addressing this question at the present time. The first is rather simple and perhaps even picayune. The second, while admittedly more convoluted and difficult to grasp, is nevertheless an important one within the context of contemporary Catholic theology. Because Hecker's name enters the literature of Catholic theology by way of his association with Americanism, no theological discussion of his ideas within a Catholic context can ignore this question and claim to be complete. If this were the only justification for pursuing this question, however, the answer would be no more than a minor footnote in the recent spate of theologically oriented literature on Hecker.

My second reason for pursuing this question flows from the nature of theological pluralism. To judge that this question is of mere antiquarian interest, or worse irrelevant, would be to misperceive the nature of theological pluralism. It is well and good— and even necessary—to contrast the neo-scholastic theological framework of *Testem Benevolentiae* with Hecker's more empirically oriented brand of American theology. We can then see that Hecker and the nineteenth-century scholastics who wrote *Testem Benevolentiae* are talking about vastly different matters when they use words such as *liberty* or *nature,* to take two conspicuous examples. At the same time, however, there must be a level at which we can discuss the mutual compatibility or incompatibility of these two theological worldviews. If such a discussion is impossible, then we are left with the "repressive tolerance" of a "lazy pluralism," to borrow simultaneously from Herbert Marcuse and David Tracy. This would not be a genuine pluralism but a form of false historicism in which questions of truth and relative adequacy cannot even arise. If such a discussion is impossible, then we can no longer speak of the many theologies as expressions of the one faith. We would simply have two of the many theologies, that of *Testem Benevolentiae* and that of Hecker.

I believe that the discussion of the mutual compatibility and incompatibility of these two theological frameworks is not only possible but even useful. Within the admittedly limited context of neo-scholastic theology, *Testem Benevolentiae* poses some very important questions to Hecker's affirmation of American culture. These are the questions which need to be asked in order to lay bare the theological foundation for such an affirmation. Further, I believe that if Hecker's theological ideas could be shown to be a form of the Americanism censured by the papal letter, then they would be examples of base culture capitulation and relatively worthless as theology, Catholic or otherwise. This is a roundabout way of saying that I do not regard as frivolous *Testem Benevolentiae*'s objections to what it describes as "Americanism."

Is the Americanism *Testem Benevolentiae* censures to be found in Hecker's own affirmation of American culture? The obvious way to answer this question would be first to describe Americanism as censured by the letter, then to describe Hecker's affirmation of American culture, and finally to compare and contrast them. We shall come to these three tasks eventually, but by the circuitous route of a detour through the historiography of Americanism. This excursion will briefly consider the presuppositions about the nature of theology which lie beneath the historical discussions of Americanism and Hecker's association with it. This detour is necessary so that the question can be asked and answered from a theological point of view which is self-consciously pluralistic and critical.

THE HISTORIOGRAPHY OF AMERICANISM

In a number of seminal essays, Bernard Lonergan has argued that Catholic theology has recently undergone a shift from what he calls the "classicist world-view to historical-mindedness."[6] This shift has led historians to revise dramatically their estimate of the Americanism episode's theological significance. With this revision comes a corresponding reassessment of Hecker's own theological significance. I believe that this shift in the understanding of the nature of theology helps explain the recent surge of theological interest in Hecker. Since the Second Vatican Council, Americanism has metamorphosed from a "phantom heresy" into a budding theological locus. By association, Hecker himself is transformed from a near theological embarrassment, about whose religious thought it would be best to keep silent, into an American theological pioneer to whom we now attribute a distinctive ecclesiology, apologetics, and spirituality.

Catholic historians and theologians have tended to view the theological aspects of the Americanism episode from two diverging points of view. The first is characterized by classicist assumptions about the nature of theology, the second by an understanding of theology more typical of historical-mindedness. We will call these two diverging perspectives the "phantom heresy" and the "revisionist" approaches to Americanism as a theological issue.

The publication in 1944 of Gibbons' 1899 reply to *Testem Benevolentiae* marked the end of a long period of silence about Americanism.[7] Gibbons' letter had argued that no one in the United States held the opinions reproved in the papal letter, hence the term "phantom heresy." This term was popularized by the appearance in 1949 of the fourth volume of Abbé Félix Klein's memoirs. It was Klein's preface to the French version of Elliott's *Life* which had triggered the Americanist controversy in France more than fifty years before. Klein's fourth volume was subtitled, *une hérésie fantôme, l'Américanisme.* An English translation of Klein's book appeared in the United States in 1951.[8] Reviews by Thomas T. McAvoy, C.S.C. and the Paulist James M. Gillis signalled the favorable reception of the phantom heresy argument by a new generation of American Catholics.[9] Following the letter, this approach distinguished political from theological Americanism. The former indicated the devotion of Americans to their political institutions, the latter referred to the opinions censured in the letter. McAvoy put the phantom heresy argument into its most sophisticated form by introducing a third sense of Americanism. He called it "American Catholicism in fact,"[10] and was prepared to admit that it had given rise to the suspicions in Europe which eventually provoked the papal letter. He refused to address the question of whether this concrete form of American Catholicism had a specifically theological dimension. He argued that since Hecker and the rest were not really theologians, this was not a proper question.[11]

The phantom heresy approach thus follows *Testem Benevolentiae* in distinguishing political Americanism from the opinions censured in the letter. Its proponents are at one in assigning the origins of Americanism in the repudiated sense to the European controversy. No one in the United States, therefore, held the reproved opinions. Whether or not Pope Leo actually thought they did is an open question. In its most sophisticated form, the phantom heresy approach admits that the Americanists may have exhibited haphazard tendencies which foreign observers generalized into the opinions which were eventually censured in the letter. These tendencies or opinions, however, could in no way be construed as theological in the strict sense.

The matter could perhaps be put into the following oversimplified form. In the classicist framework, theology as an intellectual activity pertains to doctrines understood primarily as eternal truths. Therefore, to the extent that Catholicism in the United States is American, i.e., different from Catholicism anywhere else, it cannot be theological. If it were, then it would be heretical. This is why McAvoy calls the unity among the Catholic minority a "theological" one. The specificity of American Catholicism, therefore, can be understood as extending into the realm of theology only at great risk. While the phantom heresy historians were reluctant to grant a theological dimension to Americanism, they did move the discussion of it away from the French context and carefully documented its specifically American character.[12]

In 1945, the year after Gibbons' letter had been made public, Vincent Holden, C.S.P. attempted the first theological defense of Hecker since the time of the Americanist controversy.[13] He was successful in showing that Hecker's ideas had been distorted at a number of points by Elliott, Klein, and the French translator, as well as by the rabid French monarchist, Abbé Charles Maignen.[14] Four years later in his phantom heresy book, Félix Klein himself came to Hecker's defense.

The phantom heresy approach to Americanism defined the theological boundaries for the treatment of Hecker by both Holden and Klein. They shared with the authors of *Testem Benevolentiae* a classicist conception of the nature of theology. In such a conception a plurality of theologies serves not to enrich the one faith but to threaten it. The classicist framework made it very difficult for Holden and Klein to take Maignen or the American conservatives as serious theological critics. To do so would have been to admit defeat at the outset. This meant that the legitimate theological concerns of Maignen and the conservatives could not be addressed. In spite of Holden's interpretation of *Testem Benevolentiae* as a complete exoneration of Hecker, neither he nor Klein was ever completely successful in showing that in the case of every opinion censured by the papal letter Hecker's thought had been unfaithfully represented by Elliott, Klein or the translator, or Maignen.

Instead of offering a positive exposition of Hecker's religious thought, Holden and Klein found themselves on the defensive. They failed to treat Hecker's ideas within their own native theological framework. They were forced instead to defend those ideas with a vocabulary and a conceptuality which were alien to them. Even in Holden's historical works we find him on the theological defensive. His book on Hecker's early years is overly solicitous for the possibility of Hecker's genuine religious experience, i.e., an experience of *supernatural* grace, prior to his conversion. His *Yankee Paul* (1958) spends a good part of its energy justifying Hecker's trip to Rome in 1857 and the subsequent conduct leading up to the founding of the Paulists. I find it difficult to avoid the impression that Holden worked with constant glances over his shoulder at the lingering spectre of Americanism, and specifically at Maignen's accusations of subjectivism and crypto-Protestantism, which would have haunted any Catholic treatment of Hecker during this period.[15] After Vatican II, Holden would speak of Hecker's "vindication," but for whatever reason, he never dealt with the latter half of Hecker's life.[16]

With Vatican II and what Lonergan has described as the shift to historical-mindedness, this situation changed. The logic of historical-mindedness requires the theologian to make a critical grasp of his or her own subjectivity in all its concrete dimensions, personal, social, political, religious, etc. In the United States, this has resulted in, among other things, a new fascination with American Catholicism. Historians like James Hennesey, S.J. began to educate us to the existence of an incipient, distinctively American and Catholic, theological tradition. In this reading, the Americanism episode takes on a new theological significance. The Americanists came to be viewed as forerunners of the Vatican II era church reformers.[17] Right there in the thick of these new developments, by virtue of his now familiar association with Americanism, was none other than Isaac Hecker, his previous disgrace transformed. Here was a real live American theologian.

The beginnings of this revised approach to the phantom heresy argument had been anticipated in McAvoy's third sense of Americanism and in Robert Cross's thesis about the indigenous character of the Americanists' liberalism.[18] After Vatican II it was possible to recognize and thematize the incipient theological dimensions of McAvoy's third sense of Americanism. Picking up on Cross's theme, Thomas Wangler treated Ireland's American religious liberalism under the theological heading of "ecclesiology" and the revised approach to the history of Americanism was under way.[19] James Hennesey pointed out that under the influence of the distinctive American political and religious situation, Catholics in the United States had begun to develop ideas about the Church and its government which were at odds with the ecclesiological ideas of their European counterparts who lived under a different political system.[20] The stage was set for viewing the Americanist episode as a conflict of diverging ecclesiologies, based on different political experiences. This was the approach taken by Margaret M. Reher. She numbered Hecker among the Americanists and argued that it was his ecclesiology which undergirded the entire movement. In this view, *Testem Benevo-*

lentiae constitutes a censure of authentic aspects of Hecker's ecclesiology, specifically his interpretation of the definition of papal infallibility and its corollary, the notion of a greater outpouring of the Holy Spirit.[21]

More recent scholarship has emphasized the extent to which Americanism was, in Wangler's description, an "international liberal Catholic reform movement emanating from the United States."[22] In this context, Hecker appears more as a "pawn" in the Machiavellian intrigues of O'Connell and Ireland than as the theological inspiration for their ecclesiologies, and *Testem Benevolentiae* can be read as a providential check on the uncritical culture religion of Archbishop John Ireland and Denis J. O'Connell.[23] There is little current concern with analyzing *Testem.*[24] In the interest of a more positive exposition, recent theologically oriented studies of Hecker have avoided reference to the Americanist episode. Thus Reher's conclusion that *Testem Benevolentiae* censures Hecker's authentic thought has stood unchallenged for the past decade.

To conclude, in the classicist framework, a subject's history and culture tend to be viewed as extraneous to his or her grasp of theology understood as a body of eternal truths. In this theological world-view, which the phantom heresy historians for the most part share with the authors of *Testem Benevolentiae,* it is difficult to grant Americanism a theological content without thereby admitting that it was indeed a "heresy." By contrast the shift to historical-mindedness brings into focus precisely those historical conditions of the subject's grasp of developing doctrines as true in history and culture which were previously regarded as theologically irrelevant. Revisionist historians of Americanism therefore have little difficulty in perceiving theological dimensions to the Americanist controversies. These controversies are a case study in the interaction of religion and culture bound to give rise to distinctive religious ideas.

Thus we can now speak about Hecker's distinctively American spirituality or apologetics or ecclesiology. It is a relatively straightforward though difficult historical task to sort out the influences of the American religious environment on Hecker's experience of God, his presentation of the faith to non-Catholics or his idea of the Church. If this were all that was involved, however, theology would be reduced to description. A genuine theological treatment must do more. It must provide an adequate account of why Hecker's positive affirmation of American culture should be allowed to influence Catholic theology. It is well known, for example, that Hecker shared with the Americanists the opinion that church structures should be democratized in keeping with the spirit of the age as represented by the American experience. It is both legitimate and necessary to ask, however, why this should be regarded as an ecclesiological, i.e., a theological, opinion rather than a sociological or political one.[25] This is the question which *Testem Benevolentiae* asks and the revisionist historians of Americanism have put us in a position to see its contemporary relevance.

An exhaustive theoretical answer to this question would require nothing less than a theology of theological pluralism. For this I refer the reader to the works of Lonergan, Rahner, or even David Tracy. For the purposes of the present essay we can ask whether Isaac Hecker had any religious basis for his positive evaluation of the American fact, and, if so, did he ever think about it, thereby raising it to the level of theological reflection. If he did not, then as Reher has argued, the criticisms of Maignen and *Testem Benevolentiae* may well be to the point. I will first review *Testem Benevolentiae* as a statement about the relationship between theology and culture from the point of view of nineteenth-century neo-scholasticism and then look at Hecker's religious thought as a peculiarly Catholic example of American empirical theology. Finally I will return to Reher's conclusion that *Testem* touches upon Hecker's authentic teaching.

"AMERICANISM" AS CENSURED BY *TESTEM BENEVOLENTIAE*

"Americanism" enters Catholic theology as a technical term with the publication of the papal letter *Testem Benevolentiae* in 1899. Phantom heresy historians have tended to emphasize that Americanism in the theological sense is entirely a French creation. While this is true to a certain extent, it is also true that there is a degree of continuity between Hecker and the "Heckerism" of the French controversy. This means that Hecker's association with the "Americanist heresy" is no mere accident of history.

The occasion for his posthumous return to Europe via the unlikely route of Klein's *Vie* was the latest development in a French controversy of more than a hundred years' standing. This controversy centered on the question of the attitude which French Catholicism should adopt toward the principles of '89, and specifically during the 1890s toward the third republic. The French controversy was probably the most dramatic instance of a broader question in papal policy facing Leo XIII at this time: what should be the church's posture toward the emerging European republics? This issue was complicated by the nagging presence of the Roman question about the relationship of the papal states to a unified Italy under a revolutionary government. It was the shifting balances of power between Leo's advisors on this policy that the Americanist bishops and their conservative opponents sought to interpret and exploit.[26]

It is not difficult to see how Hecker fit into this French controversy. Here was a man who, from the time of the Malines congress of 1867, through Vatican I and up until his final departure from Europe in the fall of 1875, repeatedly asserted to European audiences that America's providential mission was to solve Europe's religious problems in advance. More specifically the American religious experience had already solved the Church-State question for European Catholicism by demonstrating, in a godly alternative to the French revolution, that separation of Church and State can work toward the advancement of the church's future triumph. Hecker also believed that living under democratic political institutions tended to foster in church members precisely the qualities that European Catholicism needed to overcome its present humiliating position of weakness. When Abbé Klein presented the energetic and self-reliant Hecker to French Catholics as the model of the priest of the future, he was only echoing Hecker's own sentiments.

Liberal Catholics in Europe, and particularly in France, had long looked with hope to the United States for precisely the reasons Hecker had so clearly expressed. This was one variation on the Romantic theme of "America," the new world as last great hope and repository of old Europe's dreams. The optimism and concomitant resentment which appear in the literature on this theme find an apt summary in the French response to Klein's *Vie.* The liberal Catholic Montalembert anticipated that group's reaction when he wrote in response to Hecker's "Saint of Our Day" sermon: "I congratulate you for belonging to a country in which the Catholic cause can be freed from obstacles and prejudices which hinder its progress in a majority of European countries."[27] French *réfractaires,* on the other hand, those with monarchist sympathies, opposed *ralliement,* Leo XIII's publicly-stated policy of peaceful co-existence with the Third Republic. They regarded republicanism in any form, including the American variety, as inherently godless and chaotic. They resented appeals by their opponents to upstart Americans such as Archbishop Ireland, who, in 1892, had barnstormed the churches of Paris drumming up support for Leo's *ralliement.* The sentiments of the *réfractaires* welled up from the same deep-seated religious and political sources that now nurture Archbishop Marcel Lefebvre and his French supporters. Their reaction to Klein's near apotheosis of Hecker and O'Connell's political exploitation of it in his 1897 Fribourg speech was predictable. It achieved ultimate expression in Abbé Charles Maignen's *Père Hecker, est-il un saint?* This work collected a series of articles published separately by Maignen during the course of the French controversy over what had come to be called "Heckerism." He answered the title's question with an often tastelessly overstated negative reply. Nevertheless, beneath the excess of Maignen's *ad hominem* attacks on the Americans could be discerned standard conservative theological objections to the "theory of the immanent fact," which method Maignen believed Klein and Hecker to espouse along with arch-villain Maurice Blondel.[28] These objections, in spite of the near-hysteria of their accusations of semi-pelagianism, naturalism, and immanentism, raise difficult theological questions about the relationship between nature and grace, or, rendered into the idiom of historical consciousness, questions about the relationship between religion and culture. Most significantly, it is from Maignen's version of Heckerism, and not from the writings of any American, that *Testem Benevolentiae* takes the description of the Americanism it censures.

What is this "Heckerism" then? The pope's letter treats it in

two parts. In the terms of a more recent neo-conservative mani-
festo, *Testem Benevolentiae* accused Americanism of allowing the
world to set the agenda for the Church.[29] In its own neo-
scholastic categories which distinguished the deposit of faith
from the rule of life, Americanism was based on the false principle that adaptation to our allegedly advanced modern civilization
required not only changes in church discipline or rule of life, but
doctrinal minimizing on matters pertaining to the deposit of faith
as well. This is nothing but the standard orthodox critique of
liberals in the nineteenth century. What gives this version of
liberalism its distinctively American flavor is a proposal which
appeals to what is distinctive in the political experience identified
with the United States. This is a proposal that a certain false
liberty be introduced into the Church in base imitation of recent
developments in some secular states.[30] This proposal is supported
by the argument, deemed "preposterous" by the letter's authors,
that Vatican I's definition of papal infallibility opens a wider field
of thought and action to individuals following their natural
instincts. From this proposal follow a number of suspicious
consequences (*consectaria*) in the area of ascetical theology. The
letter goes on to censure six of these in turn: 1) that external
guidance in discerning the inner workings of the Holy Spirit is
superfluous; 2) that the present receives a more abundant outpouring of the Holy Spirit than past ages; 3) that natural virtues
are to be preferred to the supernatural; 4) that virtues can be
classified as passive and active, and that the latter are more
fitting in the present age; 5) that religious vows and religious
orders are out of date because they hamper human liberty; 6) that
old methods of bringing the faith to non-Catholics should be
rejected.

    Holden and Klein were successful in showing that most of
the *consectaria* do not represent Hecker's authentic opinions.
Nevertheless, in view of his advocacy of greater freedom in the
Church based on his affirmation of the American experience,
Reher's contention that *Testem Benevolentiae* censures his authentic thought deserves serious consideration. The reader is
asked to recall that *Testem*'s objection to Americanism is not a
completely frivolous one. It is one thing, for example, to show
how Hecker's democratic ideas get into theology, viz. through his

political experience. It is altogether another thing to show why those democratic ideas should be allowed to stay in theology. We must ask then whether Hecker's affirmation of American culture has a genuine theological basis. If it does not then it is an uncritical example of culture religion and unworthy of our consideration.

HECKER'S THEOLOGY OF HISTORY: THE THEOLOGICAL BASIS FOR A RELIGIOUS AFFIRMATION OF THE AMERICAN FACT

As we have seen, *Testem Benevolentiae* is divided into two parts, the first censuring a false way of understanding the relationship between the Church and the age, the second censuring suspicious consequences. For whatever reason, commentators have concentrated on refuting accusations related to the suspicious consequences. This is to leave unthematized the all-important question of the Church's relationship to the age which the letter discusses in its first part on general principles. Reher was the first commentator to treat systematically the profound differences of world-view between *Testem Benevolentiae* and the Americanists, among whom she numbered Hecker. She emphasized ecclesiological differences as functions of the diverging American and European political experiences.

I propose another emphasis. *Testem Benevolentiae* talks about the relationship between Church and age from the point of view of neo-scholastic theology.[31] Hecker understands that relationship within another theological framework, that of American empirical theology. I believe, therefore, that theology of history is a more fundamental theological category than ecclesiology for purposes of comparing the diverging world-views of Hecker and the papal letter. It is his view of "America" as a "providential nation" that provides the theological basis for his religious affirmation of the American fact.[32]

Hecker's affirmation of American culture developed gradually. His two books on apologetics, written while he was still a Redemptorist, tend to speak of human nature in the abstract. The ambiguity of this discussion reflects the tension between rationalism and traditionalism in nineteenth-century Catholic theology in general.[33] At this time in his life, Hecker pointed aspiring American souls away from their culture to the church's religious orders. In the closing pages of *Questions of the Soul,* however, we catch a glimpse of the Americanist themes which will occupy the writings of his Paulist years.[34] He begins to consider specifically American manifestations of human nature and their universal significance. This is a more concrete, i.e., empirical in the American sense, approach to theology than the abstract discussion of nature's powers which we find in *Aspirations of Nature* and in most of *Questions of the Soul.*

In addition to the apologetic which Hecker directed toward the New England literary and religious tradition, however, he also addressed a series of important writings to his fellow Catholics. These intra-Catholic writings, presented over a period of thirty years, proposed, sustained, and developed a new way for the nineteenth-century Catholic church in both Europe and North America to understand itself. Although the ideas expressed in these intra-Catholic writings concern the Church and the individual soul's search for spiritual perfection, they are not simply about the church question (ecclesiology) or spirituality as such. They never speak of the Church or the restless, searching soul apart from some reference to their respective roles in the realization of history's providential goal. Both individual and Church are considered precisely in their relationship to world or culture, or, in Hecker's terms, the "age."

This new vision of the relationship of Church and age centered on the messianic role of a converted America in bringing about the positive outcome of history in what Hecker called the "Church's future triumph." It was based on the providential understanding of history which Hecker had learned from New England theology via Orestes A. Brownson's personal recovery of it in the years prior to his conversion, and of which Hecker spoke in the millennialist tones of nineteenth-century evangelical revivalism. That a religious figure in the century of American progress and expansion should speak of the nation's messianic destiny or the impending arrival of God's kingdom in America was not unusual. That a Catholic priest should speak in this manner was unheard of. This was Hecker's genius.

He spoke to nineteenth-century Catholics, first in the United

States and then in Europe, in the idiom of American Calvinism in all its permutations. He presented an historically-oriented alternative, theologically grounded in the symbol of providence, to the timeless neo-scholastic self-understanding which came to dominate nineteenth-century Catholicism. In a self-consciously Catholic version of American empirical theology, he fastened his gaze on the events of history, there to discern the revealing hand of God. In a Romantic theology of history, he reached across the Atlantic for roots in the European Catholic revival. In the century of the *Syllabus Errorum* and Vatican I's definition of papal infallibility, Hecker affirmed American civilization on theological grounds and emphasized individual liberty and self-reliance based on the authentically discerned impulses of the Holy Spirit. To a beleaguered European Catholicism, increasingly preoccupied with the eternal truths of the faith, Hecker spoke of the religious significance of present historical events.

Hecker was one of the first American Catholic thinkers to bring the relationship between Roman Catholicism and American culture to reflective awareness. His intra-Catholic writings attempted to specify the theological reality of American Catholicism and to read its universal implications for both Church and world. The result was a unique Catholic form of American messianism expressed in a recognizably American idiom which Hecker had learned during the course of his lifelong conversation with American Calvinism in both its liberal and evangelical strains.

The events of Hecker's life which challenged his understanding of his own calling simultaneously elicited a statement about universal history. The first such text appeared at Rome where Hecker had just been expelled from the Redemptorists. Brownson's lectures and writings of the previous decade had exposed Hecker to the basic notion of American messianism as derived from the New England Puritans. The mid-1850s saw a surge in anti-Catholic sentiment due to dramatic increases in immigration. These outbursts of nativism and the Catholic response they evoked provided the occasion for the development and expression of Hecker's Americanist ideas. All of these factors came together at Rome in 1857 to produce two articles entitled, *The Present and Future Prospects of the Catholic Faith in the United*

States of North America.[35] Reading the signs of the times in the manner and idiom of his evangelical contemporaries, Hecker put forward his twin Americanist ideas, the impending conversion of America to Catholicism and the messianic role of a converted America in the Church's future triumph.

The Civil War Years found Hecker reaching the height of his powers as a preacher, lecturer, and publicist. His estimate of American culture in his Redemptorist apologetic underwent a profound change. The most striking feature of Hecker's sermons during this period was his strong and unambiguous affirmation of the religious value of life in this world and the progress of American civilization. This emphasis contrasted sharply with his own previous one as well as with the sermons of his contemporaries who preached the missions or "Catholic revivals." The most eloquent of these sermons, "The Saint of Our Day" (1863), presents a layman, St. Joseph, as the type of one who attained an eminent degree of religious perfection while engaged in his worldly occupation.[36] The world-affirming sermons of the 1860s constitute a religious apology for the burgeoning Hecker flour mills and the Paulist printing presses which they financed. By the end of the 1860s, Isaac Hecker had emerged as a spokesman for a class of wealthy, educated, Catholic lay people, typified by his brother George and the women with whom he corresponded as spiritual director. These were the Yankee Catholics. Most were native-born Americans. Many were converts. They, and especially George Hecker, along with Brownson and prelates like Archbishop Martin J. Spalding of Baltimore, represented the initial realization of the promise of what American Catholicism could become.[37]

The post-Civil War years occasioned two major statements from Hecker on the providential role he envisioned for a Yankee Catholicism. In the fall of 1866, he attended the second plenary council of Baltimore. On October 15, he preached a sermon to the assembled bishops entitled, "The Church's Future Triumph."[38] It remains one of the most dramatic presentations of his Americanist theology of history. In September of the following year, he returned to Belgium to attend the third Congress of Malines. This was the occasion for an address entitled, "La Situation religieuse des États Unis," noteworthy for its anticipation of his later position on America's providential contribution to Europe's religious regeneration, i.e., separation of Church and State.[39]

Two years later Hecker again returned to Europe to attend the Vatican Council, first as the procurator or representative of Bishop Sylvester Rosecrans of Columbus, Ohio, and then as theologian to Archbishop Spalding of Baltimore. Anticipation of a major providential event buoyed his spirits. He would be disappointed. Vatican I marked an important turning point in Hecker's life. It violated his innocence and forced him to integrate a monumental setback into what was, until that time, a one-sidedly optimistic and progressive view of history. It also permanently shifted the focus of his attention from the United States to Europe. Hecker experienced the definition of papal infallibility, and especially the majority's tactics in achieving it, as a step backwards towards monarchy and absolutism at a time when the providential movement of history was toward democracy. It was the destiny of the United States to be the vanguard of this providential movement. At Vatican I this destiny seemed to be thwarted and Hecker was disturbed. He left the council prematurely in April of 1870.

In late 1871 he lapsed into what his first biographer called the "long illness," which would last until his death.[40] From June of 1873 until the fall of 1875, Hecker traveled in Europe in hopes of recovering his health. His observations of religious and political conditions on the continent, along with his experience of Vatican I, led him to believe that the Church's future triumph could not come about without the religious regeneration of Europe. The providential mission of the United States would be to light the way for this. The American religious and political experience would provide a type for a form of separation of Church and State which worked to the Church's advantage rather than its ruin. At the same time as events challenged him to integrate negativity into his understanding of providence's sovereignty over history, the introspective bent of the early diaries returned and demanded to be made one with the activism of the 1860s. The closest Hecker could come in print to this healing integration was his *Exposition of the Church in View of Recent Difficulties and Controversies and the Present Needs of the Age*

(1875).[41] The correspondence and personal notes for this period reveal that Hecker was entertaining a proposal for a foundation of European Paulists who would act as catalysts for the religious regeneration called for by the *Exposition*. His prolonged absence proved a strain on the Paulists in the United States. In the fall of 1875, Hecker was called back from Europe never to return. He had traveled to Europe on four separate occasions between 1845 and 1873 and sojourned there for nearly a decade of accumulated years. In the manner of the well-worn theme of travel in nineteenth-century American literature, this experience served as a fruitful distancing which helped him to grasp the specificity of American Catholicism by contrast with its European counterpart.

A CLASH OF THEOLOGICAL WORLD-VIEWS

Hecker's religious thought is an extended reflection on the relationship between religion and culture, specifically between Catholicism and American "civilization" as he viewed them. The salient feature of this reflection is its concern to find where God is presently acting in both the larger arena of world history and the more limited topography of the individual soul. This concern was a peculiarly Catholic deviation or offshoot from the mainstream of American Protestant "experimental" religion. Hecker's interest in the theological significance of historical events is attested to by the ubiquitous presence of the symbol of providence throughout his writings.

As nineteenth-century neo-scholastics, the authors of *Testem Benevolentiae* were singularly ill-equipped to deal on its own terms with a theological frame of reference within which historical events have an inherent significance with its basis in providence, and which significance awaits discernment by the sign-seeker. At issue here is a clash of theological world-views. What is at stake in this clash can be seen in a consideration of the crucial term "nature." One of the neo-scholastics' chief objections to the theologies of their Romantic predecessors in the nineteenth century—Hecker's European counterparts—was the inability of the latter to distinguish clearly between nature and grace. Hecker's theology exhibited the same blurring between the natural and the supernatural that the neo-scholastics found in traditionalism, ontologism, and Günther. By contrast, *Testem Benevolentiae* speaks of the age as if it were a product of human nature entirely separated from the influence of grace. In the intellectual milieu which the modern scholastics shared with philosophers of Enlightenment, it was possible to speak of natural virtues, natural beatitude, separate philosophy, a purely secular state, etc. *Testem Benevolentiae*'s criticisms of Americanism as advocating natural over supernatural virtues, for example, arise from the fact that its authors understood "nature" in a sense closer than Hecker's to one in which the hypothetical pure nature of modern scholasticism is equated with historical nature. Hecker sometimes adopts the vocabulary of modern scholasticism for polemical and apologetic purposes, particularly in his interpretation of the Council of Trent on the effects of the Fall.[42] Insofar as he does this, some of the claims he makes for American civilization and human nature are open to Maignen's criticisms. In general, however, insofar as the symbol of providence is in control, Hecker's understanding of nature implies that in the actual order of providence it would be difficult to make a sharp distinction between separate philosophy and Christian philosophy, between purely natural virtues and actions performed under the influence of supernatural grace. Hecker's providential theory of history, therefore, which can also be interpreted as a form of "moderate traditionalism," involved an inchoate notion of a historically graced nature.

These two senses of *nature* find an apt illustration in diverging answers to a question with which nineteenth-century European Catholics were frequently occupied: "Is 'natural man' capable of self-government?" The Americanist controversy in France focused on a form of this question. In the context of this question, Pius IX had previously made an important political statement when he reaffirmed the doctrine of original sin in the 1854 definition of Mary's immaculate conception. As a paternalistic aristocrat, immersed in the battles of Italian unification, Leo XIII answered the question in the negative. Hecker's affirmative answer, far from sharing modernity's optimism about human prospects, rather took a page from the Romantic traditionalist critique of Enlightenment. His "theology of democracy," if you will, did not consist in the bare assertion of his optimistic interpretation of Trent's decree on justification. Hecker's positive estimate of historical human nature, and therefore of democracy, had a further theological basis. While the authors of *Testem Benevolentiae* did not share this theological basis, neither did they condemn it or censure it. Hecker read the decrees of Trent as he did because of his context within early nineteenth-century Romantic theology, and his emphasis on the doctrine of providence as inherited through Brownson from the Puritans. Hecker did not regard the founders or the inheritors of American republicanism as purely or merely natural men and women. Nor did he regard the practical virtues whose need he extolled as merely or purely natural virtues. He was a pioneering intrinsicist, but he did not arrive at his position solely through an analysis of interiority. Rather its basis is to be found in his traditionalist understanding of history.

Hecker's affirmation of the age and of modern civilization rests first of all on his acceptance of the new Romantic apologetic which, in contrast to the eighteenth century, regarded the Church as the teacher of humanity and the mother of European civilization.[43] This is the theme of the Church as civilizer which can be seen throughout his writings. Commenting on the *Syllabus Errorum,* Hecker wrote:

> So today, when the declared enemies of Christian civilization come in disguise to the Catholic Church and insist upon her reconciliation with modern civilization, she replies with Christ: Begone, Satan; modern civilization is the product of the Catholic Church and not yours. . . .[44]

In addition to this, as a moderate traditionalist Hecker could appeal to the traces of the universal memory of the Noahic revelation and write a passage such as the following:

> The written law given by divine inspiration to Moses and the same divine source as the unwritten law given to Noah and the patriarchs, and the patriarchal dispensation was the same as that received from God by Adam. There is no one rational being ever born of the human race who is not in some sort in the covenanted graces of God. It is the glory of the Catholic

Church that she exists from the beginning and in some true
sense embraces in her fold all the members of the human
race.[45]

When Hecker proposes that the Church adapt to the democratic tendency of the age, therefore, he does not do so in servile
imitation of a purely secular culture. Rather the legitimate aspirations of the age toward liberty have been inspired by centuries
of education in the school of Christianity. The age possesses in
some degree a memory of divine revelation. Fallen human nature
is not to be understood in the order of God's providence as
totally cut off from supernatural grace. It, therefore, can be
regarded as capable of self-government. When Hecker speaks of
the natural order, he is not speaking of modern scholasticism's
hypothetical pure nature nor of the unspoiled native of Enlightenment mythology.

On the other hand, as seen in his writings on Italy and
France during the 1870s, Hecker's affirmation of the democratic
age was not uncritical.[46] It included a corresponding negation.
Just as the Church, so the age too included both divine and
human dimensions. Hecker believed that in the conflict of history
the Church's divine side would ultimately become manifest and it
would unite with the age in the final triumph. Until this time he
would rely on the process of sign-seeking, informed by his lifelong submission to the authority of the Church, to distinguish the
human from the divine elements in the Church and in the age. In
terms of theological method, this would have been a less than
acceptable way of distinguishing nature from grace for the neo-
scholastics.

In spite of its manifest weaknesses, this model was more
suited to an age beginning to sense the intellectual impact of
human historicity than the doctrine-discipline alternative offered
by *Testem Benevolentiae*. Valid only in retrospect, this distinction
between matters of doctrine and matters of discipline offers no
present criterion save that of authority for distinguishing the
essential from the accidental in Christianity.[47] Hecker certainly
made numerous suggestions for changes in Church discipline,
and the papal letter, in a burst of emphatic ultramontanism,
reminded the reader that judgments about whether such changes

are required for the salvation of souls should be left to the discretion of the church and not that of private individuals.[48]

In conclusion, the principles censured in the first part of *Testem Benevolentiae* are not those held by Hecker. He did advocate adaptation to the age in the form of the introduction of greater individual liberty into the life of the church. But he did not view this as a capitulation to a purely alien spirit.

I turn now to the reading of *Testem Benevolentiae* as a direct censure of Hecker's providential interpretation of Vatican I's definition of papal infallibility and the corresponding notion of a greater outpouring of the Holy Spirit. I will argue that a comparison of the texts of Hecker's *Exposition* with Leo XIII's *Testem Benevolentiae* and *Divinum Illud* fails to support this reading. Before proceeding to the argument, it should be noted that even if we were to assume with Reher that the censure of *Testem Benevolentiae* does indeed touch Hecker's authentic thought, we would have to admit at the same time that this in itself would not be a very serious matter. The opinion which the letter censures does not deal with the meaning of the dogmatic statement, but with the interpretation of the definition's providential meaning as an historical event.[49]

The opinion on the definition of papal infallibility is mentioned in the letter because its authors regard this opinion as a supporting argument for a much more serious conclusion, namely, "that a certain liberty (*libertas*) ought to be introduced into the Church, so that, limiting the exercise and vigilance of its powers, each one of the faithful may act more freely in pursuance of his own natural bent and capacity."[50] This is to be done in order to imitate recent changes in civil society. The letter goes on to clarify the sense in which *libertas* is to be understood by a reference to Pope Leo's encyclical *Immortale Dei* (1885). Reher herself points to the fact that *libertas* as used in Leo's writings on church and state and liberty as understood in the context of American Catholicism have two divergent meanings.[51] On the basis of this fact, and on the basis of Hecker's writings, particularly those on Europe after 1875, it would be difficult to defend the conclusion that the liberty Hecker advocated for the Church was *libertas* in the sense impugned by Leo XIII. As we have seen, Hecker does not advocate liberty merely in imitation of recent changes in civil society considered as a secular or purely natural social order.[52]

This is clear from the juxtaposition of the following sentence from the *Exposition* with the text of *Testem Benevolentiae* which allegedly censures it:

For the definition of the Vatican Council, having rendered the supreme authority of the Church, which is the unerring interpreter and criterion of divinely revealed truth, more explicit and complete, has prepared the way for the faithful to follow, with greater safety and liberty, the inspirations of the Holy Spirit.

For they say in speaking of the infallible teaching of the Roman Pontiff, that after the solemn decision formulated in the Vatican Council, there is no more need of solicitude in that regard, and, because of its now being out of dispute, a wider field of thought and action is thrown open to individuals.[53]

The differences in meaning of these two texts are clear. The context of the sentence from the *Exposition* makes plain that the liberty referred to in the passage is to be understood with reference to the inspiration of the Holy Spirit rather than with reference to some form of purely natural instinct. To grasp the appropriateness of this assertion, it is sufficient to recall Hecker's fulminations against Emersonian "self-culture" and the excess of European radicals, or his defense of the *Syllabus Errorum.* Nowhere in Hecker's text do we find the censured assertion that after Vatican I there is no more need for solicitude regarding the supreme authority of the Church. Most important, however, is the conspicuous absence of any reference in the text from *Testem Benevolentiae* to the central concern in Hecker's text, namely, the inspiration of the Holy Spirit. Hecker interprets the definition of papal infallibility as providentially freeing Catholics to follow the inspirations of the Holy Spirit, not to indulge their own purely natural appetites (*suo cuiusque ingenio actuosaeque virtuti largius aliquanto indulgere*). In comparing these two texts, the central question comes down to this: does Hecker's reference to following "with greater safety and liberty, the inspirations of the Holy Spirit" mean the same thing as *Testem Benevolentiae*'s "a wider field of thought and action is open to individuals"? It is not at all clear that they mean the same thing. *Testem Benevolentiae*'s statement is more general and lacks Hecker's qualifying reference to the Holy Spirit. The authors of the letter could have clarified this question for us by citing Hecker's exact words, if that is what they wished to censure. Even if they had done this, however, it would still be necessary to put Hecker's statement back into its original context before concluding whether it was censured or not.

The conclusion that these two texts do not have identical meanings is strengthened by a consideration of the sections of the letter immediately following upon the passage in question. The letter continues by designating as "preposterous" the method of argument to which it refers, precisely because this argument would wish to withdraw or separate itself from that very infallible teaching authority upon which it grounds itself. Such a method of argument would indeed be preposterous. But we find no evidence in Hecker's conduct at Vatican I or in his writings of his wish to use the definition of papal infallibility as a way of circumventing the issue of submission to papal or church authority. When *Testem Benevolentiae* goes on to enumerate the dangers from which it interpreted the definition as providentially preserving the Church, it becomes more clear that it is not Hecker's thought to which the letter is referring. The litany *Testem Benevolentiae* recites contains many of the modern tendencies against which Hecker himself had argued in his analysis of the European scene. It is hard to believe that the letter intends to discourage people from following supernatural impulses. Although it offers no discussion of criteria for discernment, it is safe to presume that its authors shared Hecker's lifelong concern to insure that he was not self-deluded regarding what he interpreted as the supernatural impulses in his soul. The criterion which Hecker offers in the *Exposition* is the authority of the Church to which he refers in this passage as "the unerring interpreter and criterion of divinely revealed truth."

Testem Benevolentiae censures the opinion that the Holy Spirit "pours greater and richer gifts (*charismata*) into the hearts of the faithful now than in times past...."[54] Hecker's *Exposition* speaks frequently of a greater or new effusion or infusion or increased action of the Holy Spirit.[55] In judging whether this notion is the one under censure, a key word is *charismata.* The technical scholastic sense of the term regarded *charismata* as *"privilegia peculiaria Ecclesiae apostolicae et primitivae."*[56] It would require further research to conclude whether Leo used the term in this restricted sense which referred primarily to rare and extraordinary ecstatic phenomena such as prophecy, healing, glossalalia, etc. There are other Latin words used to express "gifts" of the Holy Spirit, namely *dona* and *munera.* In his 1897 encyclical on the Holy Spirit, *Divinum Illud,* Leo used all three of these words to refer to the gifts of the Holy Spirit. In one case he used *charismata* to refer to the fullness of grace possessed by the earthly Jesus, but in another case he used *charismata* as a synonym for *dona* to refer to the seven gifts of the Holy Spirit.[57] *Divinum Illud* therefore yields no consistent usage of *charismata* as a technical term. Nevertheless, with less ambiguous words available, namely *dona* and *munera,* the authors of *Testem Benevolentiae* chose *charismata.* At least one commentator has interpreted this passage of the letter as referring to *charismata* in the technical sense.[58]

It is difficult to determine exactly what Hecker meant by the greater outpouring of the Holy Spirit. The notion is found in the usage of American Calvinism. While he continued to associate it with conversions, Hecker gave the phrase a specifically Catholic twist. In his usage in the *Exposition,* for example, it refers not so much to the ecstatic phenomena of the Pauline letters or the American revival tradition, e.g., prophecy, glossalalia (*charismata* in the strict sense), but to a heightened appreciation for the doctrine of the divine indwelling and what is traditionally called actual grace. This also doubtless includes the sense that the grace of the Holy Spirit works outside the visible Church and the sacraments, which Hecker regarded as the ordinary channels of His grace. Hecker gave a clue to what he meant by the phrase in a remark made to Hewit regarding Manning's comments on the *Exposition.* Manning had written: "As to any new outpouring, as my friend P. Gratry used to hope, I have no light."[59] Responding to this, Hecker wrote: "As to the allusion to P. Gratry, I anticipate no special outpouring of the Holy Spirit—in the miraculous [*charismata?*] sense, no more than the present action, or the action of the Church in any age was miraculous—say that of these last three centuries terminating in the Vatican definition of infallibility."[60] In this text, Hecker seems to distance himself from any interpretation of the spiritual gifts to be expected for the age as the rare and marginal ecstatic phenomena referred to by the scholastic understanding of *charismata*. If this is what Pope Leo meant, then he was not questioning Hecker's notion of the greater outpouring. At any rate, there is at least enough doubt on this point to justify further inquiry before concluding that Hecker's notion of the greater outpouring of the Holy Spirit is censured by *Testem Benevolentiae*.

Whatever one concludes, it is essential to recall that Hecker's belief about the increased action or effusion of the Holy Spirit was not some kind of dogmatic assertion of the abstract superiority of modernity. On the contrary, it was the very need of modernity which prompted the belief. He was trying, in good New England fashion, to read the signs of the times. Subsequent events may prove such attempts incorrect. Church authority may judge them inopportune or imprudent. But unless what is read in the signs is patently at odds with basic tenets of the Christian confession of faith, it is difficult to imagine how individual attempts at sign-seeking could be condemned as heterodox. While its exercise is almost guaranteed to create controversy, the practice as such, i.e. reading the signs of the times, has a certified Christian pedigree going back to scriptural days.

CONCLUSION

Hecker's theology of history and the neo-scholastic theological framework of *Testem Benevolentiae* provide a study in pre-critical theological pluralism. When these two horizons met nearly one hundred years ago, instead of fusing in a degree of mutual understanding, they clashed. The language and perspective of Hecker's theology of history has obvious affinities to the millennial idiom derived from the American revivalist tradition as well as to nineteenth-century Romanticism. In this frame of reference, history becomes a book in which we read the signs of God's presence, signs of the coming Kingdom or in Hecker's terms the "Church's Future Triumph." The *Exposition*'s controversial attempt to interpret the definition of papal infallibility as a sign of the times exemplifies this characteristic concern. Some commitment to the idea that changing historical events have significance in the ultimate scheme of things is essential to an appreciation of Hecker's perspective.

Neo-scholastic theology had a quite different approach to history. As one historian has expressed it, the official face of the nineteenth-century church was firmly set against the growing sense of historicity in human affairs.[61] In theology the scholastics of the modern period dealt with New Testament eschatology and its language about the Kingdom of God in a manner quite removed from the idiom of American Calvinism. These Catholic theologians of the post-Reformation period have been described as "erudite, fairminded metaphysicians" who "could not think historically," and were consequently "unaware that their Aristotelian theological method could not handle history."[62] At the time Hecker wrote the *Exposition,* this modern scholastic theological method was on the eve of a revival of vast proportions.

With his Catholic contemporaries, Hecker believed, for example, that the saving fullness of God's presence was to be sought in the Catholic church. But he conceived of the Church in Romantic terms as the living power which animated history and pushed it forward unawares. As the nineteenth century wound down, it became more and more common for Catholics to imagine the Church as a timeless edifice standing over against history. This made it difficult to imagine the Church as something which needed to grow or progress, i.e., change. It was a perfect society in possession of the truth. In this perspective, the needs of one particular time are no more crucial to the Church's well-being than those of another. We cooperate with the grace that is sufficient to the needs of the time, but Hecker's tone of urgency is lost and comes to be interpreted as "dithyrambic" or "millennialistic." "Nature" is not treated thematically within the order of providence. Historical events, therefore, remain merely natural and have little to do with the sphere of the supernatural. At the conscious level of theory, significant interplay between Church and age, between the supernatural and the merely natural, is at a minimum.

When these two divergent, though not necessarily incompatible, frameworks encountered one another, a successful exchange and communication would have required a degree of critical sophistication which neither side possessed at the time. Misunderstanding and misinterpretation were the result. This is not to imply that such misunderstandings could have been avoided by a more careful reading of Hecker on the part of the authors of *Testem Benevolentiae,* or at least Maignen. That is not the point. At issue here is a clash of theological world-views. Successful communication in this situation would have required nothing less than a change in self-awareness. Refinement of the data would not have been enough. To bring theology's pluriform history to reflective awareness as an interplay between itself and culture, in which those who reflect are themselves involved, would have required nothing less than a shift to historical-mindedness. It was Hecker's misfortune that he had begun to bring the relationship between Catholicism and American culture to reflective awareness precisely at the time when Catholic theology had embraced on a wide scale a system of thought which, despite its acknowledged sophistication, possessed very limited intellectual tools for making that relationship the thematic core of its reflection. The point here is not only that the neo-scholastic movement was ill-equipped to deal with theological pluralism, but that theological pluralism was precisely the situation it sought to overcome by a return to scholastic method in theology.

The recent shift to historical-mindedness allows us to see these two diverging theological frames of reference with a view that was closed to Hecker and his contemporaries. These perspectives now appear as two among a plurality of legitimate but limited theoretical articulations of Christian faith. Due to the unacknowledged and unthematized relations between these two theories and the social and political interests of the groups who articulated them, we would now regard both perspectives as precritical. Neither nineteenth-century neo-scholasticism nor Hecker's moderately traditionalist theology of history constitutes adequate theological responses to our contemporary situation. Nevertheless we might allow this study in nineteenth-century Catholic theological pluralism to challenge some of our assumptions. The first goes something like this. Of course Hecker probably was censured by *Testem Benevolentiae,* but who cares? This would be an instance of the more general frame of mind which deals with Roman censures and other exercises of ecclesiastical authority by ignoring them.

It seems fitting, if only for the satisfaction that closure brings, to finally and explicitly turn and face the spectre which has haunted Hecker's memory for so long, namely, *Testem Bene-volentiae.* On the whole, *Testem Benevolentiae* fails to engage Hecker's religious thought at its center, i.e., its typically American concern for the religious meaning of history at the personal, national, and universal levels. The papal letter censures abstract statements about the relation of Catholicism and culture and their ascetical corollaries. Hecker did not speak in this way. His proposals for church reform were based on his reading of the signs of the times. He offered them not as *a priori* theoretical assertions about the ascetical life, but as concrete responses to the needs of a particular time and place.

Perhaps a more fitting way to address Hecker's thought would have been through a discussion of methods and criteria for reading the providences and discerning the Spirit. These were practices for which the neo-scholastic authors of *Testem Benevo-lentiae,* as theologians, had little inclination. At any rate, the question of whether the authors of the letter actually intended to address Hecker's authentic thought will probably continue to remain a matter of controversy. By itself *Testem Benevolentiae* can hardly be said to stand as one of history's more significant statements on the relationship between Catholicism and culture. It is worthy of discussion at least because of its influence on history's estimate of Isaac Hecker. As a warning against liberal reductionism in thinking about church reform and the relation of religion and culture, the letter must be allowed to stand or fall on the merits of its arguments. If it was ever intended as a serious attempt to interpret Hecker's religious thought, *Testem Benevo-lentiae* fell short of the mark.

In so doing, however, it serves to challenge Hecker's thought at its weakest points, i.e., where it is in danger of uncritically capitulating to American culture. Maignen was not the only one to accuse Hecker of rationalism, naturalism, semi-pelagianism, etc. These objections were raised with less hysteria during Hecker's lifetime by critics such as Brownson who did not share Maignen's irrational antipathy to republicanism. I do not think it rash to claim that, in the climate created by the condemnations of Americanism in 1899 and modernism in 1907, many—and Vincent Holden was probably among them—feared that perhaps Hecker really had been a semi-pelagian or a naturalist or whatever, that in the end his views really were indefensible.

A study of *Testem Benevolentiae* from within the context of theological pluralism makes it possible to answer these objections on Hecker's own ground. This ground is his moderately traditionalist theology of history with its hybrid idiom of American revivalism and European Catholic Romanticism. While such a theoretical framework is no longer tenable, the story of how Hecker used it in his own religious seeking remains to inspire other generations as they struggle to reflect on their experiences as American Catholics. In the face of the rationalism of the transcendentalists, Hecker's providential understanding of history affirmed the irreducibility of historical Christianity as a religious experience. In the face of his own tendencies to enthusiasm, Hecker's traditionalism affirmed the necessary relationship of personal religious experience to a shared historical community of meaning. Through the symbol of providence, he attempted to place himself under the judgment of both of these affirmations. Those who tend to see in Hecker only the man ahead of his time—the contemporary in nineteenth-century dress—might find that his millennialist dream for America's conversion stands in judgment of what may well be an underdeveloped missionary sense in the contemporary American church. Those who regard him solely as a mystic and guide in the interior life might find in his practice of reading the signs of the times a challenge to take history more seriously as a place where God speaks and acts.

On a more general plane, if present history is any indication—the movement to turn theology into a self-correcting process of public discourse to the contrary notwithstanding—Roman censures and investigations of Catholic thinkers are still very much a part of life in the Catholic church. They cannot simply be ignored. Many factors helped to generate the climate of fear in which the American church received the censure of *Testem Benevolentiae.* Those with a penchant for dialectic might have suspected that this fear would eventually give way to disdain in the reception of Roman statements. In the warm flush of

Vatican II, Roman censures took on the glow of red badges of courage. By now they have become something of an annoying interruption—sometimes of a very serious nature—in a particular theologian's academic career.

It is time for American Catholic intellectuals to take a more responsible attitude toward the Roman authority which they profess to recognize. American Catholics have always faced the problem of giving an account of their relationship as free people (theological inquirers in this case) to what appears to their fellow Christians in the United States as an arbitrary religious authority. If we can in any sense affirm that the Church has a mission to teach authoritatively in the name of Jesus—an affirmation which I believe to represent a widely-held ecumenical consensus—then American Catholic theologians must face the task of making a responsible affirmation of theological pluralism. This would demand a serious treatment of the role of church authority in the theological process as a theological question.[63] In an integralist climate, this has been and would be a difficult task. We are relatively fortunate at the present time in that a plurality of conceptual frameworks and a relatively open forum are available for the discussion of church authority in theology as a theological issue.

History testifies to the tremendous impact which *Testem Benevolentiae* has had on the quality of the intellectual life of American Catholicism. History leads us to believe that we can expect future *Testem Benevolentiae*s from Rome. While we may hope that their theological quality will improve, we must also admit that fear or disdain or annoyance is relatively inadequate as an account of our belief in the church's authority to teach through its bishops.

NOTES

1. *Le Père Hecker, Fondateur des "Paulistes" Américains, 1819–1888,* par le Père W. Elliott, de la même Compagnie. Traduit et adapté de l'anglais avec autorisation de l'auteur. Introduction par Mgr. Ireland. Préface par l'Abbé Félix Klein (7th edition; Paris: Lecoffre, 1898).

2. For the Latin text of *Testem Benevolentiae,* see *Acta Sanctae Sedis* 31 (1898–9): 470–79. For English translations, see Thomas T.

McAvoy, *The Great Crisis in American Catholic History, 1895–1900* (Chicago: Henry Regnery Co., 1957), pp. 379–91 and John Tracy Ellis, ed., *Documents of American Catholic History* (Milwaukee: Bruce Publishing Co., 1956), pp. 553–62.

3. See Joseph Wuest, C.SS.R., "Historia Separationis Paulistarum," *Annales Congregationis Ss. Redemptoris Provinciae Americanae,* III, 2 (1899), p. 6. This citation is taken from an anonymous translation at the Redemptorist Archives of the Baltimore Province in Brooklyn, N.Y. Eight decades later one can still read in passing of Pope Leo XIII's "condemnation of ITH's views." See Joseph M. McShane, S.J., "Perfection of the Life or of the Work," *America,* May 1, 1982, p. 345.

4. See, for example McAvoy, op. cit., p. 360 and James Hennesey, S.J., *American Catholics* (New York: Oxford University Press, 1981), p. 203.

5. See Robert D. Cross, "Isaac Hecker's *The Church and the Age,* or, Was Hecker a Heretic?" Paper delivered at Workshop on Paulist History and Traditions, St. Paul's College, Washington, D.C., 1974.

6. See "The Transition from a Classicist World-View to Historical-Mindedness" and "Theology in Its New Context." Both essays appear in William F. Ryan and Bernard J. Tyrrell, eds., *A Second Collection* (Philadelphia: Westminster Press, 1974).

7. *Catholic Historical Review* 30 (October 1944): 346–48.

8. Félix Klein, *La route du petit Morvandiau: Souvenirs de l'Abbé Félix Klein,* Tome IV. "Une hérésie fantôme, l'Américanisme" (Paris: Plon, 1949). Even as late as 1951, Catholic publishers in the United States were unwilling to publish a book on Americanism by one who had been involved in the controversy. The English translation, therefore, had to be done on "offset" at the Aquin Bookshop in Atchison, Kansas. See Theodore Maynard, *The Catholic Church and the American Idea* (New York: Appleton Century Crofts, 1953), p. 86. At Rome the Holy Office (now the Congregation for the Doctrine of the Faith) appointed Udalrich Beste, O.S.B. and Sebastian Tromp, S.J. as consultors. Both submitted *vota* to the Holy Office on the French original of Klein's fourth volume. Copies of these *vota* are in the Americanism file in the Archives of the Catholic University of America.

9. In the opening paragraph of his review, Gillis wrote: "The storm of 'Americanism' ought never to have happened. It was artificially produced. Its sound and fury signified nothing. There was no heresy and no schism." "Americanism: Fifty Years After," *Catholic World* 169 (July 1949): 246. John Tracy Ellis cited these words with approval in his review of McAvoy's book. See *Theological Studies* 19 (June 1958):

243. Ellis felt that the bishops would have eventually worked out their differences among themselves, and that "the sometimes careless expressions in the writings and speeches of men like Hecker, Keane and Ireland were not heresy in the theological sense." *American Catholicism* (Chicago: University of Chicago Press, 1956), p. 119. See also Ellis' *The Life of James Cardinal Gibbons, Archbishop of Baltimore,* 2 vols. (Milwaukee: Bruce Publishing Co., 1952), II, p. 2.

10. McAvoy, op cit., p. 349.

11. Ibid., pp. 354, 357. McAvoy described the unity among the various groups who made up the Catholic minority as a "theological" one. By the term *theological* he appears to have meant "those principles of faith and morals which constitute the religious basis of Catholicism" or "essential dogmatic and sacramental principles." Ibid., pp. 7, 16, 45.

12. In this connection, the work of John Tracy Ellis is of major importance. His own scholarship as well as the doctoral work he directed on almost every aspect of the controversies in the American church provides the student of Americanism with invaluable historical source material. One suspects that McAvoy, Ellis, and the church historians they trained had a much more sophisticated understanding of the Church as an historical reality than the dogmatic theologians who were their contemporaries. The theological relevance of this understanding remained of necessity concealed beneath their frequent disclaimers to theological expertise.

13. Vincent Holden, C.S.P., "A Myth in 'l'Américanisme,'" *Catholic Historical Review* 31 (1945): 154–70.

14. The publication of Klein's *Vie* generated a sizable body of newspaper and periodical literature. Clearly the most influential piece of anti-Americanist writing was Charles Maignen, *Études sur l'Américanisme. Le Père Hecker, est-il un saint?* (Rome: Desclee, 1898), translated anonymously as *Father Hecker, Is He a Saint?* (London: Burns & Oates, 1898).

15. Holden's "A Myth in 'l'Américanisme'" evidences a thorough familiarity with Maignen's accusations. Referring to the latter's book, Holden wrote, "There is no point in discussing this volume. It is known and acknowledged to be inaccurate, biased, vitriolic, libelous and venomous," p. 158. He then went on to refute four of Maignen's more overt distortions of Hecker's thought.

16. See Holden, "Father Hecker's Vision Vindicated," *Historical Records and Studies,* 50 (1964): 40–52 and, in a more popular vein, idem, "An American Ahead of His Time," *Ave Maria* 97 (June 8, 1963): 5–8.

17. An example of this shift is seen in the assessment of American-

ism by the popular historian, E.E.Y. Hales. In a 1964 review of the paperback edition of McAvoy's book, Hales described Americanism as "a generous attempt to wed the American Church with the American way of life." "1870 was too early for the Americans," Hales lamented, "1963 was too late, their flowering had been nipped in the bud." "The Americanist Controversy," *The Month* 31 (1964): 43. The tone of this review is in marked contrast to Hales's presentation of Americanism six years earlier. See *The Catholic Church in the Modern World* (New York: Hanover House, 1958), p. 175. In 1971 Hennesey suggested that it would be more advantageous "if we see in 'Americanism' not a phantom heresy to be glossed over, but the inchoate groping of Catholics formed in a tradition both indigenous and derivative, of which, like it or not, we are the continuers." J. Hennesey, "American History and the Theological Enterprise," *CTSA Proceedings* 26 (1971): 113.

18. Robert D. Cross, *The Emergence of Liberal Catholicism* (Cambridge: Harvard University Press, 1958). See p. 21 for a statement of the thesis.

19. Thomas E. Wangler, "The Ecclesiology of Archbishop John Ireland: Its Nature, Development and Influence" (Milwaukee: Ph.D. dissertation, Marquette University, 1968).

20. Hennesey, "American History and the Theological Enterprise," pp. 98–99.

21. Margaret M. Reher, "The Church and the Kingdom of God in America: The Ecclesiology of the Americanists" (New York: Ph.D. dissertation, Fordham University, 1972), pp. 192–206 and M. Reher, "Pope Leo XIII and 'Americanism'," *Theological Studies* 34 (1973): 686. Chapter III of this dissertation contains one of the most exhaustive available analyses of *Testem Benevolentiae*.

22. T. Wangler, "Emergence of John J. Keane as Liberal Catholic and Americanist (1878–1887)," *American Ecclesiastical Review* 166 (1972): 457–58.

23. R. Emmett Curran, S.J., *Michael Augustine Corrigan and the Shaping of Conservative Catholicism in America, 1878–1902* (New York: Arno Press, 1978), pp. 316, 505.

24. A notable exception is David P. Killen, "Americanism Revisited: John Spalding and *Testem Benevolentiae*," *Harvard Theological Review* 66 (Oct. 1973): 413–54. Killen argues for the revisionist conclusion that John Lancaster Spalding was a "theological Americanist."

25. In his reflections on the notion of an "American theology," Michael de Certeau gives eloquent expression to this difficulty. See "Culture Américaine et théologie Catholique," *Études* 335 (Nov. 1971): 561–77.

26. For the best available treatment of the Roman background to the Americanism episode, see Gerald P. Fogarty, S.J., *The Vatican and the Americanist Crisis: Denis J. O'Connell, American Agent in Rome, 1885–1903 (Miscellanea Historiae Pontificae,* Vol. 36) (Rome: Gregorian University Press, 1974). [See also Fogarty's *The Vatican and the American Hierarchy From 1870 to 1965.* Vol. 21 of "Päpste und Papsttum" (Stuttgart: Anton Hiersemann, 1982). See also Robert C. Ayers, "The Americanists and Franz Xaver Kraus: An Historical Analysis of an International Liberal Catholic Combination, 1897–1898" (Syracuse: Ph.D. dissertation, Syracuse University, 1981).–Ed.]

27. Count Charles de Montalembert to Hecker, April 13, 1864, PFA.

28. Maignen, *Father Hecker, Is He a Saint?,* pp. 99–102.

29. See themes 1 and 10 of the "Hartford Appeal" in Peter L. Berger and Richard J. Neuhaus, eds., *Against the World for the World, The Hartford Appeal and the Future of American Religion* (New York: Seabury Press, 1976), pp. 1, 4.

30. *Acta Sanctae Sedis* 31 (1898–9): 473. For an English translation, see McAvoy, op. cit., pp. 382–3.

31. On the authors of *Testem Benevolentiae* and their association with the neo-scholastic revival of Pope Leo XIII, see William L. Portier, "Providential Nation: An Historical-Theological Study of Isaac Hecker's Americanism" (Toronto: Ph.D. dissertation, University of St. Michael's College, 1980), pp. 637–38.

32. This is the thesis of the study mentioned in note 31 above.

33. For a discussion of this tension, see Gerald McCool, S.J., *Catholic Theology in the Nineteenth Century* (New York: Seabury Press, 1977).

34. ITH, *Questions of the Soul,* a reprint of the 1855 edition with an introduction by Joseph F. Gower (New York; Arno Press, 1978), pp. 292–93.

35. These articles first appeared in Italian translation in *La Civiltà Cattolica,* 3rd Series 8 (Nov. 6, 19, 1857): 385–402, 513–29. The English version appeared in the New York *Freeman's Journal,* December 12, 19, 26, 1857 and January 2, 1858.

36. ITH, "The Saint of Our Day," in *Paulist Sermons, 1863* (New York: D. & J. Sadlier, 1864), pp. 90–112.

37. During the early 1860s, ITH had spoken of a book on the sanctification of secular life, variously titled "The Sanctification of Daily Life" or "Common Ways to a Perfect Life." The promised work never materialized. For a brief analysis of both the positive and negative aspects of Hecker's affirmation of American civilization during the

1860's, see Portier, "Isaac Hecker and Americanism," *Ecumenist* 19 (Nov.–Dec. 1980): 9–12.

38. For the text, see *Sermons Delivered During the Second Plenary Council of Baltimore* (Baltimore: Kelly & Piet, 1866), pp. 66–68.

39. For the text, see *Revue Générale* 6 (Oct. 1867, II), pp. 348–58. This is a French translation of ITH's original English text which has apparently been lost. At the actual congress, a summary of the address was read by a native French-speaker.

40. Elliott entitled Chapter XXXII of his *The Life of Father Hecker* (New York: Columbus Press, 1891) "The Long Illness."

41. The *Exposition* appears as the first chapter of ITH's *The Church and the Age* (New York: H. J. Hewit, 1887). First published in pamphlet form at London in 1875, it was subsequently translated into German, French, and Italian. In the United States the English version appeared in the *Catholic World* 11 (April 1875): 117–38.

42. For a discussion of ITH's opinions on the effects of the Fall, see Portier, "Providential Nation," pp. 395–402.

43. For the seminal expression of this approach, see Jaime L. Balmes, *Protestantism and Catholicity Compared in Their Effects on the Civilization of Europe,* trans. from the French by C. J. Hanford and R. Kershaw (Baltimore: J. Murphy, 1851). ITH read and cited from Balmes. Another work in the same vein which had significant impact on ITH was Charles de Montalembert, *The Monks of the West,* trans. anonymously (London: William Blackwell & Sons, 1861).

44. ITH, "The Outlook in Italy," *Catholic World* 21 (October 1877): 14.

45. Ibid., p. 6 and *Church and Age,* p. 123; cf. *Lumen Gentium,* paragraphs 14–16 in Walter M. Abbott, S.J., ed., *The Documents of Vatican II* (New York: Guild Press, 1966), pp. 32–35. In speaking of Hecker as a "moderate traditionalist," it is well to recall that he resolved his early epistemological difficulties by a plunge into the traditionalism of Brownson's doctrine of life by communion. According to the neo-scholastic critique of modern thought, its weaknesses lay precisely in the areas of Hecker's early difficulties. This fact was not lost on Maignen. These areas had to do with epistemology and the establishment of first principles. Strict traditionalists had to introduce revelation in order to account for human knowledge. ITH was not a strict traditionalist. He affirmed the possibility of knowing God as creator through creation by the light of reason. As a moderate traditionalist he emphasized the insatiable character of human longings and proposed degrees of union with the divine. For a general discussion of traditional-

ism in nineteenth-century Catholic theology, see G. McCool, op. cit., Chapter 2.

46. See ITH, "The Political Crisis in France and Its Bearings," *Catholic World* 25 (August 1877): 577–90; idem, "The Outlook in Italy," *Catholic World* 27 (October 1877): 1–21; idem, "The Catholic Church in the United States: Its Rise, Relations with the Republic, Growth and Future Prospects," *Catholic World* 29 (July 1879): 432–56. These essays eventually found their way into *The Church and the Age* but in significantly abridged form.

47. In the matter of the controversy over women's ordination, for example, the question of whether this issue represents a matter of doctrine or a matter of discipline will remain until the issue ceases to be controversial.

48. *Acta Sanctae Sedis* 31 (1898–99): 472. For an English translation, see McAvoy, op cit., p. 382.

49. See Joseph Clifford Fenton, "The Teaching of the *Testem Benevolentiae*," *American Ecclesiastical Review* 129 (August 1953): 132. Fenton, an implacable conservative who regarded John Courtney Murray as a latter-day Americanist, nevertheless insisted that it would be inaccurate to designate any of the opinions reproved in the letter "heresy." In this citation he treats the particular opinion under discussion here.

50. "Libertatem quamdam in Ecclesiam esse inducendam, ut, constricta quodammodo potestatis vi ac vigilantia, liceat fidelibus suo cuiusque ingenio actuosaeque virtuti largius aliquanto indulgere." The next sentence clarifies the nature of the "liberty" under discussion: "Hoc nimirum requiri affirmant ad libertatis eius exemplum, quae, recentius invecta, civilis fere communitatis ius modo ac fundamentum est." *Acta Sanctae Sedis* 31 (1898–99): 473. For the English, see McAvoy, op cit., pp. 282–83.

51. M. Reher, "Leo XIII and 'Americanism'," pp. 686–87.

52. For a clear statement of this, see ITH, "The Mission of Leo XIII," *Catholic World* 48 (October 1888): 4–5.

53. "Aiunt enim, de Romani Pontificis infallibili magisterio, post solemne iudicium de ipso latum in Vaticana Synodo, nihil iam oportere esse sollicitos; quam ob rem, eo iam in tuto collocate, posse nunc ampliorem cuivis ad cogitandum atque agendum patere campum." *Acta Sanctae Sedis* 31 (1898–99): 473; McAvoy, op. cit., p. 383. For Hecker's text, see *Church and Age,* p. 29.

54. "Ampliora, aiunt, atque uberiora nunc quam elapsis temporibus, in animos fidelium Spiritus Sanctus influit charismata, eosque,

medio nemine, docet arcano quodam instinctu atque agit." *Acta Sanctae Sedis* 31 (1898–9): 474. For the English, see McAvoy, op. cit., p. 384.

55. See, for example, *Church and Age,* pp. 26, 28, 31, 32, 39.

56. Estevao Bettencourt, "Charism," *Sacramentum Mundi* (Montreal: Palm Publishers, 1968), Vol. I, p. 283.

57. *Acta Sanctae Sedis* 29 (1896–7): 648, 654.

58. "It might be possible to argue *a priori* that a lessening of charisms was to be expected in modern times, from some words of the encyclical of Leo XIII against Americanism." Joseph H. Crehan, S.J., "Charism," *A Catholic Dictionary of Theology* (London: Thomas Nelson, Ltd., 1967), Vol. II, p. 22.

59. Manning to ITH, February 1, 1875, PFA.

60. ITH to Augustine Hewit, February 13, 1875, PFA.

61. J. Hennesey, "Leo XIII's Thomistic Revival: A Political and Philosophical Event," *Journal of Religion* 58 (Supplement 1978): S186.

62. G. McCool, op. cit., p. 10.

63. Among others, Avery Dulles has written eloquently on this question. See, for example, his *A Church to Believe In, Discipleship and the Dynamics of Freedom* (New York: Crossroad, 1982), Chapter 8.

Isaac Hecker's Political Thought

by Edward J. Langlois, C.S.P.

INTRODUCTION

> This truth, then, if we mistake not, has been clearly shown;
> that every religious dogma has a special bearing on political
> society, and this bearing is what constitutes its political
> principle; and every political principle has a religious bear-
> ing, and this bearing involves a religious dogma which is its
> premise.[1]

These words of Isaac Hecker, taken from *The Church and
the Age,* published in 1887 shortly before his death, summarize a
lifelong attempt to understand the relationship between politics
and religion. Hecker had long insisted that there could be no
separation between the two, and that the mix necessitated a
political theology. This is the apology for an essay on Hecker's
political thought.[2] Without an analysis of his political thought, its
origin in American political language and values and their shaping by his early political involvement and search for truth,
Hecker studies remain incomplete. Not only would Hecker studies remain incomplete, so would the general study of American
politics and the Catholic input in particular.

The importance of Isaac Hecker in American political
thought is that he was the main source of the apologetical bridge
between Catholicism and American nationalism. Until Hecker's
attempt at providing an American Catholic political theory,
Catholics saw America as a Protestant-inspired and ruled country alien to the church. Its separation of Church and State
seemed to relegate the authority of Christianity to a minor role in
politics, while simultaneously emphasizing the importance of
Protestant theology and denominationalism to American liberty.

Hecker and his mentor, Orestes Brownson, reassured Catholics about the legitimacy of their citizenship and helped them not only accept the basic goodness of American government, but encouraged them to demand assertively their rightful place in liberal democratic politics. They insisted that it was Catholicism, not Protestantism, that was the real basis of American government and history.

While American Catholic studies link Hecker and Brownson in the formulation of this assertive Catholic optimism toward America, Hecker must take precedence over Brownson in the formation of American Catholic political thought. Although they shared a similar formative experience in radical Jacksonian politics and a similar vision of the mix between politics and religion both before and after their conversion to Catholicism, Brownson grew pessimistic and bitter about American democracy after the Civil War. He questioned whether a democratic society could provide the necessary foundation for Catholicism, and hinted that the Catholic church in America should formulate a criticism of American institutions.[3] It was Hecker, not Brownson, who insisted consistently on the positive relationship between Catholicism and Americanism. It is to Hecker, not Brownson, that the credit must go in formulating the first optimistic Catholic political theory of liberal democracy. The word "liberal" has two meanings in this essay. Primarily it refers to the current of political philosophy beginning with John Locke that sought to narrow the scope of government by legitimizing the invisible hand of laissez-faire capitalism. Rejecting the classical search for the naturally best polity, it rested on the artifice of state of nature and not natural right. Politics was not natural to human beings, but a barely-tolerated artificial prop necessary to protect what was really important—the competitive individualism necessary for economic relationships. Both this English stream of liberalism and its continental expression, a militantly anti-clerical republican nationalism, criticized religious interference in economics and politics. In turn, Catholicism was suspicious of liberalism, and Pius IX condemned it specifically in the *Syllabus of Errors* in 1864.

It was Hecker's optimism about the possibility of reconciling liberalism and Catholicism that influenced the next generation of

Catholic leaders such as Cardinal Gibbons, Archbishop Ireland, and Bishop Keane. He thereby helped form the American tradition of social liberalism, a term used by Catholic commentators to indicate a movement (eventually successful) within American Catholicism that was optimistic about American politics, encouraged Catholic political participation, and supported public welfare legislation. Thus Hecker stands at the beginning of a line of Catholic liberals that will extend through Msgr. John A. Ryan and Msgr. John J. Burke at the beginning of the twentieth century to the Rev. John Courtney Murray, Msgr. George Higgins, and the liberalism of the American Catholic church at midcentury and beyond.[4]

Hecker's political task was to reconcile the Roman church to America, proving to Catholics that their country was not Protestant at its ideological roots, and to Protestants that Catholics were not inherently anti-democratic. Hecker's political theory was forged in the radical Jacksonian politics of his youth. His political language was based on the once pervasive belief that America was the Redeemer Nation ushering in the Kingdom of God on earth. This belief was called millennialism, and its tenets shaped Hecker's political theory as it did the ideas of his contemporaries.[5] Hecker's conversion to Roman Catholicism strengthened his belief that God had chosen America for a special task in salvation history.

Hecker's political theory argued that Catholic natural law in the Thomistic tradition and American natural rights in the Lockean tradition were linked. Locke and the English liberal tradition had rejected Thomistic theory arguing that politics could not be understood by natural laws. Politics was artificial, not natural, and the less politics the better. The important thing for humans was economic relationships and the right to pursue these relationships with as little government interference as possible. Therefore the English liberal tradition posited a set of natural rights that were pre-political, existing in a "state of nature" prior to politics and which could not be jeopardized by political action. Hecker rejected this state of nature argument, reverting back to a natural law view that politics was a good and natural part of life and part of God's plan for the world. Grace built on natural laws; religion influenced politics; and therefore the Church was the school for political virtue. This institutional authority for liberal democracy was antithetical to the English liberal tradition.

Hecker set out to prove that Protestantism could never support liberal democracy. It was fundamentally un-democratic because of its stress on predestination, the inherent degradation of nature, and the corruption of humanity, and its minimizing of reason and free will. Hecker formulated an optimistic Catholic view of liberal democracy by showing how Catholic belief in works as well as grace, the inherent goodness of nature and humanity, its respect for reason and free will and the ability of reason to discern the natural law all would buttress the American constitution. Only Catholicism could fulfill America's God-given role as Redeemer Nation. Protestant denominationalism exacerbated America's political divisions. Its theology inhibited the flowering of its natural virtues. Catholicism would encourage political unity, providing natural community bonds and training in civic virtue so necessary for a republic.

While Hecker succeeded in incorporating American Catholics into the mainstream of American politics and debunking Protestant prejudice, the radical potential of Hecker's political theory—the outpouring of the Holy Spirit over a Catholic America—did not materialize. America did not convert. Instead, with the unwitting help of Hecker's theory, American Catholics became subservient to civil religion. Because Catholics learned so well an optimistic view of the links between their faith and their flag, their faith lost any potential for dissent until the post-Vatican II period. Hecker's combining of Catholicism and Americanism led to an acceptance of interest group liberalism. Political scientist Theodore J. Lowi describes interest group liberalism as the American public philosophy that emerged from the wreck of laissez-faire capitalism toward the end of the nineteenth century.[6] It amalgamated capitalism with the positive use of government power in public policy and recognized the increasingly pluralistic nature of American society. This pluralism manifested itself in a plethora of groups that organized various areas of American life from business associations to labor unions to church groups. Almost every interest organized itself and sought to influence public policy. Historian Aaron Abell has documented the meteoric growth of Catholic organizations at the beginning of the twentieth century, culminating in the formation of an umbrella organization, the National Catholic Welfare Conference, in the 1920s.[7]

Hecker's dream of a unitary Catholic society failed. America did not convert in mass. Pluralism was the reality of the American future. Once conversion failed, the potential for change in Hecker's political theory was lost. The Roman Catholic church could not become the national community-builder, translator of political values, and school for justice and republican virtue that he hoped for. Increasingly, Catholic demands were for equal rights for its interest within a pluralistic society. This failure of Hecker's politics should not minimize its importance to American Catholic studies. His advocacy of Catholic political involvement, his support for liberal democracy, his emphasis on the indwelling of the Holy Spirit and its implications for political initiative, his desire for more democratic church structures and the need for differing cultural expressions of Catholicism, helped prepare the church for Vatican II.

This essay's method places Isaac Hecker's ideas about religion and politics in the framework of general American political theory. In order to understand properly the American Catholic experience, studies of American Catholicism must link specific Catholic themes with the general themes of American politics and history. This essay is a work in political theory. It is not concerned primarily with the details of historical context, although these details have some bearing in providing settings and connections. Its primary focus is with ideas and arguments—symbols and language—that give rise to a theory about politics. Specifically, it studies the way Isaac Hecker translated American symbols into Catholic language (and vice versa) through his books, articles, sermons, letters, diaries, and editorial policy. This essay works under the premise that political language, how people interpret political symbols, how they articulate that interpretation into words and actions, can explain the stuff of politics. The political theorist cannot speak an esoteric language. As a member of a specific political community, the theorist must use the commonly used symbols that judge value and authority. Hecker is a legitimate and powerful American political theorist

because he knew how to use the important symbols of American
political language—Christianity and democracy. Hecker was able
to describe the connections, and we know more about America
by an analysis of the language of a nineteenth-century American
Catholic priest.

HECKER'S POLITICAL FORMATION

Isaac Hecker received his political formation through his
activity in the Locofoco Party, his friendship with Orestes
Brownson, and his association with the Brook Farm Transcendentalists. This formation occurred in the second quarter of the
nineteenth century, that period of American history known as
the Age of Jackson.[8] It was a time of intense political activity and
social reform where democratic impulses and evangelical revivals
mixed with utopian socialism and Shaker communes—a time
that Alice Felt Tyler has aptly called *Freedom's Ferment*. Americans were marching in a great crusade to reform everything from
drinking habits to slavery.[9] It was also a time of unabashed
demands for pure laissez-faire capitalism, where anti-monopoly
cries for equal rights for the little man masked cut-throat competition and eager entrepreneurship. It was also the height of anti-
Catholic bigotry.[10]

Hecker's German artisan background was perfect soil for
radical Jacksonian politics. One estimate maintains that German
immigrants supported the Jacksonian Democracy by eighty per-
cent.[11] Although the Heckers were successful bakers and were
moving during this period from the status of skilled workers to
business entrepreneurs, they never forgot the plight of workers.
Perhaps their father's failure as an independent tradesman enabled them to empathize with the less fortunate. The Heckers
saw political answers in the reform movement within Tammany
Hall, New York City's version of the Jacksonian Democratic
Party, known as the "Workingman's Movement." The particular
group that the Heckers joined became known as the Locofoco
Party because of their use of "Locofoco" matches to light up one
of their meetings.

It was here that Isaac received his political formation. He
learned to think politically as a radical Jacksonian, and these

political ideas remained with him for the rest of his life.[12] The fundamental idea of the Locofocos was that government should protect the equal rights of all citizens in person and in property guaranteed by the Declaration of Independence and the Bill of Rights. Special rights granted to the few, especially the growing monopolies, abridged the right of equal opportunity for all. The Locofocos were angry at any favoritism shown by government to "aristocratic elements."[13] They wanted a return to a primitive Jeffersonianism with absolutely equal rights to life, liberty, and property, with as little government involvement as possible.

The Locofoco dissent was steeped in evangelical terms, for along with the egalitarian tendency in politics, the Age of Jackson witnessed a concomitant desire for religious levelling. The Locofocos combined their laissez-faire liberalism with a belief that America was the Redeemer Nation, and they were God's saints chosen to establish His Kingdom on earth. Religion was not only a matter of personal renewal, but political renewal as well.

The Locofoco party began to disintegrate in 1837 over the issue of whether to return to Tammany Hall and regular Democratic party politics. Modern observers would agree that while the party was small, its influence was considerable.[14] It did succeed in democratizing to some extent the Tammany machine and had its influence on the national party as well. There is no doubt that the Locofocos were a radical party. They severely challenged the emerging industrial class structure in America and the type of economy that fostered it. This was not the radicalism of the later Marxists. It was, in Louis Hartz's terms, "petit-bourgeois" dissent—the dissent of small businessmen, tradesmen, and artisans against bigness at all levels. It was radical because it sought to go back to the laissez-faire roots of American society and claim its legitimacy over the growth of monopoly capital. It did not challenge Locke and the foundations of English liberalism, but claimed Locofocoism as its true heir. There was no chance that later Marxists like Daniel DeLeon or Gene Debs could capture this dissent, for it was a dissent that looks backward to a radical libertarian agrarian republic and not forward to the realities of the emerging entrepreneurial, industrial republic. Hecker's Locofoco dissent in the 1830s, as his Catholic dissent would be in the 1880s, was based on a religious impulse and a conservative return to America's mythical roots in the vigorous yeoman republic of Jefferson. Hecker might have been a Jacksonian radical, he certainly was not a Marxist.

Not able to translate dissent into political activity, the American radical became discouraged. The Lockean laissez-faire pragmatism was too entrenched. The religious vision of America as Redeemer Nation was too amorphous to provide concrete political alternatives. The radical's political energy was channeled elsewhere. In 1858, shortly before founding the Paulists, Hecker mirrored this disenchantment with practical politics.[15] He told his superiors that after several years of political activity he discovered that the "evils of society were not so much political as social, and that not much was to be hoped from political action." His experience showed him that "politicians were governed more by selfishness and a thirst for power than by patriotism and the desire of doing good to their fellow citizens."

The path from Locofoco Democrat to Roman Catholic priest led Isaac Hecker from New York Jacksonian party politics through Brook Farm utopian socialism. The guide along the path was Orestes Brownson. Brownson in his own right was one of the giants of American philosophy and one of the leading Catholic apologists of the nineteenth century. Hecker probably heard Brownson lecture in New York City in the late 1830s, but met him for the first time in 1841, when Brownson was lecturing in New York on "The Democracy of Christ" and "The Reform Spirit of Our Age." Brownson changed Hecker's life. He introduced the young man into a new world of philosophical and religious ideas. Primary among these was the idea that there could be no separation between politics and religion. Brownson himself had travelled a long way from Calvinism to Unitarianism, and, at the time he met Hecker, he had formed his own church in Boston for working people. His belief in the close link between American politics and the religious view that America was Redeemer Nation was not phrased in the traditional evangelical language of American Protestantism, but in the rational, humanistic categories of New England Unitarianism. This is evidence that millennialist ideas spread across the entire spectrum of American religion. Brownson combined this religious view of America with a scathing indictment of emerging industrial society and its concomitant treatment of workers.[16] He called for a type of Christianity that would make the Kingdom of God real, here and now.

The Hecker brothers were very sympathetic to Brownson's views. Reflecting back on this period in 1887, Isaac claimed that he and his friends had a "profound appreciation and sympathy" for Brownson personally. They were excited about his presentation of the compatibility between Christianity and democracy. "Christ was a social Democrat, Dr. Brownson maintained, and he and many of us had no other religion but the social theories we drew from Christ's life and teaching. . . ."[17] The Heckers were so enthused that they invited Brownson to give a Fourth of July oration in New York City, and, at their request, he returned to give another series of lectures in 1842. During his visits Brownson lived with the Heckers and had many long discussions with young Isaac over the failure of the "Workingman's Movement."

Discouraged at the failure of the "Locofoco party," Isaac began to look less to the electoral process than to what he called "social" reform. In 1858, he reflected that upon his perception of the failure of party politics to solve problems, he began to analyze the "social" evils of the day. This analysis led him deeper into religious questions. "The many miseries and the great wretchedness which exists in modern society sprang, in my opinion, from the want of the practical application of the moral principles of Christianity to the social relations between men."[18]

Upon Brownson's advice, Isaac sought to further his ideas on social reform and deepen his spiritual journey by living at Brook Farm. His entry there in April, 1843, thrust him into the center of Transcendentalism, the radical branch of New England Unitarianism. Brook Farm was a "Transcendentalist missionary and educational enterprise".[19] Isaac was popular at the Farm, and he met such luminaries as Ralph Waldo Emerson, Nathaniel Hawthorne, Henry David Thoreau, Theodore Parker, Margaret Fuller, Robert Owen, William Ellery Channing, and Horace Greeley. Charles Dana, later managing editor of the *New York Tribune,* Assistant Secretary of War, and editor of the *New York Sun,* was Isaac's roommate. Hecker became the community baker, and his simple, straightforward (if not somewhat naive) search for "Truth" endeared him to all. George Curtis, later a journalist for *Harper's Weekly,* nicknamed him "Ernest the Seeker" after Channing's essay of the same name.

Hecker quickly became disenchanted with Brook Farm. True, the ethereal atmosphere widened his intellectual horizons as he attended the many lectures on European philosophy, but he did not see the experiment in community life as providing a suitable paradigm for "social" change. The Brook Farmers' quest for natural, spontaneous bonding in small communes did not suffice. Increasingly, Hecker saw the need for institutional religion. The utopian voluntarism of the Farm would not provide the authority needed for change. Hecker could not decide which church was closest to the one that Christ intended, but he saw the lack of "Church" (not churches) as the great deficiency in America.[20]

For all his personal asceticism and mystical contemplation, for all his rejection of electoral solutions, Isaac's interest in "Church" did not mean that he rejected an interest in practical affairs. He was determined not to be an "arm-chair" theorist, but an activist in helping establish God's Kingdom on earth. The Locofoco rhetoric and Brownson's discussions had not been lost on the young man. Writing in his Brook Farm diary, he stated that he must feel as if he were "acting out the will of God, hence establishing the kingdom of God upon earth." Personal religion was not enough, mere "church-going" was fruitless. Real religion involved action in the present world. "The earth is to be His kingdom and your prayers must be deeds and your actions must be music ascending to heaven...." In a phrase that would summarize his life work as a priest, he stated that "God must be planted."[21] The utopian communities were not fertile ground for this planting, but impractical schemes for social betterment. While the Transcendentalists were sincere, they were not grasping the reality of which they talked. They were not able to translate their ideas into action. In a biting criticism, Hecker wrote in his journal that the Transcendentalist "would have written a critical essay on the power of the soul at the foot of the cross."[22] The only real translator of ideas into action was the "Church."

As Isaac Hecker drew closer to the Roman Catholic church,

he did not reject his political formation in the Locofoco Party, the ideas of Brownson, nor the search for community of Brook Farm. His political ideals continued to be the Equal Rights Democracy of Jackson and the natural community of Brook Farm. He had fought for the rights of the little man, opposing all big interests and monopolies. He had advocated the extension of democratic principles into economics through the free market of laissez-faire capitalism. He sought the natural bonds of community that would bring people together in peace and justice. He perceived the social effects of Christianity. That Hecker was true to these ideas for the rest of his life is an example of the power of Jacksonian political schooling. Hecker was able to reflect in 1887 that his political ideals in 1837 were just as valid as ever.

Hecker's political formation shows that Jacksonian political symbols were not only political in the narrow sense, but religious as well. Characteristic of the spirit of American millennialism, Hecker's political education taught him that America was the Chosen Nation, the Redeemer Nation, where God was ushering in the promises of the New Jerusalem. Hecker and his contemporaries took these promises literally. The Kingdom of God on earth would be made real through the political effort of Americans like himself. The organizing ability of this religio-political language was so powerful that even after his conversion to Catholicism (a religion thought to escape millennialist influence because of its hierarchical institutionalism) he continued to use millennialist themes.[23] Hecker is an example of how millennialism went far beyond the usual American Protestant evangelical channels to embrace religions much more heavily liturgical and institutional.

Hecker's experience shows that at the same time that these symbols were powerful rhetorically, they were difficult to translate into political reality. The translation of political symbols into a political language capable of engendering political action is one of the essential functions of the political theorist. It is a difficult task for an American because of the very amorphous religious character of American political symbols. Hecker felt this difficulty. He recognized that liberal democratic political activity by itself did not satisfy the human quest for truth and justice. The ideals of Equal Rights Democracy could not be made real by political methods alone. The extension of the franchise, the removal of monopoly privilege, attacks on the national bank would do only so much. Corruption and compromise—sin—were too prevalent. Contemporary studies support the reality of Hecker's disenchantment with Jacksonian politics. The high-blown rhetoric of the "Democracy" often masked a frenetic scramble for economic advantage. Equal Rights Democracy too often meant the right to get rich at any cost.

Hecker was frustrated with an American political language that said one thing and meant another, that spoke to a mythical return to Jeffersonian roots, but was blindly groping for a way into the industrial future. Yet he was not disenchanted with politics in general, for he insisted that his conversion to Roman Catholicism was the fulfillment of his reform zeal and not its negation. It was a heady time for a young political theorist when the symbolic language in use was out of joint. Hecker was struggling to make sense out of a world he desperately wanted to reform. He found that sense in the Roman Catholic church and not in New England Transcendentalism. Hecker's criticism of the Transcendentalists as arm-chair theorists spoke directly to the poverty of the American political theory he felt was incapable of true analysis. Even those Americans most committed to the quest for truth were incapable of action. Instead of acting, they were always looking for new facts. They excited nothing but curiosity. He felt that it was his responsibility to formulate a new political theory that would build on the past but be equal to the future, one that would be capable of praxis.

Hecker sketched his frustration with the current social and political reform ideas in his diary of October 17, 1843.[24] He drew a triangle with the words "personal," "political," and "social reform" on the three legs, and "religion," "church," and "unity" in the middle. This was the beginning of his new formulation, for it was his expressive attempt to organize the various facets of human experience into some sort of understandable paradigm. At this early stage the connections were not precise, but Hecker had discovered both the problem and the cure. He had cut through to the essential difficulty in American politics, one that Alexis de Tocqueville in *Democracy in America* had made so familiar: American life was separated and fragmented.[25] The connections between individuals were weak. The task was to formulate a political theory that would bring these isolated individuals together while at the same time preserving liberty. This was an important task, for the problem of unity, as Tocqueville recognized, might be solved in America by the tyranny of public opinion, a leveling equality so destructive of liberty that Americans might not even sense their slavery.

Hecker's triangular diagram indicates that his search for personal truth, social reform, and community had come to rest in the "Church." Conversion was the cure. Again, like Tocqueville, Hecker discovered in America that the Roman church far from being the enemy of democracy was really one of its foremost supporters. Hecker would develop his political theory in an attempt to make graphic the relationship between religion and liberal democracy, specifically, to show how the Roman Catholic church was the real guardian of American freedom. The church provided the unity and moral direction that liberal democracy lacked. As in the triangular diagram, it was the center of personal, social, and political reform. It provided community, a connection among individuals that fostered mutual respect, trust, and responsibility. It nourished liberty, not tyranny. The deciding point in Hecker's conversion had been the idea of community—the Community of Saints, a traditional Catholic dogma.[26] This community was so powerful, so binding, so real, that it transcended human time and space. It preserved the uniqueness of each individual's spiritual journey, but linked that spiritual journey to temporal realities as well.

Isaac Hecker never rejected politics by entering the church. His political formation had served him well. He would remain throughout his life a political man. What he did reject was a type of politics that later political theory would call alienating, one that separated people from each other, from nature, from their work, from the very act of political decision-making that allowed them to forge their futures. Hecker's political theoretical task as he entered the Roman church would be to find a way to destroy this alienation, fulfill the American dream, and facilitate the coming of God's Kingdom on earth.

PRIEST AND POLITICAL THEORIST

Shortly after his conversion to Rome in 1844, Isaac Hecker decided to become a priest. He studied in Europe, was ordained in 1849, and returned to the United States in 1851. By becoming a priest, he did not abandon his earlier interest in formulating a political theory combining his belief in Roman Catholicism and his analysis of the social problems in America. Instead, he saw his conversion and priestly vocation as the fulfillment of his earlier reform zeal and the basis of his future analysis of America. Publishing two books in the 1850s to further his theories, Hecker insisted that religion was essential to politics—it was prior to and inclusive of it.[27] Politics, in turn, was an integral part of any Christian vocation. Hecker's political theory would be an attempt to show how his own journey to the Roman church fulfilled his Jacksonian aspirations and the community dreams of the Brook Farmers. He would provide an example for other Americans to follow. His primary audience was the Transcendentalists and like-minded intellects. He believed that they were symbolic of many others who were in the same struggle he was during his own search. He hoped that a recounting of his salvation history would be instructive for them. His salvation history was also a political history, an account of how religious and political salvation go together. A natural searcher, Hecker assumed that all other Americans were searching too. Perhaps this was naïve in an America whose liberal tradition minimized the political philosophical search for the ideal polity and maximized practical entrepreneurial activity.

Hecker was confident that he would be heard, and once heard, accepted because of the logical power and natural truth of his argument. The first task both of the missionary and the political theorist was to catch the listener at crisis points in life. So Hecker's first book, *Questions of the Soul,* spoke to the common human problems of life, and the natural longings for unity and truth. It quoted from secular poetry and novels. Hecker hoped that if he could catch his audience's attention in this first book, he could then lead them naturally to conversion through his second book, *Aspirations of Nature.* The first book spoke to the heart, the second to the mind. He realized that political theory must combine both mind and heart, fitting the American experience of pragmatism with Christian ideals.

Religion was the key to the mind and the heart.[28] It was the key that other nineteenth-century theorists such as Comte, Weber, and Durkheim also recognized. Hecker's advantage was that religion's importance in the political sphere was an accepted truth in American life. The separation of Church and State in the American mind never meant a rejection of Christianity as the necessary moral foundation of American government. Hecker built his theory on an accepted American idea. Moreover, as a Catholic he had another advantage, for the Catholic tradition prided itself on being able to combine reason and faith, mind and heart, religion and politics. Hecker looked at America with Thomistic eyes. Secure in the Catholic natural law tradition, he used that strength to criticize the weaknesses in the American liberal democratic tradition of natural rights without seeming to denigrate it. He linked American natural rights with Catholic natural law theory.

Hecker's link between natural law and natural rights is unique in American political theory, for he was able to perceive one of the fundamental problems in the English liberal tradition—its lack of institutionalized authority to protect and foster individual rights and liberties. The English liberal tradition rejected church and king, classical philosophy and "noblesse oblige." It would trust no political power with the authority to form liberal consciences and mold justice. The placing of individual rights in a pre-political state of nature was fundamentally different from the concept of nature in classical political philosophy and in the natural law tradition. In these, politics itself was a natural part of life. Individual rights were part of the political process. They were based on what was naturally right about life, a complementary system of rights and duties that could be discerned by correct reasoning. The right use of reason could provide the authority for justice necessary to make political rights a reality. Catholic natural law posited the church as the institutional arbiter of rights and duties. The church protected these rights and duties by interpreting the natural law through right reason and the formation of individual consciences. It could interpret rights and duties in specific situations. For Hecker,

America's conversion to Catholicism would ground her quest for individual rights and liberties in an institutional framework, a school for liberalism that would form the consciences of individuals in democratic virtue.

Protestantism could not guide America to her destiny. It could not be the school for democratic virtue. It negated reason, free will, and the inherent good of nature. It did not provide a creative role for liberal democratic people to shape their political destiny. Human nature in the Catholic tradition was inherently good (although tainted by sin). Depraved human nature prevented the reconciliation of democracy and faith. Protestants would remain forever alienated, their hearts forever separated from their minds. If people were to be God's instruments for the reconstruction of the world, then it was necessary to see the world as a good place, a place where (to use Hecker's own words) God could be planted. Only by seeing creation as good could people work in that world through reason and free will. Ultimately, Protestantism was un-American. "One would believe that according to the great light [Luther] of Protestantism, the great purpose of Christianity was to make every man an abject slave, and to make him hug his chains which fetter his free limbs."[29]

Protestantism, rather than answering questions of the soul and aspirations of nature, thereby leading people to natural unity, led them instead to anarchy. It was fundamentally incompatible with American government. There was an "antagonism which exists between it and the spirit of our institutions." The American Constitution, liberal democracy, presupposed reason and free will and the inherent goodness of nature. Since Protestantism negated these, it was weakening and destroying America.[30] Hecker emphasized that it was not God alone who worked for human redemption, rather it was a combination of human and divine effort. Humans were not predestined, nor justified by faith alone. Through faith and works they were God's instruments in the world. They needed the Catholic church to direct and fulfill their aspirations. The church connected people with God and with each other. It unified a geographically and socioeconomically diverse nation. It spoke the natural rights language of the Declaration of Independence, the Constitution, and the

Bill of Rights, but grounded those rights in a foundation of natural law.

Just as the individual soul needed a religious guide, so too a polity needed to find its common soul. Hecker's guide for both was Catholicism. It gave a person the opportunity for becoming Christian "without violating the laws of his reason, without stifling the dictates of his conscience. She alone is capable to guide man to his destiny. . . ."[31] True, the Roman church was maligned and misrepresented in America, but that would change when Americans saw how the church could help fulfill their dream.

Hecker did not stop at investigating the destiny of the United States, for America's destiny was the world's. The future of humanity depended on what course Catholicism took in the United States. Hecker posed the fundamental question of the day: "Whether the Catholic Church will succeed in Christianizing the American people as she had Christianized all European nations, so that the Cross of Christ will accompany the stars and stripes in our future."[32] Hecker painted a picture of the religious role of America in millennialist terms common to his contemporaries. In the millennialist view, political and religious time would meld. America would redeem the world. The Kingdom of God would actually come down to earth. America's history was salvation history. America's history was theodicy. There is one essential difference between Hecker's argument and the Protestant millennialist's. Now, the great outpouring of the Holy Spirit would occur after America's conversion to Catholicism. This conversion would reinvigorate Christianity with an abundance of spiritual and material riches. The American people, "once Catholic, can give a new, noble, and glorious realization to Christianity, a development which will go even beyond the past in achievements of zeal, in abundance of saints, as well as in art, science, and material questions." America would be Redeemer Nation only as Catholic nation, for the church "alone is able to give unity to a people, composed of such conflicting elements as ours, and to form them into a great nation."[33]

Hecker elevated the actions of the present into cosmic significance: "The promises of the past, the hopes of the present, the interests of the future, are bound up and vitally connected with our efforts and successes." God was guiding the United States to a glorious destiny, and his earthly saints were instruments of his will. "America is the country of the future. The living God is above us, and the blessings of heaven are with us. Let us then go forward trusting that our convictions will bring us to the realities which they foreshadow."[34] This was similar to Protestant self-conceptions of the saintly politician. The difference with Hecker's argument was that the American saint ushering in the millennium was no longer the Puritan or the awakened Protestant evangelical of Jonathan Edwards, but devout Roman Catholics.

The Roman Catholic church would translate American ideals into political reality. It would connect people institutionally and would make unity a political reality. It would give flesh and direction to political theory and policymaking. Justice could now be defined, and once defined, actualized. The question centered on the difference between Protestant and Catholic principles, between individual interpretation and institutionalized sacrament. Hecker dismissed as politically dangerous nonsense the argument that Protestant denominationalism fostered liberal democracy, that somehow competition of diversity would arrive at the truth. However, he was straining at the limits of liberalism as Americans knew it by positing an institutionalized translator of political language as a unifying force. To the liberal democrat such power smelled of aristocracy and divine right, traditional American fears of Papism. Surely the connections between people such an institutional power would forge would be destructive of freedom.

Hecker had a defense against such a charge. It was essential to remember that Hecker was a confirmed liberal democrat. At no point in his life or in his theory did he advocate an aristocratic liberalism. Brownson, on the other hand, did sour on liberal democracy after the tragedy of the Civil War and the failure of America to convert as a nation to Catholicism. Hecker's political solution for the problems of American liberal democracy never involved a European solution, the introduction of clergy privilege into government, or the formal linking of Church and State. For example, in an article written in Rome shortly before the founding of the Paulists, Hecker praised the Catholic church in America for refraining from pulpit politics during the Know Nothing period.[35] Pulpit politics was not the fruit of his political theory. Instead, Hecker proposed a type of political power for the Roman church compatible with the invisible hand of liberal democracy—the supposed self-regulating, automatic society. The church would be another invisible hand along with the invisible one of the marketplace. The church would not get involved in the details of electioneering, in the formation of public policy, or in bureaucratic maneuvering. The church would not meddle in politics; in a converted America it would not have to. Conversion was the answer to every problem. Once there was a unified Catholic citizenry, then political theory ran automatically into political action as the result of faith, a faith that would give rise to action for justice. At the same time that Hecker provided an institutional guide for liberal democracy, he also tried to preserve Equal Rights Democracy. Forever the Jacksonian, he did not desire a centralized political power that would be the community-binding agent and translator of values. Instead, he advocated a non-governmental power—Catholicism—that would perform the same task.

The problem was that religio-political language in a Catholic America might remain as amorphous and unrelated to practical decision-making as it did in Protestant America. By the church keeping to her distinct role of preaching the Word, teaching morality, and administering sacrament, of not meddling in politics, there would still be the problem of individuals interpreting their consciences differently. It also assumed that each member of the church would be saintly. Granted that the Catholic missions that the Paulists began preaching called Catholics to repent and prepare the way for the Kingdom, Hecker's argument nonetheless collapsed the Kingdom of God into nineteenth-century America. It was too optimistic about human nature and the role of the Holy Spirit in individual Christians. Too often the institutional church did not criticize itself. Catholicism's emphasis on natural law too often forgot the reality of sin. It placed too much emphasis on the work of individual Christians and not enough on God's work. It baptized too readily human conceptions of what the Second Coming would be like. Perhaps God was not a Jacksonian Democrat after all.

THE CIVIL WAR

Isaac Hecker popularized his political theory by means of parish missions, sermons, spiritual direction, and the press. While Paulist missions and pamphleteering did not focus directly on practical political topics, Hecker viewed this kind of missionary work as pre-political activity, for it revived Catholic faith, formed consciences, built enthusiasm, and led to politics. The mission aimed at developing better Christians. In turn, these revived Christians would be more responsible citizens. Paulist mission activity was essential in providing Hecker with an opportunity to understand and communicate with the American clergy and laity. He became a popular figure. Years later Cardinal Gibbons could reflect on how a Paulist mission inspired him to become a priest. One of the reasons Hecker's theory lived is that he was a good organizer. He travelled extensively, acquainting himself not only with the mood of Catholics throughout the nation, but with that of the non-Catholic population as well. Coming to Rome as a convert, Hecker was at ease with Protestant audiences. In a pre-ecumenical age, he at least took their arguments seriously and was willing to debate them. Through his travel and lecturing, Hecker was able to picture the totality of the American experience in its geographical and socio-economic diversity.

As Hecker and his fellow Paulists were darting about the United States preaching and lecturing, the Civil War broke out. In a sermon written in April 1861 (the month the Confederates attacked Fort Sumter), Hecker was convinced that the root of the problem was a lack of common religion.[36] He had already discussed the tensions of the pre-war period in his Roman articles.[37] There he claimed that the church was the friend of both master and slave. Catholics, unlike the fanatic and divisive Protestant Abolitionists, favored union and reconciliation. In the sermon, he maintained that it was not enough for America to be Christian, but its Christianity had to be unifying and morally authoritative. Hecker used the political issue of the day to exemplify his political theory. There must be a "Church" in America and not denominations, for only this kind of religion could prevent sectional and political differences from leading to hostility. The church would provide common religious convictions "to which in time of violence and discord an appeal can be made which will be regarded, and bring forth from the bosom of the people a response that renders them forgetful of private interest and makes peace take the place of discord and violence."

The impending war was a perfect example of how the Catholic church would prevent hostility. In a situation directed by Catholicism, both parties would have to compromise. The church would be the moral instructor, truly being Mother Church settling amicably an internal family dispute. The present conflict was slavery, an issue that the church was trained to deal with. "Slavery under the benign influence of Catholic principles and legislation, voluntarily and insensibly disappears, just as serfdom was made to give way to modern society without violence or bloodshed."

Strangely, Hecker was not at all despondent at the thought of war. While claiming that it "is indeed a pitiable sight to see an intelligent and professedly Xtian [sic] community forced (in this boasted age of civilization) by a few stubborn narrow minded fanatics into a fratricidal war," he maintained nevertheless that it would have a salutary effect on the country. It would make Americans realize their dependence on God, and it would show them the poverty of a religion (Protestantism) without a "divine sanction." In other words, it would show that Protestantism was wrong. The war could even be a "great national blessing" if it caused Americans to appreciate the Catholic church. God might even be using it to prepare the American people to see the truths of Roman Catholicism: "Who can tell, God in his inscrutable providence may in our present trial and sacrifices be preparing our people to see the necessity to acknowledge the truth of His Holy Catholic Religion."

Hecker's language in dealing with the Civil War fitted closely with the way most Union supporters were dealing with it—in religious categories. The belief that Americans were a chosen people had reached a peak in the pre-war period, and the outbreak of war by no means shattered this millennialist vision. Instead, the war was proof that the apocalyptic drama was about to begin. Millennialists had forecast that the chosen people would have to undergo more extensive trials than other peoples and suffer more at the hand of God's enemies, so that they might emerge all the more fitting vessels of God's election. Witness the trials that the chosen people of the Old Testament had to bear. God was planning a future for the United States so magnificent that mere reform was not enough. It would take a conflagration such as the Civil War to prepare the ground for the millennium prefigured in Holy Scripture. Time would no longer be out of joint, but religious time and political time would meld as the promises of the Kingdom of God would unfold in the United States. The Civil War was more than just another skirmish over moral reform, it was the most important crisis in the history of the world.[38]

The flavor of this thinking affected Hecker's views on the Civil War, as his previous quotations indicate. Yet for him and like-minded Catholics there was a very important step before the millennium was to occur—America's conversion to Rome. For Protestant Americans in the North, the Civil War was God's work, a sacrament of history where humans were finally encountering God prior to the Second Coming. For Hecker, an orthodox Catholic, the church was the sacrament. The Civil War was preparing Americans to accept the church. By itself the war would not prepare Americans for the future promises of peace and justice, but it still was an example of God's direct intervention in American history in preparation for a glorious Christian future.

Hecker summarized his analysis of the Civil War in a sermon preached at the Second Plenary Council of Baltimore where the American Catholic hierarchy had gathered soon after the peace. Appropriately, the title was, "The Future Triumph of the Church."[39] Hecker began by interpreting for the bishops the cosmic meaning of the war. While no one could determine the exact date when "the fulness of the glory of Christ's Church upon earth" would come, yet "if it be allowed to interpret the signs of the times, its harbingers [had] already appeared." Hecker's purpose in appearing before them was to map out the reasons for "indulging the hope of the future triumph of the Church upon earth, and the means by which it will be brought about." He specified this future triumph by painting a picture of Christian hope: "In the history of the earth, in that of political society, in that of religion, there is a gradual and steady progress towards the realization upon earth of the Good, the True, the Beautiful—God." Hecker tried to dispel the false notion that Christianity was concerned only with the after-life, with the spiritual as opposed to the material. Catholic doctrine did not "divorce God from man and nature." It aimed at the union of body and soul, material and spirit. Human happiness was not exclusively spiritual, nor was it exclusively in the beyond. "Hence, also, the ultimate aim of the Church is not to people heaven with souls alone—this is but a stage in their progress. She looks forward to that day when the soul and body shall again be united, and man's happiness be complete and perfect."

Hecker supported this millennialist vision by quoting from Isaiah 9:1–18, Matthew 3:2 and 10:7—all passages proclaiming that the Kingdom of God is at hand. He stressed that in the Lord's Prayer we say "Thy Kingdom come. Thy will be done on earth as it is in heaven." In true Catholic eschatological fashion he pointed out instances in church history where the Kingdom had been realized, however briefly. Early Christian communities and contemporary religious orders were examples where selfishness had been abolished and "the reign of the common brotherhood of man and the supreme love of God was begun." He made explicit historical links between religious and political time to show that the church "is silently and persistently pushing society toward its true ideal." Feudalism was a progression over barbarism, hired labor over serfdom. "The tendency of our times of substituting common interests for private and personal selfishness, is a still nearer approach to a common brotherhood. . . ."

Only the Catholic church aimed for "the establishing and realization of God's kingdom among men." The world would be much closer to this goal if it were not for the Protestant Reformation. Thankfully, Protestantism was on the run. The church had been strengthened by the Counter Reformation; strict Calvinism was being rejected; and liberal Protestantism, based on reason alone, had no future. Even the pagan worlds of Turkey and China were being conquered by Christianity. In addition to these internal and external factors which doomed Protestantism, the progress of reason and science was preparing the world for "the approaching triumph of Christianity." As people drew closer together through the wonders of modern inventions, they would draw closer together in appreciation of the truth. "Remove the barriers that separate men from each other, and you facilitate the triumph of universal truth, and prepare the way for the reign of universal brotherhood among men."

All of these portents of the triumph of Christ's Church were centered in the United States. Hecker, preaching to the American hierarchy at the end of the war, insisted that the future of the church, the future of the world, was America. Isaac Hecker had baptized America Catholic:

> Nowhere is there a promise of a brighter future for the Church than in our own country. Here, thanks to our American Constitution, the Church is free to do her divine work. Here, she finds a civilization in harmony with her divine teachings. Here, Christianity is promised a reception from an intelligent and free people, that she will give forth a development of unprecedented glory. For religion is never so beautiful as when in connection with knowledge and freedom.
>
> Let us, therefore, arise and open our eyes to the bright future that is before us! Let us labor with a lively faith, a firm hope, and a charity that knows no bounds, by every good work and good example, for the reign of God's kingdom upon earth.[40]

In the years immediately after the Civil War, Hecker continued his priestly activity of preaching, sacramental ministry, spiritual direction, and giving missions. He added to this work increased writing, publishing, and lecturing, for he felt that he must reach a wider audience. If America were to be converted to Catholicism, if the church were to come closer to being triumphant, he would have to reach the non-Catholic. He already felt a kinship with them. A convert himself, he knew the arguments non-Catholics posed. He wanted to build on the grounds which Catholics and Protestants shared; their love for America and their common Christian heritage. Catholics did not have to break Protestants down to unbelief in order to rebuild true belief. Catholics should build on what was good in Protestants, what was already Catholic. Individual Protestants had to be made to see that their core was Catholic just as the core of America was Catholic.

Hecker felt that the church could convert the Protestants in mass if it could develop a distinctive American spirituality. "Our American character is suitable for a certain type of spiritual perfection."[41] Any attempt to force another type of spirituality on the American people "will be unsuccessful, if not fatal in many instances." Progress toward the conversion of America would occur only when Catholic apologetics attempted to synthesize elements of Catholic faith with "what is good and true in our type of character." There could be no foppish attempts by Yankees to be super-Romans. Rather, a strong American Catholic faith would have to be rooted solidly in Yankee characteristics. "Our faith must take root in our national characteristics, and we find ourselves entirely at home in it. My wish is to help my fellow countrymen and women in this work."

Hecker was not satisfied with remaining even on this level of recognition of the links between American culture and Catholic spirituality. The next step in his argument was that America presented the best ground for the development of Christian spirituality. "I believe that our civilization presents to Christianity a broader basis to rear a spiritual life upon, than any other form of civilization."[42] He claimed that he "can be all the better Catholic because I am an American; and all the better American because I am a Catholic." Hecker's claim that Catholicism and Americanism were mutually self-reinforcing produced a dilemma. On the one hand, it had the healthy impact of helping individual Catholics experience their country as a good place where they could work for their own salvation by contributing toward the common good. It also allayed the suspicions of Protestants over Catholic allegiance toward the American government. This worked toward an integrated spirituality where national pride would be balanced by Christian faith. Unfortunately, this synthesis risked falling into an uncritical civil cult where religion and politics were collusive and uncritical. For Catholics, this meant moving from a Catholic spirituality based on American ideals yet able to criticize the bad parts of the American dream to one that accepted uncritically everything

"American" as superior to others. This uncritical acceptance of American nationalism would be the dark side of the success of Hecker's attempt to make Catholics feel proud of their faith and their flag.

The Church and the Age

During the last two decades of his life, Isaac Hecker worked not only at preaching the truths of Catholicism to an American audience, but at lessening the fears of the European church toward liberal democracy. He felt that providing an American Catholic political theory for Americans was insufficient; he had to bring the American spirit to the universal Church. As cogent as his arguments were in showing the relationships between Catholicism and liberalism, and as ready as American Catholics were to accept them, non-Catholics continued to perceive the church as a prop for European aristocracy. As Protestant millennialist dreams of the Civil War faded into the economic growth of the Gilded Age, so did Hecker's Catholic dream fade for the conversion of America. The American Catholic church was increasingly an immigrant church, not a Yankee one. Protestants did not heed the call to come home to Rome. Yet Hecker remained eternally optimistic. The *Catholic World,* the Catholic Publication Society, the indefatigable missions and lectures, were all instruments to spread his political theory. The Holy Spirit, infallibly guiding the church, would eventually reconcile it with modernity. Hecker hoped that the Ecumenical Council called by Pius IX in 1869 would hasten that reconciliation.

Many in the American church, and some liberal Europeans, believed that Hecker would be the champion of democracy at the Council, showing that the church was compatible with liberal democracy.[43] Unfortunately for Hecker, he and the other champions of church reform underestimated the strength of the conservative ultramontane faction. Hecker had always supported the papacy, but he felt that a definition of infallibility would be disastrous both for the universal church and especially the American. As late as the opening of the Council in December 1869, he was positive that it would not discuss infallibility. He felt that to define the pope's power would actually lessen it. It would be best not to articulate the complex relationship between pope, bishops, and councils. In a personal memorandum, Hecker claimed that the controversy showed the difference between the "Italian" and the "Western" minds. The Italian mind tried to make a declaration without looking to "consequences, in touching points of history, etc." The "Western" mind examined "critically all its bearings," presenting "perplexing difficulties."[44] Despite his opposition to the definition, there was never any doubt that once defined, Hecker would accept it. Writing to his brother George he maintained that if the question be fairly settled, all dispute should end: "The rule of faith is in the authority of the Church, and to dispute that is not to be Catholic." He ended by warning George that going "into any details in my position would not be prudent, and I fear no practical good."[45]

The infallibility definition was a setback for Hecker's political theory, for it seemed to contradict his claim of the church's inherent support of democratic rights. Hecker's response was to return to America and try to show all the more clearly the compatibility between America and Catholicism. He felt that once the definition of papal authority was defined, the institutional authority question in the church would recede, and the role of the indwelling of the Holy Spirit would take precedence. He was certain that the anti-democratic spirit of the ultramontanists could not survive, for the effort to increase what he called the "Monarchical" element in the church would be the "last flickering of an expiring candle," with "the complete overthrow of that party in the Church."[46] The Paulists should continue to work toward reconciling the church with the modern spirit of the Age, not only in America, but in Europe as well. The focus on the role of the Holy Spirit in the lives of individual Christians would overbalance with democratic spirit the monarchical spirit of the Vatican Council.

Hecker's optimism shined through in his last book, *The Church and the Age,* a collection of articles published in 1887 and containing pieces dating from 1875.[47] The sub-title, "An Exposition of the Catholic Church in View of the Needs and Aspirations of the Present Age," indicated the wide scope of the book and the more universal audience Hecker addressed. It was a sober, reflective collection, one summarizing and analyzing the ideas of an entire career. It reflected the continued optimism of the missionary that the Holy Spirit would bring all things to the good and the continued enthusiasm of the Jacksonian radical, grown slightly out of date in the "Gilded Age," but still advocating equal rights for all. It was the work of a churchman who believed that the Catholic church, despite her human failures, was the Body of Christ continuing to minister to the world. It was also the work of an American political theorist, analyzing the various streams of American experience into a unified theory.

Many of the arguments were familiar. Hecker defended the church, maintaining that far from being a reactionary force in world politics, it was actually radical, for it went to the root problem of human destiny—religion. He stated the familiar attacks on the inherently undemocratic nature of Protestantism and the role of the Catholic church in unifying America and building on her natural rights foundation. He painted a glorious picture of America's future, re-emphasizing the role of the Holy Spirit. Here was the synthesis between Church and State, religion and politics. The Holy Spirit worked first in individuals, converting and renewing them. This internal working of the Holy Spirit inspired individuals to work toward the conversion and renewal of the entire world. The radical remedy for the problems of modernity was increased attention to the indwelling of the Holy Spirit. First came the religious work of the church, the "science of Christian perfection," through the "exercises of prayer, spiritual reading, sacraments, the practice of virtues, and good works." All of these helped "remove the hindrances in the way of the action of the Holy Spirit." Once this religious work began, then came political action as the individual, attentive to the voice of the Holy Spirit, made actions consonant with beliefs. "The radical and adequate remedy for all the evils of our age, and the source of all true progress, consists in increased attention and fidelity to the action of the Holy Spirit in the soul."[48]

Hecker was absolutely confident that the church would remedy the defects of the modern age, for he saw an infallible progress toward perfection guided by the Holy Spirit working through the church. The Christian task was to recognize this divine work in history and then conform life to its prompting. By so doing, the Christian was linked with the external work of the

Spirit through history—the church. This was the way that historical and political time melded with religious time. By listening to the indwelling Spirit and adhering to the external authority of the church, the Christian naturally linked religion and politics. There was no formal separation of Sunday and workday obligations, neither was there an amorphous mix, nor a formal union. Instead, there was a conscious realization that one's personal salvation is coterminous with communal salvation. Over time individual religious action linked with political action. There would be a natural union between religion and politics only when neither institutional church nor government sought domination over each other. Union would come when each adhered to its sphere of natural competence. The individual Christian, prompted by the Holy Spirit, made the link.

While Hecker insisted on the same providential role for the United States in *The Church and the Age,* there seemed to be a recognition in some of his other writings that America was not about to convert in mass to Catholicism. This was particularly true in Hecker's discussion of the "School Question" in the *Catholic World.*[49] When a political crisis came (the justice of public schools which are really Protestant supported by Catholic taxes) Hecker resorted to the hard-hitting, practical language of his Jacksonian training—equal rights, fair play, anti-monopoly. It was not fair that Catholic taxes should support Protestant-inspired public schools. Gone were the arguments for conversion and the coming of the Kingdom on earth. Instead of becoming America's school for republican virtue, the church became another interest group vying for political power through the electoral process. The saintly work for the coming of the Kingdom was reduced to protecting the Catholic share of the pie.

The problem was that the most important part of Hecker's political theory, conversion to Catholicism, had not worked. When faced with a problem in public policy, he had to resort to the pragmatic American insistence on fair play. He reduced his theoretical concern for the ends of political life to a practical concern for the means. This was the fate of American political theory. Consensus was possible on the means. Agreement over the specific ends was much more difficult. However, Hecker's political theory cannot be dismissed as a total failure. One very important result was to link Catholic interest with other American interests. During the Know Nothing period of anti-Catholicism, there would have been serious doubt whether Catholics even had a right to enter the American political process. Half a century later there was no question that they had that right. Hecker can take much of the credit for that change in opinion. He worked to convince Catholics that America was compatible with their faith, therefore that they should demand their political rights. In addition, his theory worked to convince Protestants that they had nothing to fear from Rome. They should perceive, like Tocqueville, the American church's wholehearted support of democratic institutions. By insisting how American Catholics were and how Catholic America was, Hecker succeeded in including Catholics within the American political system.

The problem was that by including Catholics into the mainstream of American politics, Catholics inevitably became less "Catholic" and more "American." This began with Hecker's orthodox attempt to base his political theory in a natural law discernible to all Americans and not necessarily specific to Catholic faith. Instead of leading to an acknowledgment by the American public of the need for conversion to Catholicism, the recognition of the commonality of political principles led to a Catholic acceptance of "common denominator" Christianity. Hecker's argument for proportional public aid to parochial schools, for example, rested on the assumption that Protestants and Catholics shared a common opinion on American fundamentals. Where his original argument would then have shown why Protestants should become Catholic if they wanted to fulfill these principles, his argument now was that you can control *your* group if you let us control *ours*. We agree on enough to allow us to be different. This common opinion with its patriotic and religious trappings—civil religion—became increasingly powerful in American Catholicism. For example, Dorothy Dohen has documented almost a century later how the Catholic hierarchy's language was much more American than Catholic.[50]

Hecker hoped to mobilize this common agreement on basic Christian principles against unifying attempts by a centralized government. Any plan for centralized, federally-controlled attempts to rebuild unity after the Civil War frightened him.

Centralization was not the answer for the lack of connections among Americans. His theory had posed the Catholic church as the unifying, connecting force in liberal democratic society. The political reality of the closing decades of the nineteenth century was that Americans were not accepting the Roman church as that community builder. Hecker's analysis of the school question showed that he had to revert to more commonly accepted American "connecting" language—the traditional demands of liberty, fair play, and equal rights.

If the common translator of political language and community builder was not to be the church, then Hecker was willing to support civil religion—a common agreement on Christian fundamentals combined with patriotic support of democratic procedures. Out of necessity, civil religion would have to be the unifier of America and translator of values. His argument for parochial schools, for example, spoke to a broad American audience and reminded them of the necessity of Christianity in fostering virtue. The argument no longer was, now that we can agree, look how the Catholic church best expresses this argument and come and join us. Instead the argument was, now that we agree that Christianity is basic for American democracy, let us together support our individual interests, our right to be different. If not, then a greater evil looms ahead—a government enforced unity.

Hecker was willing to lower his vision in the face of an increase of centralized democratic power that he feared would have an anti-Catholic bias. Seeing the education question as a "test question" not only for education but for other policy as well, he stayed with his Locofoco fear of bigness. The consequences of Hecker's theory, then, were to reject centralized administration and promote interest group bargaining. They would lead to a Catholic liberalism supporting the social welfare policy and interest group liberalism of the New Deal. It would not challenge the fundamentals of the American liberal tradition, for its support of interest group liberalism was an attempt to retain the invisible hand. Now the competition was between interest groups, not individuals. The American Catholic response to politics would not be an aristocratic reaction, nor a formation of a specifically Catholic political party, as in Europe. The American Catholic answer was the organization of Catholic interest groups and political bargaining. At the same time that it protected its own interests, the Catholic political response was assertive on social reform. One of the results of Hecker's political theory has been the consistent impetus for Catholics to move beyond an individual response to social problems to political ones, from charity to public policy.

CONCLUSION

Isaac Hecker remained optimistic throughout his life about the necessity of reconciling the church with the democratic spirit of modernity. He saw reconciliation as essential not only to the success of his political theory, but to the triumph of the church. One of Hecker's most important contributions to political theory was his recognition that different religious beliefs necessarily had different political results. Politics, in turn, affected religious belief. If the future were to be democratic, as he believed, reconciliation between the church and democracy would be essential. If the church's political theory were to remain skeptical or even antagonistic toward this political reality, it would be forever fighting a rearguard action. This was unnecessary, for the church had nothing to fear from democracy. The Catholic principle and the democratic were mutually supportive.

During the last two decades of his life, Hecker worked at lessening the church's fear of democracy by widening his audience to include European Catholics. The task was difficult, evidenced especially at Hecker's rebuff at Vatican I. He went to the Council as the champion of the democratic spirit, hoping to throw open the church windows in a way Pope John XXIII did a century later. The European church, still smarting from attacks by anti-clerical revolutionary forces, was suspicious of any movement to democratize the church. Hecker's formation of a Catholic liberal democratic political theory, however, was prophetic— the monarchical element in the church was doomed to fail. Within two decades Leo XIII was opening the church to the realities of modern politics, a process that would continue throughout the twentieth century, accelerating at Vatican II.

Disappointed at the definition of papal infallibility and the negative Roman attitude toward church reform and democracy,

Hecker was not discouraged. He continued to view the American church as the healthiest daughter of Rome and the liberal democratic separation of Church and State as the most fruitful for the Catholic future. America was Europe's teacher. Hecker was solidly in the American political tradition of understanding the New World as a special place free from the corruption of European history. In Perry Miller's description of the Puritan enterprise, Americans saw themselves on an "Errand into the Wilderness" that would serve as a guide for Europe.[51] This understanding worked closely with American millennialism with its belief that Americans were a Chosen People in the Redeemer Nation. The irony was that an understanding that originally served to picture America as free of corrupting Papist politics now was used by a Catholic leader as a criterion to reform Catholic politics. It was a conception, parenthetically, that rarely instructed Europeans as much as it threatened them. This was especially true for European Catholics toward the end of the nineteenth century when Americans (Catholics included) exulted in their splendid little war to rid the Western Hemisphere of Spanish control. Viewing America as providentially founded and governed, Hecker exhibited a type of patriotism that verged on the chauvinistic, a type that would lead Catholics to an uncritical acceptance of American civil religion—a patriotism, however, that was not unusual for his time.

Hecker's mature political thought, as collected in *The Church and the Age*, built on his earlier theory and placed him securely in the reform tradition. If the future of the world were democracy, then there was no turning back to aristocracy. The choice was reform or revolution. The church had to stop fighting democracy and realize that it had everything to gain by being on the side of liberal democratic change. The religious renewal within the Catholic church supporting this reform effort was the increased attentiveness by individual Catholics to the indwelling of the Holy Spirit in their lives. The Holy Spirit, working through the ministry of the church, continually called individuals to conversion and renewal. It necessitated an openness to political activity by its stress on working for the coming of the Kingdom on earth.

The synthesis between religion and politics depended on the

individually-committed Christian making the connections between belief and practice. The emphasis on the individual both
religiously and politically worked out to be akin to Equal Rights
Democracy. Hecker's life shows the incredible power of Jacksonian ideas throughout the nineteenth century. When he discussed
the superiority of liberal democratic government he stressed that
by governing as little as possible it allowed room for individuals
to work out their own destinies. By the separation of Church and
State, liberal democratic government gave freedom to individual
Christians to cooperate with the Holy Spirit. Far from de-Chris-
tianizing politics, the separation of Church and State opened it
all the more to the power of grace. Liberal democracy invigorat-
ed Christianity by tearing away all the artificial props and aristocratic privileges and letting the church rely on its only real
strength—individuals who make up the Body of Christ.

Hecker, the missionary priest, had unquestioned faith in the
work of the Holy Spirit. The Holy Spirit did and would continue
to work through the church to convert and renew. Conscientious
Christians would work for the coming of the Kingdom. The
problem was that Hecker's theory operated on the basis of faith,
a dynamic not easily transferable from religion to politics. It
spoke too much of the heart and not enough of the mind. Hecker
had to face the accusation that his theory was not political at all,
but one fundamentally religious. Even if there were a common
ground between Catholic natural law doctrine and American
natural rights theory—a common ethic discernible by reason
quite apart from faith—the central point of Hecker's argument
still was that the de-alienating connections a liberal democracy
needed had to come from agreement on more than an ethic. They
had to come from unitary religious belief. If America as a nation
did not convert and become a unitary instead of a denomination-
al society, then the implications of Hecker's theory would be
quite different. The Catholic church would be only one denomination among others. Political survival would depend on all
denominations agreeing on a basic set of Christian principles
laced with American patriotism—American civil religion. The
radical energy that a unitary Catholic polity would engender by
providing community and moral leadership faded into an inertia
supporting the political status-quo.

Evangelical and liberal Protestants rejected conversion. Skeptics remained indifferent. Catholics themselves were divided. Increasingly the church's energy was spent caring for the immigrant instead of reaching out to potential Yankee converts. European Catholics were suspicious of a Catholic political theory that was so open to the separation of Church and State, so encouraging of democratic reform, and so attentive to the indwelling of the Holy Spirit. Hecker had to wait almost a century for vindication, for as Sydney Ahlstrom in *A Religious History of the American People* states, "No nineteenth-century Roman Catholic in America so clearly foreshadowed the *aggiornamento* which Pope John XXIII would begin to call for when he became pope—on the centenary of the Paulists' founding."[52]

NOTES

1. ITH, *The Church and the Age—An Exposition of the Catholic Church in View of the Needs and Aspirations of the Present Age* (New York: Catholic Publication Society, 1887), p. 79.

2. This essay is a summary of my doctoral thesis, "The Formation of American Catholic Political Thought: Isaac Hecker's Political Theory," (Ph.D. dissertation, Cornell University, 1977).

3. For evidence of Brownson's post-Civil War pessimism on liberal democracy see "Dr. Brownson," *Tablet* (Brooklyn), June 18, 1870, from a copy in the PFA. See also the Hecker-Brownson correspondence from August to October, 1870, in The *Brownson-Hecker Correspondence,* Joseph F. Gower and Richard M. Leliaert, eds. (Notre Dame, Indiana: University of Notre Dame Press, 1979), pp. 291–297.

4. For a thorough analysis of the role of liberal political philosophy in America, see Louis Hartz, *The Liberal Tradition in America* (New York: Harcourt, Brace, and World, 1955). He claims that political theory in America is a recurrent variation on a liberal theme. For a discussion of Catholic social liberalism, see Aaron I. Abell, ed., *American Catholic Thought on Social Questions* (Indianapolis: Bobbs-Merrill Company, 1968) and Charles E. Curran, *New Perspectives in Moral Theology* (Notre Dame, Indiana: University of Notre Dame Press, 1976).

5. For an analysis of millennialism, see H. Richard Niebuhr, *The Kingdom of God in America* (New York: Harper Books of Harper & Row, 1959); Ernest Lee Tuveson, *Redeemer Nation* (Chicago: Universi-

ty of Chicago Press, 1968); and Cushing Strout, *The New Heavens and New Earth, Political Religion in America* (New York: Harper & Row, 1974).

6. Theodore J. Lowi, *The End of Liberalism* (New York: W.W. Norton 1969), pp. 29–37.

7. Abell, *American Catholic Thought on Social Questions.*

8. See Arthur M. Schlesinger, Jr., *The Age of Jackson* (Boston: Little, Brown and Company, 1946); Lee Benson, *The Concept of Jacksonian Democracy* (Princeton: Princeton University Press, 1961); and Marvin Meyers, *The Jacksonian Persuasion* (New York: Vintage Books of Random House, 1957). For a discussion of the Hecker family's involvement, see Walter Hugins, *Jacksonian Democracy and the Working Class* (Stanford: Stanford University Press, 1960), pp. 103–105.

9. Alice Felt Tyler, *Freedom's Ferment* (New York: Harper Torchbook of Harper & Row, 1944).

10. The best analysis of anti-Catholic bigotry during this period is Ray Allen Billington, *The Protestant Crusade, 1800–1860* (Chicago: Quadrangle Books, 1964).

11. Benson, *Concept of Jacksonian Democracy,* p. 185.

12. ITH, "Dr. Brownson and the Workingman's Party Fifty Years Ago," CW 45 (May 1887): 203.

13. A good analysis of Tammany and its reformers can be found in Jerome Mushkat's *Tammany* (Syracuse: Syracuse University Press, 1971). A contemporary history of the Locofoco Party was written by its recording secretary: F. Byrdsall, *The History of the Loco-Foco or Equal Rights Party* (New York: Burt and Franklin, 1967). This was originally published in New York City in 1842.

14. Hugins, *Jacksonian Democracy,* p. 32.

15. ITH, Document submitted to his superiors, January 6, 1858, PFA.

16. In 1849, Brownson had published a pamphlet supporting the Democratic party entitled "The Laboring Class." It is one of the most devastating indictments of social inequality in America. It may be found in *The Brownson Reader,* Alvan S. Ryan, ed. (New York: P.J. Kenedy and Sons, 1955).

17. ITH, "Dr. Brownson and the Workingman's Party," p. 205.

18. ITH, Document submitted to superiors, January 6, 1858.

19. Tyler, *Freedom's Ferment,* p. 176.

20. By April 24, 1843, ITH was contemplating entering the Roman Catholic Church. See his early diary of that date, PFA.

21. Early diary, June 26, 1843.

22. Ibid., June 14, 1844.

23. For an example of ITH's continued use of millennialist language at his conversion, see his letter to Brownson, March 15, 1844, *Brownson-Hecker Correspondence,* pp. 86–87.

24. Early Diary, October 17, 1843.

25. Alexis de Tocqueville, *Democracy in America* (New York: Vintage Books of Random House, 1945), Volume II, Part II, Chapters V, VII, and VIII. Also, Volume I, Chapters XII and XIV.

26. Walter Elliott, *The Life of Father Hecker* (4th ed.; New York: Columbus Press, 1898), p. 64.

27. ITH, *Questions of the Soul* (New York: D. Appleton & Co., 1855) and *Aspirations of Nature* (New York: James B. Kirker, 1857).

28. ITH, *Questions of the Soul,* pp. 55–56.

29. ITH, *Aspirations of Nature,* p. 133.

30. Ibid., p. 185.

31. ITH, *Questions of the Soul,* p. 29.

32. Ibid., p. 292.

33. Ibid., p. 293.

34. ITH, *Aspirations of Nature,* p. 47.

35. ITH, "Present and Future Prospects of the Catholic Faith in the United States of North America," *Civiltà Cattolica,* 3rd ser., Vol. 8, No. 184 and 185, (1857):II, p. 6. In these Roman articles, Hecker summarizes the ideas in both *Questions of the Soul* and *Aspirations of Nature.*

36. "Sermon on Disintegrating Political State of Union," April, 1861, PFA. The copy states that the sermon was never delivered.

37. ITH, *Civiltà Cattolica,* II, pp. 6–8.

38. See Tuveson, *Redeemer Nation,* Chapter VI, "The Ennobling War."

39. "The Future Triumph of the Church," October 16, 1866, PFA.

40. Ibid.

41. Hecker to Mrs. Jane King, June 26, 1863, PFA.

42. Hecker to Mrs. King, July 12, 1863, PFA.

43. See, for example, the following letters in the PFA: Father B. Cochrane to ITH, September 2, 1869; Richard Simpson to Lord Acton, November 6, 1869 (copy); Bishop Döllinger to Lord Acton, November 22, 1869 (copy).

44. Personal Notes, December 30, 1869, PFA.

45. Hecker to his brother George, March 11, 1870, PFA.

46. Personal Notes, January 5, 1870.

47. ITH, *The Church and the Age.* (New York: Catholic Publication Society, 1887).

48. Ibid., pp. 24–26.

49. For an excellent overview of Hecker on this issue see: Joseph F. Gower, "A 'Test Question' for Religious Liberty: Isaac Hecker on Education," *Notre Dame Journal for Education* (Spring 1976):28–43. For articles in CW on the topic see: "The Catholic View of Public Education in the United States," CW 8 (Feb. 1869):691; ITH, "Catholics and Protestants Agreeing on the School Question," CW 31 (Feb. 1881):700; ITH, "A New but False Plea for Public Schools," CW 36 (Dec. 1882):416; ITH, "What Does the Public-School Question Mean?" CW 33 (June 1881):88; and ITH, "The Impending Issue of the School Question," CW 36 (March 1883):849.

50. Dorothy Dohen, *Nationalism and American Catholicism* (New York: Sheed and Ward, 1967).

51. Perry Miller, *Errand into the Wilderness* (New York: Harper Torchbooks of Harper & Row, 1956).

52. Sydney E. Ahlstrom, *A Religious History of the American People* (New Haven: Yale University Press, 1972), p. 554.

An Evangelical Imperative:
Isaac Hecker, Catholicism,
and Modern Society

by David J. O'Brien

For two centuries, Christians have attempted to find the proper expression of their faith in a world transformed by the revolutions of industrialization, urbanization, and secularization. Some have favored an approach, usually called liberal, by which the Church would affirm progress, liberty and reason, and adapt its forms, if not its substance, to the demands of modernization. Others, more conservative, have taken the opposite approach, denouncing modernity as fundamentally illegitimate and calling for the restoration of a coherent, unified social system, integrated and sanctioned by a single religion, even a single church.

The religious history of the last several centuries, especially in the United States, has been written largely within this dualistic framework of liberalism and conservatism, accommodation and resistance, modernism and fundamentalism. These histories often reflect less the real choices available to people in the past than continuing ideological debates within the churches and the culture at large. Certainly in the United States there were few if any believing, serious Christians, Catholic or Protestant, who favored all out surrender or all out withdrawal from "the modern world." Most were simply attempting to balance multiple convictions, loyalties, fears, and hopes in order to construct personal lives and social institutions appropriate to complex experiences. Liberals in general hoped to reduce the distance, and the tension, between religion and other spheres of life by reinterpreting religion, in part because they believed that values and symbols in the broader culture had originated in and were compatible with

Christianity. Conservatives may have wanted to clarify, perhaps expand, the boundaries between the Church and the world, in part because they feared for the health of the Church but also because they believed that a healthy Church, in the long run, could not but contribute to a healthy community and nation.

Isaac Hecker was an American Catholic convert and evangelist who never accepted, probably never even understood, the liberal-conservative alternatives. Like most Christians, he wished both to uphold traditional doctrines and affirm modern possibilities. He devoted his life to building up the oldest and apparently most conservative of Christian churches, and to affirming and championing the claims and hopes of the world's newest and apparently most liberal nation. He probed the depths of both and emerged with the outrageous proposition that, in the most profound sense, the origin and destiny of each was the same. Misunderstood and rejected by most Catholics and Americans of his generation, Isaac Hecker remains in many ways not only the "model priest" his admirers saw, but a witness to the most challenging possibilities of American Catholicism, possibilities more evident, and more endangered, a century later than they were during his lifetime.

I

In 1789, as France embarked on its revolution, the United States launched a new government based on its recently ratified constitution. Two years later the Bill of Rights was added, providing that Congress should make "no law respecting the establishment of religion or prohibiting the free exercise thereof." Disestablishment and free exercise, separation of Church and State, and religious liberty fixed and affirmed the pluralistic context for religious life which had come to prevail in colonial America and spread throughout the Western world during the next two centuries. Previously, churches had contested to control the State; now they were to conduct their affairs apart from the State. In theory at least the State would not favor any church, perhaps not even favor religion as such; the Church, on its part, could not enlist the aid of the State to uphold its doctrines, enforce its judgments, or coerce consciences. Each man and woman would be free to consider the claims of the several churches and select that which best suited his or her needs and aspirations. A non-political church was supposed to be a better church because it was composed of members who had freely chosen its doctrines and freely accepted its discipline; it could be God's people, pure and undefiled by the contamination of power and self-interest. A non-religious state would be a better state because it would be free of the divisive passions of religion. Confined to temporal concerns by an explicit recognition of fundamental human rights, it would be capable of enlisting the loyalty of all, regardless of religious persuasion. No wonder many a contemporary regarded the achievements of the American Revolution in the long-contested religious arena as its most significant accomplishment.

Of course the situation proved more complex than this. In European nations, with longer histories and more unified populations, the practice of separation and liberty was long in coming; even in America their full understanding and practice evolved gradually and are still far from complete. It was one thing to deprive the Church of political and the State of ecclesiastical power; it was another to construct a nation and a system of government able to enlist the loyalty of its citizens without benefit of religious symbols and sanctions. Must not a society, to be a true society, have some common ideas, taken for granted by the people, which encourage them to subordinate personal to common interests, and engage when necessary in common actions? Furthermore, for many persons religion involves the most profound personal commitment; can religious persons live comfortably and securely in communities whose common life makes no reference to the symbols which embody ultimate meaning and value? Many thought not in 1789; many are not sure two centuries later.

Retrospective analysis of nineteenth-century thought on these matters stumbles regularly over the ingrained twentieth-century preference for liberty and separation. Despite considerable evidence that the desire for unity and transcendence at the heart of orthodoxy and religious uniformity remains deeply rooted in the human heart, most observers still regard the liberal solution of the First Amendment as both inevitable and appropriate. Nineteenth-century people were far less sure; even in the United States, where practical considerations made separation and freedom the most workable option, many worried about its consequences and sought ways to avoid its implications. What was necessary might not be ideal, or even right; legitimacy was both a theoretical question and a practical one, a source of social and cultural conflict and of personal anxiety and stress. The optimistic affirmations of Thomas Jefferson remained for many years a distinctly minority position; more common was the conviction so apparent in evangelical enterprises and Nativist outbreaks that America was and must remain a Christian nation. If that could not be accomplished through the State, and most doubted that it could, it would have to be accomplished outside the State, in that realm of social activity which intervened between personal life and the formal institutions of government. Thus Christian social action, ranging from efforts to strengthen the Church and the faith of the people to vigorous struggles to make society in all its dimensions correspond to the perceived demands of the Gospel, was intended to set the limits of pluralism and freedom, and maintain some rough, general correspondence between personal religious beliefs and the symbols, style, and moral tone of public life.

Evangelical religion, it seems, was more than a branch of Christianity or a movement within the churches. All churches necessarily became more evangelical the more they became modern and American. As the external freedom of the churches became an inner freedom to find God and create a personal religious life, as legal freedom of conscience became a living freedom to read and make one's own the Holy Bible and the book of nature, as the Church of habit and outward conformity, in Puritan New England, Catholic immigrant neighborhoods, or rural Baptist counties, gave way to the Church as a self-constructed, voluntary community, evangelical assumptions and styles proved irresistible. The more freedom became an external fact and an internal experience, it seemed, the more the Scriptures became the only legitimate authority, the person became the object of evangelization and the subject of religious history, and the Church became a voluntary community of "like hearted and like minded" believers. Presbyterians, Methodists, and Episcopalians, later Catholics, Lutherans, and Orthodox, all eventually faced the inescapable imperative of adopting the forms and much of the substance of the evangelical tradition, not to replace, but precisely to preserve, their own distinctive doctrine, authority, polity, and mission.

Evangelical Christianity in the nineteenth century placed its greatest emphasis on the preaching of the Gospel, aiming at the conversion of men and women away from a life of sinful indulgence and selfishness to a new birth of grace in the soul. In the United States, the forms and methods of evangelism changed, but the goal was always the same: to reach the individual sinner, rich or poor, bring him or her to an acknowledgement of sin, an awareness of dependence upon God, and a new commitment to Jesus Christ. The very action of evangelizing thus had social, cultural, and political significance. On the frontier and in the city were thousands who had not heard or heeded the saving message of the Gospel. By bringing it to them, the revivalists not only won converts to a now voluntary church, but they bridged the gap between social classes, brought a sense of discipline to the dissolute and moral obligation to the respectable. By spreading the Gospel, evangelical Christians believed they could help Americans govern themselves, developing the internalized moral restraints necessary for a democratic society.

Beyond the social impact of evangelism itself, there was a more direct social action message, as Timothy L. Smith has demonstrated. Revivalists of all persuasions were never satisfied simply with personal conversion. Their theology emphasized individual salvation through faith in Jesus Christ, and did not feature a notion of works as gainful toward salvation. Nevertheless, faith, if honest and genuine, would manifest itself in benevolence, in a willingness to do the Lord's will by combatting sin and pursuing a life of personal holiness and perfection. The evangelical stress on a changed life, expressed in works of mercy and a commitment to walk in the Lord's way, was a major, perhaps the major, source of reform energy in nineteenth-century America. The fact that revivalist ministers generally believed that America was God's special nation and its people his chosen ones meant that the energy to do his will flowed through personal reform to charity and to active efforts to purge the nation of sin, remove those blemishes which cost it the Lord's favor, and eliminate those sinful obstacles that stood in the way of its millennial promise.

In other words, among the fruits of conversion was inevitably a social message, an effort to measure society against the standard of Jesus and work to make social and cultural practices conform to those standards. By the 1830s and 1840s this evangelistic zeal was intensified by the spread of holiness and perfectionist enthusiasm. Conversion and commitment generated a crusading zeal to purge the nation of sin and bring it to fulfillment of its divine promise, indeed to clear the way for the advent of God's Kingdom, felt by many to be close at hand on these shores.

Evangelistic social Christianity, then, responded to the problems posed by modern freedom by seeking to convert a free people to the Gospel, establishing the Church on a voluntary basis, and sending forth converted persons to renew society, and bring the nation to God; Christian social action aimed not at capturing the government but at controlling or influencing social institutions, the family, the school, the forms of social interaction, and the symbols of common life. In time, this approach found its moderate form in a temperate Gospel of private Christianity, in which salvation was simply a personal matter and religion confined to the private world of family and friends. But it never lost its prophetic strain, nor its ever-present desire to apply the Gospel to society and form men and women determined to do the Lord's will in the world.

There was another response to the problems posed by the democratic revolutions, one especially marked among those drawn from the world of established churches. For such persons, the new separations of religion and life were simply unacceptable departures from divinely constituted institutions and authorities. This approach was most dramatically presented by nineteenth-century Catholicism, with its official denunciations of civil and religious liberty, Church-State separation, amoral economic organization, and scientific and cultural work devoid of explicit Christian content or reference. Because such a worldly world simply should not exist, its source must be found outside the church, in demonic forces, conspiratorial intrigues, and such basic evils as human pride and greed. While not opposed to converting individuals, the church placed its highest priority on its own institutional integrity and survival. It must hold firm to traditional doctrines, firm lines of authority, and its own understanding of how society should be organized. Only a return to the church would alleviate social evils and restore order and true liberty. In such a stance lay the sources of the Ultramontane movement in Roman Catholicism, which combined concrete efforts to strengthen papal authority within the church with clarification of the yawning gap that existed between the church and the "so-called modern world."

Evangelical Christianity and Roman Catholicism both embraced a fairly clear understanding of the social role of religion. Each adopted specific strategies for dealing with society, the one seeking to renew social and cultural institutions by converting individuals to Christ, the other by recapturing social and cultural institutions for that agency which alone connected heaven and earth, the Church. Catholics (and many Anglicans and Lutherans) set out on various crusades to alleviate the suffering of the poor, to combat social evils and vices, and to win a greater degree of justice in society, all with the intention of strengthening the Church and bringing about a restoration of established Christianity. In France, for example, Frederick Ozanam persuaded a generation of young Catholics to turn away from the endless struggle to control the State and concentrate instead on "the social question." Through acts of charity inspired by the Gospel, they would witness to the charity and love of Jesus and eventually overcome the hostility of the poor and restore a Christian culture and society. Later a Christian social movement arose among paternalistic employers and aristocrats bent on bringing back a benevolent royal government which would protect the poor and insure justice, all under the inspiration of Christianity and the authority of the Church. Similarly, in Germany, Emmanuel von Ketteler, Bishop of Mainz, organized working-class Catholics to redress injustice through workers' organizations and a Catholic political party. His program, which won papal endorsement in *Rerum Novarum* in 1891, was moderate and reformist but, like the encyclical, it regarded secular society as fundamentally illegitimate and argued for the restoration of "a

Christian social order." This intense desire to "restore all things in Christ," to prove the moral depravity and practical failure of modernity, and persuade nations, classes, and governments to resume their rightful role in Christendom remained the major stance of orthodox Roman Catholics through the first half of the twentieth century.

For Catholics, it was less the preaching of the Gospel than the spread of the church which would discipline the people, limit the dangers of immorality and vice, and allow for an orderly freedom. Organized efforts to combat poverty, drunkenness, and injustice would bring apathetic Catholics back to regular church attendance and Christian practice. Directed at those beyond the church, it was a kind of pre-evangelization, based on the assumption that the saving word of God would not be heard if the stomach was empty or the heart filled with bitterness. In its extreme form, this approach to social action in the context of freedom was linked to a view of history. Once there had been Christian societies in which persons recognized their social obligations and expressed their mutual rights and responsibilities through a range of private and public institutions supported by the moral power of the church. The Reformation had broken people's loyalty to the church, unleashing individual energies and eroding bonds of community and mutual obligation. The end product was the hyper-individualism of liberalism, with no personal recognition of social obligation, leaving only the State to protect the weak. Disestablishment and religious liberty were ultimately self-defeating; only a return to the church could restore civil authority and social harmony and alleviate class conflict. For evangelicals the agents of social regeneration were regenerated individuals; for ecclesiastical reformers the agency of social regeneration was the church itself.

II

Isaac Thomas Hecker was an evangelical Catholic. The substance and style of Catholic resistance to modernity remained alien to Hecker's experience and imagination. As alert to the failings of Protestantism and modern culture as any born Catholic, he was insensitive to the creative power of evangelical Christianity to maintain its own strength and continually occasion protest and reform in the larger society. Nevertheless, the imperatives arising from personal freedom and popular democracy were so much a part of Hecker's life and experience that they became self-evident, taken for granted, like the water in which the fish must swim. His profoundly mystical experience of God's presence in his own life and in history, his instinctive dedication to freedom and human dignity, his confidence in the American people, and his deep personal commitment to the Roman Catholic church combined to form a uniquely American, and therefore necessarily evangelical, understanding of faith, church, and mission.

At an early stage of his religious development Hecker concluded that religion was the key to social as well as personal questions. As a young man, Hecker was active in the Workingman's Party of New York, posting handbills of meetings, working on campaigns and even, at the age of fifteen, proposing at a ward meeting a set of resolutions on the money question. In this setting he first met Orestes Brownson, then the leading champion of radical social democracy in the country. The object of their efforts, Hecker recalled years later, was "the amelioration of the conditions of the most numerous classes of society in the speediest manner." There was little of religion in their politics, as Hecker remembered it, but they often referred to a generalized Christianity: "Christ was the big Democrat and the Gospel was the true Democratic platform." While Hecker was never again so directly involved in causes, he did not regret the experience. They were "guileless men absorbed in seeking a solution for the problems of life," he wrote a half-century later. Nor were they, as social reformers, "given over to theories altogether wrong"; if adopted, they might have prevented "some of the problems" which later threatened "public order."[1]

In 1840 Hecker was shaken from his life of bakery work and reform enthusiasm by a powerful religious experience which led him to embark on a search for religious truth and a new direction for his life. As his biographer, Vincent Holden, put it, "the focus of his attention, interest and concern shifted from social reform and the physical problem of the universe to the intensely personal problem of himself and his creator."[2] Hecker, like many of his contemporaries, saw his own early life as a progression from political reform to social reform, then to a consideration of first principles which in turn led to basic religious issues. "I had gone through the different heresies of Protestantism and the different social and political theories which assume to take the place of religion," he recalled near the end of his life. "Oh! how long did I try to make politics serve for my religion!"[3]

At Brook Farm Hecker tried to find answers to his personal needs to understand and ground his experience of God and to orient his life in an idealistic, positive direction. It had become clear to him that social evils were "not so much social as personal, and it would not be by a social reform that they would be remedied, but by a personal one."[4] In his diary in 1843 he expressed this schematically in a triangle with the three sides labelled personal reform, social reform, and political reform and within the triangle the words "Unity, Church, Religion." For personal, political, and social fulfillment, one thing was needed: religion, a religion that was certain, unifying, and present in an organized way through a church. Protestantism was too divided and divisive, and too negative in its view of human nature to provide the answer, while Transcendentalism proved too abstract, too cold, too detached from the real world.

Hecker was also preoccupied in these years with his own loneliness and inability to find stable, intimate relationships. He regretted as well the manner in which American society separated individuals from one another. What could bind them together into one nation and create forms of authority, self-discipline, community, and mutuality? Only religion and only a religion which was universally recognized as true. One key to such a religion he found in the Catechism of the Council of Trent:

> Every true Christian possesses nothing which he should not consider common to all others with himself, and should, therefore, be prepared promptly to relieve an indigent fellow creature; for he that is blessed with worldly goods, and sees his brother in want, and will not assist him, is at once convicted of not having the love of God within him.[5]

The social problem became a very personal problem for Hecker as he struggled to determine how to deal with his own worldly responsibilities. During his sojourn at Brook Farm he occasionally referred in his diary to the conflict between riches and worldly responsibilities and the total dedication to the life of the Spirit to which he felt himself called. Nurtured on biblical Christianity, he regularly referred to the dangers, to the "curse" of riches, and to the "well of love and gratitude" which opened before those who were stripped of possessions.[6] Filled with the romantic passion of the day and place, Hecker looked with disdain on the world's work and searched for something better, echoing his friend Thoreau in his yearning for a fuller and richer life. Thinking of the work that awaited him at home with his brothers, he spoke to them through the diary:

> This is not work to me, it is death, it is no work, nay worse, it is sin, hence damnation, and I am not ready to go to hell yet, friend, I would rather beat my head against the wall, die in the battle, than accept practically, indolently, the slow, lingering annihilation of my soul. . . . Your work gives *me* no activity, no action, I am not *in* the work you set before me. It is dead, lifeless work for me, and to starve if I must, is better than to do the profane, the sacrilegious labor you place before me. . . . I want God's living work to do. My labor must be a sermon.[7]

Failing to find "God's living work" at Brook Farm, he went to Fruitlands, which promised a life of labor and self-denial which would sanctify work and integrate principles of truth with an entire way of life. Arriving there, he wrote his family that "if the people are what they seem to be, they will be the means of bringing out and fixing that which has led me of late and been dimly foreshadowed in my speech and action."[8] He was quick to note that on the first day he worked more than he would at home, as it was harvest time. Hecker lasted only two weeks, however; Fruitlands lacked what he thought was the proper balance between work and reflection. Now, there was nowhere to go but home. For the next few months he tried to readjust to his "old life" at the expense of his brothers, demanding, with some arrogance, that as owners of the business they renounce profits, live simply, and practice in business the law of love.[9] Despite their efforts to accommodate him, he remained unsatisfied, returning finally to Concord, professedly to study languages, but in fact to reflect and finally to make his choice to enter the Catholic church.

While Hecker's direct contact during his quest with evangelical or revivalist Christianity was limited, evangelical assumptions permeated the atmosphere. Blending uneasily with the current of Romanticism in New England, Bible Christianity and emphasis on personal conversion was omnipresent. Men and women at Brook Farm sought religious perfection and, converted to purity and high ideals, sought to change their lives to conform to their new inner disposition. Hecker was totally bound up with this culture and this understanding of human life. "It is no use to attempt to reform society with human regulations," he wrote, "for these are no more than the rules of human beings and it is they who need reform."[10] For the individual this meant the pursuit of the "divine life within the soul," seeking first the Kingdom of God, to be found not through "nature, philosophy, science, art or by any other method than that of the Gospel, the perfect surrender of the *whole* heart to God."[11] All persons must seek conditions of life necessary for that inner divine life; wordly activity, which Hecker shunned so passionately, reflected and reinforced a worldly spirit. Total submission to God, a submission Hecker felt increasingly could only be found in the church, demanded a change in each person's way of life, not by retreat to monastic isolation or sectarian righteousness but by directing one's life and work to the extension of that one way of life which alone answered the religious needs of men and women and the social needs of peoples and nations.

III

The universality of the church, its reach through history, across social classes and across national boundaries, its integral identity with the whole of humanity, was a major attraction to the young convert desperately in search of solid ground for his own personal experience of the Holy Spirit. He was a romantic

Catholic, one converted to the idea of the Church, its doctrines, traditions, and symbolism. Before he made his decision to enter the church his association with Catholics consisted of one rather unsuccessful conversation with Archbishop John Hughes of New York and one more inspiring visit to a small chapel in West Roxbury for an Easter Service.

With decision came new associations, and the experience could be disillusioning. Hecker was largely unmoved by Bishop John Fitzpatrick, who, instead of seeking the reasons that led the young searcher to Rome, began testing him for dangerous views, particularly on private property.[12] Back in New York, the gentle, educated auxiliary bishop John McCloskey was more sympathetic, but discovery of the time-bound church of real people continued. "It never can be too often uttered that Catholicism means the universal Good and True and Beautiful," he noted in his diary, but he learned that ideals and practice often did not coincide. In January, 1845, for example, he noted his concern over the practice of pew rentals. As a Protestant he never sat in such pews "from principle: how much less would one tolerate it as a Catholic." He spoke with McCloskey, who presented the prudential reasons for the practice, but Hecker "felt the providential and unconditional faith in God would be the sure and only course for the church to pursue." However, as the practice, though "rather repugnant to the spirit of the Church," was temporary and not permanent, he decided to "rest awhile" but he wrote Brownson that there was "temporally speaking, much to be done and undone in the Church as it now is."[13]

This tension was especially severe because of Hecker's strong sense of patriotism and confidence in the special character of American society. Hecker admired the strong sense of independence and honest endeavor which characterized his generation, traits he often summed up under the word "manly." Catholicism might appear to emphasize the subordination of individual to authority and thus be foreign to the temperament of the American people, but Hecker concluded, on the contrary, that Catholicism provided a solid objective foundation for those human qualities. The church could guide persons toward full independence, giving them a real destiny toward which to aim and a means of achieving that destiny which need not compro-

mise their personal dignity or independence, yet in practice this
was not always self-evident. When he visited Archbishop Hughes
before his conversion, he came away with concerns that continually reoccurred in his life. Hughes "said that the Church was
one of discipline ... he seemed to think I had some loose
Protestant notions of the Church," Hecker noted in his diary. "I
feel not in the least disinclined to be governed by the most rigid
discipline of any church, yet I am not prepared to enter the
Roman Catholic Church at present. The Roman Catholic
Church is not national with us hence it does not meet our wants
nor does it fully understand and sympathize with the experience
and dispositions of our people."[14]

Later, among the Redemptorists, he experienced an arbitrary authority which he was prepared to accept himself, though
he thought it reflected attitudes and assumptions repugnant to
the American character, thus limiting effective missionary work.
His resentment of such "foreign" attitudes burst forth in a letter
to his brother George while in Rome in 1858:

> In my opinion you will not obtain from any foreigner a
> manly support in our favor. It is not *in* them; and more, their
> national feeling of jealousy must be conquered to do it. *They
> will not and do not trust us Americans,* for they have the same
> suspicions that the superiors of the Congregation entertain,
> and they dare not expose these, for these are but fears of our
> influence and future predominance. I know what I am say-
> ing; the Irish hierarchy in the United States would keep us
> under the German domination and servitude on the same
> grounds. They will both unite against any Catholic American
> movement, and make it a common cause. Our hope is in the
> American portion of the hierarchy. . . . I tell you my present
> sentiments. I go in for emancipation from foreignism in the
> Catholic Church in the United States and take a Catholic
> American position.[15]

Hecker thus never felt a close identity with the immigrant,
working class people who constituted the bulk of the church's
membership. During the Redemptorist period, he avoided presenting the major sermons which sought to arouse a sense of sin
and repentance and bring persons to the sacraments. Instead,

while sharing the work of the confessional, he preferred to give the instructional talks and to explore ways to reach those non-Catholics whose interest was aroused by the mission. The new community he founded was similarly intended to address the needs of the more educated American laity while directing its major energies toward intelligent non-Catholics. In 1856, he wrote: "Up to the present time the Church has been almost exclusively devoted to provide for her own children, and this has been almost too great a task for her, as the immigration from Ireland was so great" but, he added quickly, "this has to some extent ceased and we can be thinking of extending our holy faith among the American people."[16] Eighteen months later he wrote to his colleagues from Rome that he was more sympathetic than they to the establishment of a "new company more aimed at non-Catholics than the great mass of poor Catholics."[17] At a conference for Paulist seminarians in 1878, Hecker began by dividing "our audience" into three parts: (1) "Catholics from the old countries" whose faith rested on tradition; "all that they require for their salvation is the faithful administration of the ordinary means of the Church," by implication available through the diocesan clergy; (2) "their children born here," who from their education and "the influence of their surroundings" have had their intelligence awakened and "require for their perseverence in the faith, and their satisfaction, a further, more explicit, knowledge of their religion"; and (3) the non-Catholics among whom "the inroads of sectarianism, infidelity, and atheism" have rendered "the present moment opportune to present to them the truths of Catholicity." For the Paulists, conferences on religion, that is public instruction and lectures, "should be chiefly addressed to these last two classes."

Hecker went on to outline the approach which had by then become standard for him and, as Joseph Gower has pointed out, constituted a major advance in apologetics. He emphasized that the "dominant tendency of our times" was reason, "the only element which is admitted by all as the criterion of truth." Reason was capable of posing questions about the purpose and end of life but not answering them, Hecker argued. Only religion could provide the answers, and among Americans two religions claimed to do so, Protestantism and Catholicism. The former failed to meet the test of reason because its answers were multiple and uncertain; only Catholicism offered certainty based upon divine revelation and passed the tests of Scripture and tradition. "A man who would not yield up the gift of intelligence and be a Christian must needs be a Catholic," Hecker concluded. Therefore, Paulists should seek topics "before the public mind," accept the "civilization, political institutions, of the people" among whom they labored and should assume that "everyone loves the truth and is seeking it out with sincerity and would embrace it if he could only see it clearly."[18]

Hecker's understanding of the relationship between Church and society, arose from this profound affirmation of human intelligence and liberty. For Hecker, as for most Americans, a political society, or a church, composed of men and women who were participants by accidents of birth or by ignorance of alternatives was of lesser value than one composed of people who had made free and intelligent decisions.

> The more a civilization solicits the exercise of man's intelligence and enlarges the field for the action of his free will, the broader will be the basis it offers for sanctity. Ignorance and weakness are the negation of life; they are either sinful or the consequences of sin, and to remedy these common evils is the aim of the Christian religion. Enlightened intelligence and true liberty of the will are essential conditions of all moral action and the means of merit.[19]

How were free and intelligent people to arrive at the one religion, the one Church, needed for the success of the democratic experiment? Hecker, confident in the truth of Catholic claims, was convinced that those claims need only be presented clearly, forcefully, detached from the accidental and non-essential features of European and traditional culture which surrounded them. Like the non-separatist Puritans of New England who believed that the Bible taught one message, so that its authority was sufficient to secure a uniformity of faith and morals, Hecker believed that Christianity had one whole, complete, and readily available expression, the Roman Catholic church, which combined the best elements of Protestantism with those elements which Protestantism had lost: "She is the center at which all aspirations meet, the answer to all the wants of the human heart . . . she is the source of true life, and the true element of progress."[20] If Catholicism failed to convert America it could only be because of a lack of faith and confidence among Catholics or a lack of honesty and intelligence on the part of non-Catholic Americans. His work was a work of clarifying perceptions by removing the cultural barriers that prevented communication. If this could be done, Americans would become Catholic, Catholics would endorse the claims of democracy and make them their own, and the Kingdom of God would be at hand.

In 1866, at the Second Plenary Council of Baltimore, the time seemed right. A united hierarchy with promising leadership, an apocalyptic civil war which had clearly revealed the limitations of Protestantism and the relevance of Catholicism's unique qualities, and a lessening of prejudice all seemed to promise "The Future Triumph of the Church." Noting the dramatic improvements in communications, transportation, and scientific knowledge, Hecker told the assembled prelates that the signs of the times pointed toward the removal of barriers between peoples and the opening of history toward unity and brotherhood.

> Nowhere is there a promise of a brighter future for the Church than in our own country. Here, thanks to our American Constitution, the church is free to do her divine work. Here she finds a civilization in harmony with divine teachings. Here Christianity is promised a reception from an intelligent and free people, that she will give forth a development of unprecedented glory. For religion is never so beautiful as when in connection with knowledge and freedom. Let us, therefore, arise and open up our eyes to the bright future that is before us! Let us labor with a lively faith, a firm hope, and a charity that knows no bounds, by every good work and good example, for the reign of God's Kingdom upon earth.[21]

One source of Hecker's optimism was a positive anthropology, as several students of Hecker have noted. From his warm, supportive mother and brothers, the openness, hospitality and friendship he experienced in New England, perhaps from the intensity of his experience of God, so often expressed in feminine images, Hecker drew a positive, optimistic understanding of human possibility. Frustrated by lack of understanding, even from those he loved, frustrated, too, by the abstractions and philosophical confusion of the Transcendentalists, he knew the limitations that existed in reality. Nevertheless, the hopeful Christian humanism expressed while at Brook Farm held firm even after his entry into a Catholic church whose dominant theology and pastoral approach arose from a far more pessimistic outlook:

> Man is not aware of his Godlike capacities. . . . Man, thou hast thy creation in thy own hands. . . . Men are not fully awakened to the responsibility that rests upon them, to the deep eternal importance of every act of life, even a word, a thought. . . . Man gives being to that which had no being. He creates something where there was nothing. He is a Creator. A God in God. Every man I meet is an unconscious prophecy to me. I would awaken him to the wonder of his being.[22]

Like his American generation Hecker imagined that the reason this greatness did not show forth was because of the weight of tradition and prejudice; reform was always the removal of impediments. The conviction that the hopes and aspiration of people, that creative potential grounded in the spirit, was not a vain illusion, but had a real object, guided Hecker throughout his own quest. Man had a "destiny." Attracted to the Transcendentalism of New England, he despaired of it because it failed in the end to ground human hopes in reality. As he wrote years later, Brownson "was firmly persuaded, and so am I, that the greatest fault of men generally is that they deem the life of their souls, thoughts, judgments and convictions, yearnings, aspirations and longings, to be too subject to illusion to be worthy of their attentive study and manly fidelity; that even multitudes of Catholics partly undervalue the divine reality of their inner life. . . ."[23]

This self-doubt, this failure to trust the instincts of human nature, accounted for many social evils. "The secret cause of dishonesty in public life and frivolity in private personal conduct in the case of men and women of good natural qualities," Hecker argued, "is their hesitation and uncertainty concerning the reality of the objects of their higher aspirations."[24] Thus in apologetics, evangelism, and reform, Hecker was determined to ground his approach on the foundation of human capacities and human hopes, giving rise to an inwardness reflective of evangelical religion and Transcendentalist humanism:

> Human Nature alone can be taken for granted. The Religion, therefore, that is to meet the wants of the age, and answer its demands, must take its starting point from man's nature. It is, therefore, upon the essential and indestructible elements of Human Nature that Religion, particularly in this country, has to raise the foundations of its temple. The sanctuary of Religion must be restored to the place where the God of nature placed it, in the human soul.[25]

Hecker's spirituality was intimately related to this vision of human possibility. By the 1860s he had become convinced that providence was providing special opportunities in America to exemplify the new type of Christian who in turn would evangelize the nation.

> Our American character is suitable for a certain type of spiritual perfection. An attempt to bring out any other or impose any other upon it, will be unsuccessful, if not fatal in many instances. Besides, our faith can make no great progress until we present the ideal of life as conceived by our best minds. To do this, requires the identification of our faith with what is good and true in our type of character. Our Faith must take root in our national characteristics and we find ourselves entirely at home in it. My wish is to help my fellow countrymen and women in this work. I believe our civilization presents to Christianity a broader basis to rear a spiritual life upon, than any other form of civilization. I wish to see advantage taken of this, and prevent a narrow and repugnant form of spirituality from taking its place: one which we cannot adopt and will not accept generally. It is my conviction that if there were everywhere souls presenting a type of Christian perfection consistent with our faith, and its doctrines and teachings, and in harmony with our American character, this would go a great way in reconciling our religion to our people. I have the conviction that I can be all

the better Catholic because I am an American: and all the better American because I am a Catholic. This shewn [sic] many obstacles in the way of the conversion of our people will be removed.[26]

It was through a thoroughly evangelized people that this new form of Christian Americanism and Americanist Christianity would become visible. At its deepest level, it indicated the way in which Hecker saw, in light of divine providence, the special qualities of the nation.

The nature of the work to be done is plain to my mind and has been for years; and for years I have been approximating to it. I look forward to the union of all that is divine in our holy faith with the increased activity of intelligence and freedom of action in our country, as destined to recast *all* things and give birth to a new and higher form of civilization.... In regard to spiritual matters, the same views and convictions actuate me. I aim in bringing the intellect and will into complete union with Divine Truth and under its guidance will be brought about, in the individual, that which eventually will be developed in Society. Given the union of the soul with God, preserving at the same time all that is true and genuine in the American character, and you have the special object I aim at in personal direction. Now where this identification of our religion with all that is genuine in our character is made, we shall have in such persons a model character, the type of what we may anticipate in the future, when our religion has become universal in our country. This type of character will be superior to any that can be produced by a false or incomplete form of Christianity, hence attractive, and the means of bringing the truth of our Religion to bear on the minds of our countrymen. *Personal perfection* is a means for the conversion of our country.[27]

Hecker's positive view of human nature served another purpose as well, one central to his overall objective. His large task, as Edward Langlois has pointed out, was to show Protestants that Catholicism was not anti-democratic and Catholics that American democracy was not necessarily Protestant. More, he had to show that Catholicism was more suited to American democratic aspirations than was Protestantism. One way he did this was to identify Protestantism with Calvinism and to argue that Calvinism's pessimistic assessment of human nature was in the long run incompatible with self-government. Catholicism, upholding the importance of both nature and grace, good works and faith, while maintaining that human reason and free will remained intact after the Fall, blended positively with the nation's aspirations. Accepting the prevailing notion of a special mission of America in light of the coming Kingdom of God, Hecker argued that only Catholicism could provide the positive affirmation of human possibility, the training in civic virtue and discipline, and the political and cultural unity necessary for the fulfillment of the nation's promise. It could play this role, however, only if it moved beyond its preoccupation with externals and returned to its evangelical origins, preaching the Gospel and restoring faith, and destiny, to their primacy in the inner world of spirit. Beyond Catholicism and Protestantism was Christ and his Revelation, the object of which "was to establish the Kingdom of God in human souls and through them to the rest of the world."[28] The object of man's inner and outer aspirations, the destiny of persons and nations, was the same: the Kingdom of God. The way to that destiny, for people and nations, was the true Church of Christ, which grounded converted persons in a universal community and provided nations with the only way to assure unity, freedom, and purpose.

IV

Unlike his European Catholic contemporaries, Hecker never fully internalized a radical separation of the Church and the modern world. Unlike liberal Christians, he never accepted a separation of religion and culture which would make of the Church simply one agency of goodness among many, a kind of pluralism which rested content in a culture based on secular principles and operating by processes beyond the reach of any religion. Unlike some evangelical Protestants, he could not accept a sense of social obligation and responsibility that was largely personal; redeemed persons could not make a just or happy world by themselves; they needed an organized body, the Church, for the security of their faith and for the full realization of their shared humanity. Conversion to Catholicism, for Hecker, was a reconciliation of man with God and with himself, a reconciliation that would ultimately bring about both a united, universal Church and a fully human culture. Both his method of preaching and his hopes for its results reflected this integration of the religious and the social.

In a letter to Bishop Bayley of Newark in 1863 Hecker described the enthusiastic response he was receiving to his public lectures in a way which clearly expressed this approach to evangelization. His method was that set forth in his two books, "searching for the element in man's nature to which the doctrine or sacrament for the lecture addresses itself," then seeking the religion "which recognizes this element and is responsive to it." "By the authority of the premises in their own bosoms," he reported, the audience is led to see the failure of Protestantism and to see that only the Catholic religion is "true to their intelligence, the voice of conscience and the instincts implanted in their nature by the hand of God."

> The power and reach of this method is much greater than I ever dreamed of. It does away with opposition and silences objections. What can a man do, deny the deep necessities of his nature? Shall he say that God implanted these in his soul, and with no intention of satisfying them? I avoid by this plan entirely, the old system of controversy, and everything personal. I throw off everything professional, preach from the platform or stage in my secular dress, extempore, I tell them frankly that I come among them not as an advocate of the Catholic Church, but as a man who owes supreme allegiance to Truth and if I advocate the Catholic Church, it is because I am convinced that she is the true church, and for no other reason.

Lest there be any doubt of the implications of Hecker's approach, he drew them out for the bishop, and his words indicated the problem that would arise in his later career, first with Brownson, then with the church of Vatican I: " . . . Religion will never regain its ascendancy over the minds of men, Catholics or non-Catholics, by imposing it upon them by way of authority, in this country at least, and I think it would be well if they understood this same thing in Europe. Religion to regain its ascendancy must find its foundation in the elements of our nature, and on these appeal to men, and awaken their minds to its necessity, beauty and glory."[29] In a eulogy for his friend Jeremiah Cummings in 1866 he sounded a similar theme:

> He did not regard Catholic truth as a weapon to beat down an opponent with, but rather as the food of the soul, and he sought to prepare it with such skill that would entice those who were ahunger for it to taste its sweetness and be satisfied. He did not anticipate the gaining of erring souls by threatening denunciations, but like St. Paul before the Athenians, he began by admitting the truths that they partially possessed already, leading them on to their full possession, and to other kindred truths until the whole Catholic truth took captive their understandings and won their hearts.[30]

For Hecker, then, the future of the American church, and perhaps the whole church, would be assured only by vigorous evangelical efforts to convert persons and through them the whole of society. The church could not grow simply by perpetuating old world ways; these would fade in the second and third generation in any case. Nor was it to grow simply by rescuing persons thrown from the decks of a floundering Protestant ship, though he certainly believed it was floundering. Such images reflected a separation of religion and culture he never admitted, perhaps never understood. For Hecker religion and human civilization, for the good of both, must eventually be integrated and that goal must inform all the work of the church. While in Rome in 1857 he noted that he was "for accepting the American civilization with its usage and customs" because, "leaving aside other reasons, it is the only way by which Catholicity can become the religion of our people." The mind set of those European and immigrant leaders who wished only to enable the church to survive in a hostile world seemed always to Hecker a fearful withdrawal from the essential task of reconciling religion and human culture, for religion was nothing more than one side of the entire human experience. Openness to American life was more than a tactic for expansion, it was an indispensable attitude if the church was to fulfill its mission of meeting the needs of persons and affirming and grounding human destiny. In these terms Hecker was clearly right to believe "The character and spirit of our people and their institutions must find themselves at home in Religion in the way those of other nations have, and it is on this basis that the Catholic Religion alone can make progress in our country."[31]

V

Hecker was a democrat in the sense that he understood and appreciated the new freedom consequent on the American experiment. He was not a radical political democrat, for a basic ambivalence about democratic politics plagued his commentary on public affairs. Nor was he a social democrat in any sense other than in having a faith in equality of opporunity. As early as 1844 Hecker had repudiated any simplistic view of democracy. The notion that the voice of the people was the voice of God, he wrote, "would be true in a political sense if all citizens were members of Christ's body in full communion with God, filled with his grace, and being Christians in every deed." Indeed, the Church was infallible precisely because it was such a body. The State, however, populated by Christians and non-Christians, "is apt to commit mistakes as well as individuals."[32] Accordingly, the direction of the Church's effort should be to awaken and guide consciences, seeking to restore faith and love in the inner life of men and women, showing that if, and in the end only if, they would face the needs of their hearts could they find the fulfillment of their social and political aspirations.

Still, Hecker trusted people, individually and collectively. He was prepared to work in the context of freedom, to deal openly and affirmatively with popular opinion. For this reason he seemed sometimes naïve, even heretical. Brownson came to regard Hecker's optimism as dangerous, questioning particularly his view of original sin and "exclusive salvation" through the church. At one point he wrote that "Father Hecker is semipelagian without knowing it."[33] Worst of all was Hecker's confidence in popular judgment. Brownson in 1870 wrote his son that "Father Hecker's notion that Democracy is favorable to Catholicity is worse than foolish. Democracy rests on popular opinion and never looks beyond and no people that makes popular opinion its criterion of right and wrong is or can be Catholic. Catholicity spreads among a people only in proportion as they habitually act from the law of God which is above kings and peoples alike, above popular opinion and the pleasure of the prince."[34] Hecker would have agreed, in principle, but his own experience led him to the conviction that men could be persuaded to accept Catholicity only from within, that their adherence to "the law of God," in principle above them, must be voluntary in the new democratic society that was emerging. This did not disturb him as it did Brownson precisely because Hecker believed that God's law was in fact conducive to personal happiness and social well being. By 1870 the disillusioned Brownson was prepared to bombard the public with its failures, hoping, but not expecting, that they would recognize their need for the church's authority and submit to it. Hecker, in contrast, persisted in his confidence in reason, in human nature, and in the church, accepting the reality of voluntarism and, unlike Brownson, celebrating it as indeed the best context for the church because it alone assured that adherence to Christ and his Church was free, honest, and deeply rooted.

Hecker's understanding of the voluntary character of religion in modern society went further, for he acknowledged that the Church's ability to exercise authority, even over its own members and even on matters of faith and morals, depended on the willing consent of its members. "The divine authority of the church . . . possesses no practical value and effect except what is voluntarily given to it on the part of the faithful," he told a congregation.

> The Church does not ask you to accept her authority in the management of your secular and temporal affairs. These you know as much about as priests, and likely more. What, however, regards the eternal welfare of your souls, on these interests she was divinely commissioned to speak. Here she expects the cheerful and voluntary obedience of all her chil-

> dren. Is that asking too much? I think not . . . loveful obedi-
> ence to divine guidance is not only the primary want of man's
> heart, but one that he gives cheerfully, and while giving it, he
> is ennobled, exalted and made free.[35]

Many evils persisted in the world which the church was against
but she depended on the free support of her members. "She does
not, and cannot force submission," Hecker said. "Forced submission can make slaves, but not Christians."

A further reflection of Hecker's evangelical approach was
his realization that social and political action must be the work of
the laity. Clearly there was a problem here. On the one hand,
Hecker had argued that Catholicism could supply the authority,
unity, and sense of community which could enable the nation to
fulfill its promise. On the other hand he also realized that this
could only be accomplished in freedom, for intelligence and
liberty were premises for the church, the nation, and even for the
Kingdom of God itself. The church could teach, and exercise
authority, on specifically religious matters, but even here, it
depended on the free consent of members. If the State failed to
understand the importance of freedom, revolution was inevitable;
if the church failed, "apostasy" was equally assured. On "secular" matters of moral significance, the church could teach but
could only act through its members, who, cooperating with their
priests, promoted temperance, charity, education, and the amelioration of social ills, while working as enlightened, instructed
individuals in business, government, and other secular areas.
More than any other Catholic of the period, in Europe or
America, Hecker respected the independence of the laity and saw
the layperson's work in society, in family, neighborhood, factory,
counting house, and government hall, as morally significant and
central to the mission of the church. He influenced a later
generation to view the educational, political, and economic advancement of the Catholic laity as good, not simply because it
made greater resources available for church activities or en-
hanced the prestige and status of all Catholics, but also because it
made Catholic influence possible in the midst of contemporary
American society. The church of the future would be "a church
of energetic individuals," as John Ireland called it, in which

educated, intelligent, and "manly" laypeople worked to Christianize the social order and bring 'more and more Americans to see the value and necessity of the church for the fulfillment of their personal and national aspirations.

In a sermon in 1863 Hecker noted that each age had its characteristic forms of spirituality and sanctity: martyrs in the early days of the church, the hermits and desert fathers in a time of cultural collapse, the cloistered life in the age of faith, the militant vigor of Ignatius Loyola and the Jesuits in the age of the Counter Reformation. "Each class of men did in their day what their age required. Each was true to its time, its wants, its promises, and therefore had its peculiar beauty and charm." What should characterize Christian presence in the nineteenth century? The age claimed to be one of "advanced civilization; to be marked by unprecedented diffusion of intelligence and liberty." In such a civilization the ideal of sanctification would be "the union of religion with a fully enlightened intelligence and an entire liberty of will, directed wholly to the realization of the great end of our being." In this setting he pointed to the example of St. Joseph, who found God and spiritual perfection in the midst of daily life:

> To find God and to be one with God, a solitary life in the desert was not necessary to St. Joseph. He was in the world, and found God where he was. He sanctified his work by carrying God with him into the work-shop. St. Joseph was no flower of the desert, or plant of the cloister; he found the means of perfection in the world, and consecrated it to God by making its cares and duties subservient to divine purposes.

St. Joseph practiced virtue in his home, which was "his cloister" and while working contemplated divine truths, achieving a degree of perfection "in society and human relationships" as great as the martyr, the monk, or the missionary.

> Our age is not an age of martyrdom, nor an age of hermits, nor a monastic age. Although it has its martyrs, its recluses, and its monastic communities, these are not, and are not likely to be, its prevailing types of Christian perfection. Our age lives in its busy marts, in counting rooms, in workshops,

in homes, and in the varied relations that form human society, and it is in these that sanctity is to be introduced. . . . This, then, is the field of conquest for the heroic Christian of our day. Out of the cares, toils, duties, afflictions, and responsibilities of daily life are to be built the pillars of sanctity . . . of our age. This is the coming form of triumph of Christian virtue.[36]

The entire church faced the evangelical imperative to reach out in mission for the conversion of men and women. "Every Catholic, whatever may be his station in life, is called to cooperate in the work" of evangelization, Hecker told a lay audience in St. Louis. "Wherever you see a Catholic true to his religion, where you see a Catholic setting his face against the reigning vices of his time, there you will find a missionary." The signs of the times visible in private immorality and public corruption required a religious response, aimed at producing good Christians who would both resolve social problems and win converts for the church. "Honest men in commerce, unbribed legislators, upright lawyers, just judges, honest mechanics and servants, these are the apostles of the laity here and now."[37]

Hecker's concept of social action remained heavily evangelical, with converted persons exerting a benevolent impact on society. Of course, as an expression of its own solidarity and faith, the church would always reach out to the poor and needy; in doing so it would make clear the shortcomings of a secular approach and the potential of Christian benevolence. In May 1865 Hecker wrote that he had long thought about the question: "How is modern society to be saved from pauperism?" The State, aided by voluntary assistance, had proven inadequate to the task, because public charity was inefficient, overly expensive, and degrading to the poor. The only remedy, he believed, was the association of individuals who would visit the poor and the inmates of prisons and all those in need, receiving funds from government and voluntary charities but carrying out the work "for no other pay than the love of God and of their fellow-men." This remedy only the church could supply. Not only would it prove effective, but it would also "be a new phase in the demonstration of the Divine Origin of Catholicity . . . that modern man will not be slow to understand."[38] St. Paul the Apostle parish accordingly had an impressive array of charitable activities.

Hecker was shocked by the case of Edward McGlynn, pastor of St. Stephen's parish and one of a group of activist priests who gathered regularly to discuss problems facing the church in New York and in the nation. Hecker was on the fringe of this group, whose members apparently regarded him with the greatest respect. There are hints that Hecker found the conversation arising from McGlynn's "copious hospitality" mildly disturbing and when McGlynn's support of Henry George in the 1886 mayoral campaign led to his suspension from exercising priestly faculties and eventually to his excommunication, Hecker was appalled. He saw McGlynn's actions as arising from an extreme idealism and intense passion which drove him first to identify with the Georgite agitation and challenge the church's support of private property in land and then, most horribly to Hecker, to surrender his priesthood. Hecker believed that poverty and class conflict could be solved only on Catholic principles of reconciliation, harmony, and mutual responsibility. Frederick Ozanam, the French founder of the St. Vincent de Paul society, had shown the way "by bringing the wealthier classes in immediate contact with the poor," whereas McGlynn aimed to alleviate the condition of the poor without the help of the other classes, abolishing classes rather than bringing them into contact with one another. No more efficacious instrument of such reconciling reform existed than the priesthood according to Hecker. When McGlynn abandoned it, and began attacking the "ecclesiastical machine" and "slandering" priests and nuns, Hecker hoped that it was passion and not heresy. He noted that McGlynn claimed to resist the church's efforts to deprive him of his rights of citizenship, but then used his citizenship to attack the church, thus furthering the divorce of religion and politics. This was wrong, Hecker believed: "All free institutions stand in need of the support of religion, and the love of country needs for its life the love of God." Nevertheless, the McGlynn episode, and the problems of social justice it highlighted, left Hecker troubled.[39]

As a young man, Hecker concluded that the social question was at its source a religious question requiring a religious response. What was true for individuals caught in the whirlpool of contending schools of philosophy, movements of reform, and churches of all sorts was also true for the nation: a religious conversion was needed, and needed immediately. As he wrote in *Aspirations of Nature:*

> This moment is a crisis, the greatest crisis in our history. . . .
> Our destiny as a nation hinges on this moment. . . . For no
> nation, as no individual, becomes fully conscious of its capac-
> ities, discovers its divine destination, until it is wholly under
> the influence of religious inspiration. No people becomes
> properly a nation, acts as one man; unfolds its highest capa-
> bilities, displays its true genius and utmost strength, until it
> becomes not only politically and socially, but religiously, of
> one mind and heart. Religion ever was and forever must be
> the highest source of inspiration, and the most powerful
> engine of progress in every department of human activity.[40]

From his own experience Hecker concluded then that the source and solution of the social problem was to be found in religion. "There is no denying the fact that the religious problem sums up all the problems," he wrote in 1881. "In the last analysis it is religion which shapes, and by right ought to shape, among intelligent men, all institutions."[41] But the resolution, for Hecker, in contrast to most European Catholics of the day, lay less in an argument about the beneficial social role of the Catholic church than in a clearer, more positive, more intelligent proclamation of the basic religious truths on which Catholicism rested. Social vices, like personal ones, arose not from bad persons or bad institutions but from the inability of good persons to honestly believe fundamental Christian truths: "The secret cause of dis-honesty in public life and frivolity in private personal conduct in the case of men and women of good natural qualities is their hesitation and uncertainty concerning the reality of their higher aspirations."[42]

Still, for all Isaac Hecker's evangelical reliance on convert-ed, benevolent individuals, his Christianity could not be a purely individualistic religion through which converted people alone would make a perfect world. Nor could it be a purely corporate religion in which men and women surrendered their will and intelligence to the leadership of a divinely inspired and guaranteed church. The former approach he saw as ultimately sentimental and powerless, unable to ground and direct the power of individual regeneration toward historically significant objectives. It led to the chaos of Protestant sectarianism, the jumble of discordant voices, and the ultimate collapse of religion under the weight of what would later be called social sin. The latter approach, on the other hand, required the compromise of intelligence and liberty, producing feeble men and women and a church closed in on itself, leaving the world to apostasy and revolution.

Early in his life Hecker recognized that the social problem was at its heart a religious problem. Later he understood the paradox that the religious problem was itself a social problem, as Catholicism languished, tied to the styles of the past and to the cultural experiences of Latin nations and cultures. Gradually, he came to see that the way out, for non-Catholic Americans and for non-American Catholics, including those in the immigrant church, was the way of perception rather than judgment or action. There was no lack of clear and often correct judgments on both sides: non-Catholic Americans were correct in judging the church as they saw it as somewhat backward and hostile to their aspirations. Non-American Catholics were correct to judge America as they saw it as overly individualistic and in danger of collapse into religious chaos and social revolution. Nor was there any lack of action; both sides were probably too energetic in their projects for the conquest of the other. What was missing was clear perception, an ability to see clearly what was going on. Nothing exasperated Hecker's friends and critics more than his constant desire to reinterpret what was going on, and to do so in what seemed a hopelessly naïve way. Where Catholics saw Americans as sectarian and obsessed with liberty, Hecker saw them as sincere searchers after truth. Where Americans saw Catholics as hopelessly foreign and authoritarian, Hecker saw them as custodians of divine promises which brought the Holy Spirit to life in the world. Neither the Civil War nor the First Vatican Council shook his optimism; both were providential events which would bring good results. All that was needed was to probe the depths and see what was really going on.

So Hecker spent his life trying to correct perceptions, re-

move barriers of prejudice and ignorance which blinded both
Catholics and Americans to their common humanity, which
obscured the central truth that both Church and society were
historical expressions of a single human nature headed toward a
single human destiny. Possessing a nineteenth-century version of
the twentieth-century notion that religion is the heart of culture
and culture the form of religion, Hecker resisted the separation of
religion and culture while accepting and affirming for now the
separation of Church and State. He would urge Protestants to
look beyond the present forms of Catholic culture to find their
source in history and in the human soul, to see sacraments, for
example, in terms of the human needs from which they arose and
which they were designed to meet. He would urge Catholics to
look beyond the confusing variety of American experiences to
their sources in human freedom and human intelligence, each a
gift of the Creator.

Hecker attempted, but never completed, a highly creative
integration of American evangelical style with the substance and
form of Roman Catholicism. He understood that a democratic
society required a democratic religion; that the substance and
form of religion could not remain aloof from the society that
surrounded it and, if the principles on which that society were
based were sound, it should not do so. Conversely he believed
without doubt or hesitation in the truths of the Catholic church,
truths ultimately not only compatible but identical with the
truths of the American experiment. The solution lay not in any
superficial accommodation of the church to American culture,
nor in any surrender of American integrity and independence to
the sovereign sway of Catholic ecclesiastical power. Rather both
church and nation need only plumb their own traditions to their
depths, as he believed he had done, and they would find there the
same spirit, the same God, the same foundation in creation,
redemption, and salvation. Hecker wanted America to be Catholic because only in Catholicism could it find the fulfillment of its
deepest and noblest aspirations. He wanted Catholicism to become American because the United States revealed the deepest
aspirations of nature and posed the most profound questions of
the soul.

While institutions of Church and State remained separate,

the men and women who composed them met on the common ground of society and culture. Here he believed pluralism reached its limits. Customs and traditions met and clashed, religions contested with one another, social classes fought each other for power and gain. Neither democratic political institutions nor reasonable religious ones could survive if people differed and fought over every inch of power, privilege, and prestige. How to limit conflict, channel the enormous human energies unleashed by modern civilization, find ways of human living which bound people together on the basis of their common humanity rather than divided them around superficial divisions of ethnicity, class, and race; these were the issues of the day. America said to Hecker that a resolution could only be found in freedom; it must exert its claim on the reason and the heart of man. Thus his apologetics and his spirituality: Christianity must renew society from within. Learning this, he saw the limits of modern Catholic social thought, with its emphasis upon a reorganized social order. Such institutions must express changed consciousness; they cannot create it. Catholicism must probe behind the forms of monarchy and guilds and paternalistic benevolent aristocracy and find the spirit which animated them, a spirit of faith, in Man as well as in God, of hope, focused on a providential view of history, and a spirit of love expressed in community, liturgy, sacrament, and fellowship.

Thus through much of his career Hecker dreamed of carrying his evangelical message to the thousands of young Americans adrift amid rapid social change, left standing alone, manfully independent, clear-headed, and pure-hearted, waiting to hear the truth. If he could reach that audience and show them that their personal, social, and political aspirations all found their answer in Catholicism, he could convert the Americans, and thus the Americanizing Catholics as well. But something stood in his way: the church itself in its immigrant and parochial form in the United States and far worse in its Latin and Jesuit form in Europe. Just as he had dreamed of preaching the old faith to the new man in America, he eventually realized he must preach the new good news of America to the old church in Europe. If his early evangelical work had aimed at drawing Americans to the deepest recesses of their hearts to ask the seldom-faced questions of meaning and purpose buried there, so later in his life he dreamed of evangelizing European Catholicism, drawing it to consider the spirit which lay behind its forms and explode the dynamite of the Gospel long buried within.

VI

Out of his own disappointment and frustration, Hecker forged a vision of church history and the current prospects of the church. By the 1870s his highly American approach to renewal, removing the impediments from the innate disposition to seek "destiny" and associate with that church best able to promote it, had been supplemented by a growing realization that inner motivation among Catholics was needed. The church must turn away from its understandable post-Reformation concern with external dangers and consequent "restriction of personal action" in order to bring about "an expansion of individual action" appropriate to present opportunities. The new age would belong to Catholicism "not by the suppression of authority and discipline, but in fortifying individual action and greater fidelity to the action of the Holy Spirit in the soul."[43]

If the needs of a growing immigrant church in the United States restricted Hecker's hopes, the growing alienation of the church from modern culture had the same effect abroad. At home, pastoral and social needs prevented most Catholics, and most bishops, from attending to the basic Christian truths which could open the church to authentic evangelization of American culture. In Europe, the hostility of secular states and the consequent conservatism of Catholic leadership had the same effect. While in Rome for the Vatican Council Hecker wrote his brother: "The life of the members of the Church everywhere appears to be drawn not directly from the primary truths of divine faith but from the secondary; and this tendency looks as if it were on the increase. This begets weakness and instead of replacing the primary truths in a newer light, others are proposed to be added. This foreshadows decadence and deterioration."[44]

Preoccupation with externals lay at the root of the church's weakness. Yet, the very attacks upon her external power which confined the church "to the soul and the sanctuary" also provided "the direction of her recovery and future triumph." In the immediate past, Catholics lamented the loss of external power and consequently looked for external sources of renewal, in greater discipline in the church and alliance with reaction in society, an attitude which in Hecker's view, "enfeebles the Christian character." Ever optimistic, Hecker argued that Vatican I completed the work of defense; a new era lay on the horizon, its emergence "coincident with the recent changes in the political world, the predominance of the Saxon race and the more recent development of republican tendencies among the Latin-Celtic races." The latter had furnished the "human elements" for the completion of the church's authority and external government; the former would now "furnish the human elements necessary for the development of her internal character, her relations with reason, conscience, individuality, resulting in the ideal type of man—the most exalted faith united with the most thorough manhood. The earliest example will be the product of the most complete expression of the Saxon elements in the political order united with Catholicity in the United States."[45]

Hecker saw public events in a similar light. The movement toward freedom required greater popular political participation, making the church's responsibility to instruct the people concerning their new duties doubly important. Public opinion, not kings and princes, was now central to political affairs, making separation of Church and State inevitable. "The Church will necessarily . . . be called upon to assume her rightful independence and look for her chief support to the voluntary offerings of her faithful children," resting religion, as in early Christianity, on the foundations of "the conviction of each individual soul and upon personal sacrifice." Yet Hecker clearly did not regard such separation "as the normal and more perfect condition of Society. Religious dogmas are the basis of political principles, whether we recognize the fact or no, and sooner or later an intelligent people will see they harmonize, and seek a union. Europe is now in the act of temporary separation . . . necessary to a transition to a more perfect union."[46]

By the 1870s Hecker had worked out a complex understanding of the historical relationship of the church to modern society. The period which began with the Reformation climaxed with the

Vatican Council. The need then had been to strengthen the external defenses of the church against assault, and the agents for this external combat had been the Jesuits. Now, for Hecker, that work was completed, for the Council had guaranteed the inner discipline and external strength of the church by perfecting her governance under the Pope and insuring the maintenance of doctrine through infallibility. The stage was set now for the reconciliation of church and society by recalling that each arose ultimately from the depths of the human spirit and each reflected profound yearnings of human beings for truth and for a clear sense of destiny. It would not be too much to say that Hecker blended American evangelical social Christianity into the ecclesiastical social Christianity of Catholicism. The goal indeed was the restoration of Catholicity, the means were evangelical, bringing first Catholics and then all persons to awareness of the presence of the Spirit within which could not but result in their affirmative response to the Spirit present in the church. Together converted persons and a mission-oriented, evangelistic church would reconcile the false tensions of the age and create a new era in human history. Now the church could return to "her normal course of action":

> With the divine external authority of the Church completed, fixed beyond all controversy, her attention and that of all her children can now be turned to the divine and interior authority of the Holy Ghost in the soul. The whole church giving her attention to the interior inspirations of the Holy Spirit will give birth to her renewal and enable her to reconquer her place and true position in Europe and the whole world.[47]

As an American, Hecker had long before come to understand the voluntary nature of religious association, the need for a form of evangelization which enlisted the free, rational consent of the whole person, and the possibility that a confident, open Catholicism could enter deeply into the heart of modern society and bring it to the realization of its human promise. Most of the time, his natural modesty restrained his enthusiasm and restricted his conviction to the immediate circumstances of the United States. While in Europe for the Vatican Council, however, he began to elaborate his vision to encompass the universal church as it struggled with internal issues of authority and external relations with the secular world. In January 1870 he noted:

> Ideas that have for a long time been confusedly before my mind become distinct; regarding the state of things in Europe and remedy.... Europe may find not only her political regeneration in the civilization on the other side of the Atlantic, but also the renewal of Catholicity. Europe needs men who from a fresh view and contemplation of truth, and a deeper love springing therefrom, should consecrate themselves to the propagation of the faith and the good of humanity, men who are, from this higher view of truth, free from all parties, schools, or prejudices; who are neither ultramontanes nor Gallicans, ontologists or psychologists, ancien regime or '89, conservative or radical.[48]

He also expressed his enthusiasm about the mission of American civilization to renew Europe and the church to his brother George, noting that the Paulists, "as the first religious foundation based on it," had a great work before them. "The people demand a larger share in political government; religion must become a matter of greater personal conviction; extension of suffrage and voluntary support of religion are necessary correlatives," he wrote. "The sooner political governments, and the church government, prepare for these changes, the better. Resistance to these will bring revolution and apostasy."[49] In February he was already planning the Paulist extension to Europe. "The work that Divine Providence has called us as a religious community to do in our own country, were its spirit extended throughout all Europe, it would be the focus and element of its regeneration. For our country has a providential position in view of Europe, and our baptizing and efforts to Catholicize and sanctify it, gives it an importance in a religious aspect of a most interesting and significant character. Were there a sufficient number of Paulists I should like to see a community established in every center of Europe, in London, Paris, Vienna, Madrid, Berlin, Florence, Rome. They would be an element of reconciliation of past and future and of reconstruction."[50]

This vision, which he would preach if he could to the whole world, came together only a short time before illness and depression were overwhelming him. On the one hand he felt the need for utter surrender to the will of God, even when it meant the abandonment of all activity, while on the other he was sure of his insight into the needs of the moment and anxious to see the Paulists spread the word not just in America but in Europe. Yet, what he saw in Europe were "antagonistic parties," with none of whom he had any sympathy, and already antagonisms were spreading among American Catholics. In 1872 he had written, in words that seemed prophetic amid the controversies which beset the church around the turn of the century: "My face is turned toward a rising sun, and I catch the gleams of a promise of a brighter future for the church and humanity; while in Europe men's faces are turned toward a setting sun. We are looking in opposite directions."[51]

If Hecker's dreams were doomed in the context of his generation's approach to Americanization, they had even less hope abroad. Hecker argued that infallibility finally grounded the defense of the church and a new era lay ahead which would be marked by confidence in the Holy Spirit, the emergence of energetic, independent, apostolic people identifying their faith with the work of human progress. John Henry Newman saw things more clearly. "Whereas you infer 'we are so bad we are sure to get better,' " Newman wrote, "I feel there is another inference conceivable and possible; in fact 'we are so bad off that we are likely to be worse.' When a man's head is under water, we may therefore prophesy that he is on the way to swim safe to shore, but it is open to us to fear on the contrary that he may be sinking to the bottom." The more pessimistic view seemed self-evident to Newman:

> The main point, the one point (as far as I have the means of knowing) which the Holy Father has insisted on as the condition of a prosperous state of the Catholic religion is not an effusion of Divine Influences whether among Catholics or in the circumjacent Protestantism and infidelity, but the maintenance of the Temporal Power . . . The Temporal Pow-

er then being a first principle at Rome, and the prospective movement of the races of Europe and America being, as you say, "expensive and popular," I do not see how Catholicity is likely to "attract," as regards those races, "sympathy and cheerful cooperation."[52]

The problem went deeper than that, so deep that it lay almost beyond the intelligible. During his lifetime and especially in the controversies which raged around his ideas after his death, Hecker's friends argued that Hecker's ideas of providence, spirit, and evangelization were all simply means to the greatness and glory of the church. Even during his lifetime Hecker complained that few had understood him, perhaps only Baker among the Paulists themselves. Elliott, devoted and persistent in his love, must have been hurt by Hecker's depressed murmurings of his lack of disciples. Yet, Hecker was right. For even Elliott, like other liberal Catholics of the post-conciliar period, saw the church as the primary, even sole, agency of human betterment. Returning to the church was the object of evangelization and however much they might praise modern accomplishments, it was always simply a tactic, to win acceptance, a hearing, to be men of their age. Perhaps once church and culture were so intimately related that one did not have to think of the distinction. By the 1880s it had become so pervasive that it need not even be acknowledged. But that distinction was never part of Hecker's understanding or sensibility. Church and society each expressed something deep in human experience, longings for truth, for happiness, for love, for destiny. Church and society offered distinct but integrally related answers to the aspirations of nature and the questions of the soul. There was no moment when there was church, constituted separate and apart from the world, so distinct that it could plan its strategy of reconquest. Rather church and world evolved together. One wished to make men Catholics for the sake of those persons, not for the sake of the church; one wished to reconstitute Catholicism as the religion of society not for the sake of the church but for the sake of those human communities and human works which man desired to build.

VII

Pervasive in Hecker's historical interpretation of modern Catholicism was the conviction that the church, perhaps inevitably, had concentrated on its external authority at the expense of the inner power of the Holy Spirit and had thus helped to create the very antagonism from which it suffered. Much of modern Catholicism, including its social teaching, seemed aimed at such an external reconquest, a reestablishment of Christendom through negotiation with the state or by appeal to the fears of social classes. For Hecker, the church was an agency of human development and fulfillment, it was for the sake of man and not the reverse. It was this humanism, with its optimistic sense of human possibilities, that led to disagreements with Brownson, to Hecker's seemingly idiosyncratic interpretation of Vatican I, and to his later depression, and it informed the controversies about Heckerism and Americanism in the years that followed his death. Hecker wished to affirm America because there the elements of freedom and progress so central to human destiny were manifest on behalf of the entire human family; that idea in the hands of more churchy and less spiritual men easily slipped into "Americanism," an ideological elevation of American experience as normative for church and society.

It is in this context that the creative if incomplete theology of Isaac Hecker takes on significance. As a nineteenth-century American he was sometimes tempted toward a too optimistic view of human nature and a too benign view of human history. As a nineteenth-century Catholic he was equally tempted towards a Catholic triumphalism and imperialism. Situated for better or worse in the midst of an immigrant church in a basically Protestant country, he sought to overcome non-Catholic suspicions of Catholicism and Catholic suspicions of America, with only limited success. Only Newman of his English-speaking contemporaries was more misunderstood; like Newman, too, his ideas provided useful ammunition for mid-twentieth-century reformers who selected elements of their thought but rarely confronted the profound demands of their Christian humanism. For Hecker, Catholicism and American "civilization" were not separate entities, constituted apart from one another and therefore in need of either negotiated truces or eventual surrender of one side or the other. Hecker indeed wished to convert America, not for the sake of a triumphal church but for the sake of America and Americans, who could find in Catholicism their own deepest meaning. He wished to Americanize Catholicism, not in the cheap sense of adapting to American ways but in the far deeper sense of entering fully into that process of humanization at work in contemporary history and revealed most fully in the United States. For Hecker the Kingdom of God, the end of human history, was not a great big Catholic church presided over by John Hughes and Pius IX, nor was it an age of American empire, when American culture became the culture of the world. The Kingdom of God was that point in history when man came once again to reconciliation with himself, when the God revealed in Jesus was known by whole, free, intelligent men and women to be their God, when they knew that there were answers to the questions of their soul, fulfillment for the aspirations of their nature. To fulfill their legitimate human and divine mission, he told Americans, they needed a church and a religion, one church and one religion. To fulfill their divine mission, he told Catholics, they needed to see the theological and spiritual significance of freedom and intelligence. They had to learn that a church composed of men and women who had made personal decisions of faith based on intelligent examination of Catholic claims and free decisions to affirm and make their own the teachings of the church, was a better church, better because closer to the human nature God had created, better because closer to the Kingdom of God which He intended.

The social mission of the church for Hecker was redundant, then. The mission of the church was social in its very nature, to redeem all of human life by reconciliation in love with the Creator. Of course the church attempted to alleviate the plight of the suffering, of course it fought against social evils like drunkenness, unequal educational opportunity, or class oppression, but these actions flowed directly from its self-understanding and were integral to its evangelical mission. Just as it was better to help the poor help themselves and become self-sustaining, so it was better to enable the non-Catholic Christian to make a free decision of faith by presenting Catholicism whole, and depending on their fairness, intelligence, and good will. That very process of evangelism was social, for it was the means whereby a new society, a new humanity, could be created in freedom and in truth.

Here Hecker's social theory breaks down, as it always seems to among evangelicals. He seemed to suggest that better men and women at one with the spirit without and within, achieved through the Catholic church, would place the problems of society on the road to solution. Responsible capitalists, sober and industrious workingmen, highminded political officials, an active and disciplined citizenry, together would place the superficial problems of injustice in perspective and, through mutual charity and forebearance, solve them. In the later years of his life, his church and his nation became increasingly fascinated with power. The "steam priest" ignored it. While corporations, trade unions, and governments erected massive systems of centralized control and rational direction, Hecker focused in on the spirit and the person. From his almost mystical perspective the brutality of the Civil War and the glaring injustices of industrial cities were secondary and largely irrelevant. Only change hearts, bring persons into touch with their destiny, and things would right themselves.

Was he then wrong? For the generation of the 1890s and for those who succeeded them it seemed so. Not wrong in a fundamental sense, but naïve; useful for the church, but still essentially naïve. Yet the problem Hecker addressed remains, postponed again and again by abundance and growth, but regularly recurring. How is a democracy to persuade men and women voluntarily to accept the disciplines required to make a just and peaceful society, much less a prosperous one? How can the church uphold the truth about God and man among a people conscious they can choose? As a Christian and as an American, Hecker believed that coercion was wrong and that the only church and society worth living in were those that were free. For those who still believe that, Hecker's central demand remains inescapable: men and women must find a basis of community in their shared humanity and make of it a community which answers their most profound human needs. The church's role is to bear witness to that possibility in word, fellowship, sacrament, and the quality of its presence among its fellows. On that basis alone the intelligence and imagination can be engaged, not in finally resolving issues of economic justice, social harmony, and world peace but in the never ending struggle to give form and shape to human existence in ways which express the dignity of the human person. Hecker's call thus remains timeless and prophetic, the highest of idealisms and the wisest of realisms.

For Hecker's understanding of church and society to find a receptive audience required the emergence of a new kind of church, one prepared to abandon the external uniformity of the past, of Christendom, and still not content to accept a simply marginal role in society and culture, as was expected by liberal pluralism. That was not the church which existed in the nineteenth century. In a moment of frustration, Hecker wrote his colleagues in 1857 that "the Pope and the rest have no appreciation of the condition of things with us, and are filled with the ideas of monarchy and imagine there is no stability among us. Worse, they have an idea that we do not even understand what Christian virtue is, especially obedience and humility, simply because we have not the stupidity and servility of their own people." Apologizing the next day for his impatience, he nevertheless insisted that "servility is taken in great measure for obedience and the habit of servility is considered humility."[53] The church after Vatican II was a different church, struggling in diverse human situations to discover the most appropriate forms of life, and rejecting in principle the docility and servility Hecker noted. In Communist Eastern Europe, a post-Christian Western Europe, in emerging nations of Africa and Asia, and in revolutionary situations in Latin America, Catholics are detaching themselves and their church from unhealthy dependence upon the forms of the past in order to enter more fully into the lives of peoples, communities, and nations. For all its diversity, several things seem more and more consensual in the post-conciliar church: that religion enters culture through the person, that freedom, freedom for the church to evangelize and for the person to respond, is indispensable to authentic evangelization, that freedom is both a condition of civil rights, protected by law and political process, and social and economic rights, liberating persons from the slavery of poverty, ignorance, disease. Catholicism increasingly regards evangelization as a process of announcing the Good News of Jesus Christ among "all the strata of humanity and through its influence transforming humanity from within and making it new," as Pope Paul VI put it. His definition of evangelization echoed themes central to Hecker's life and work, lending new relevance to his efforts to open the church to the realities of modern history and enlist religion in the central struggle of that history: the fulfillment of age-old hopes for justice, peace, liberation, and a destiny that transcends the limits of time and history itself:

> ... there is no new humanity if there are not first of all new persons renewed by Baptism and by lives lived according to the Gospel. The purpose of evangelization is therefore precisely this interior change, and if it had to be expressed in one sentence the best way of stating it would be to say that the church evangelizes when she seeks to convert, solely through the Divine Power of the Message she proclaims, both the personal and collective consciences of people, the activities in which they engage and concrete milieux which are theirs.[54]

For today's American Catholics, the process of social and religious change of a generation has sapped confidence in the divine power of the Message; they are no longer sure that their country has a distinctive mission to the world or that their church has a special role to play in the nation. Yet, signs persist that confirm Hecker's notion that the nation, to fulfill its destiny, needs a religion capable of overcoming selfishness and endowing public life with noble purpose and that there is enough power left in the Gospel, and wisdom enough in the contemporary teaching of the universal church, to allow one to believe with some reason that Catholicism might assist in providing that religious dimension to American culture. In any event, Hecker's faith and hope stand as a sign of American and Catholic possibility; only the future will provide evidence of whether his basic insights were correct, whether a church of free men and women can enable a nation of free men and women to be a power for good in the world.

NOTES

1. "Dr. Brownson and the Workingman's Party Fifty Years Ago," CW 45 (May 1887): 200–208. Brownson's religious views were far more complex than Hecker recalled; see Thomas P. Ryan, *Orestes Brownson: A Definitive Biography* (Huntington, Ind., 1976) Chap. 11–15.

2. Vincent Holden, *Yankee Paul* (Milwaukee, 1958), p. 25.

3. Walter Elliott, "Notes Toward a New Life of Father Hecker," undated, PFA.

4. ITH described this change in "Document Submitted to Superiors," January 8, 1858, PFA. It is discussed in detail in Edward Langlois, "The Political Theory of Isaac Thomas Hecker" (Ph.D. dissertation, Cornell University), p. 48.

5. Quoted in Langlois, p. 52.

6. ITH's early diary, July 28, 1843, PFA.

7. Ibid., May 26, 1843.

8. ITH to "Kindred," July 13, 1843, PFA.

9. Diary, June 24, 1843.

10. Diary, notes, undated. On the pervasiveness of evangelical themes, even among the Transcendentalists, see Timothy L. Smith, "Transcendental Grace: Biblical Themes in the New England Renaissance," a yet unpublished paper. I am indebted to Professor Smith for sharing this essay with me and for giving the present paper a careful reading.

11. ITH to Friends, June 14, 1844, PFA.

12. "Dr. Brownson and Bishop Fitzpatrick," CW 45 (April 1887): 3.

13. Diary, Jan. 20, 1845.

14. Ibid., March 22, 1844.

15. ITH to George Hecker, Jan. 2, 1858, PFA.

16. ITH to Father Douglas, July 29, 1856, PFA.

17. ITH to Fathers, Jan. 1, 1858, PFA.

18. "Notes for Conferences on Religion," Oct. 2, 1878, PFA.

19. Quoted in Langlois, p. 112.

20. *Exposition of the Church in View of the Recent Difficulties and Controversies, and Present Needs of the Age* (London: Basil Montague, 1875).

21. "The Future Triumph of the Church," PFA.

22. Diary, July 27, 1843.

23. "Dr. Brownson's Road to the Church," CW 46 (Oct. 1887): 5.

24. "Life is Real," CW 46 (Oct. 1878): 137–38.

25. ITH, *Aspirations of Nature* (New York, James B. Kirker, 1857), p. 28.

26. ITH to Mrs. Jane King, June 26, 1863, PFA.

27. Ibid., January 18, n.y.

28. *Exposition,* PFA.

29. ITH to Archbishop Bayley, Feb. 27, 1863, copy in PFA.

30. Sermon reported in *New York Tablet,* Jan. 13, 1866.

31. "Notes in Rome," Feb. 21, 1857, PFA.

32. Diary, May 7, 1844.

33. Orestes Brownson to Henry Brownson, March 15, 1871, copy in PFA.

34. Ibid., Nov. 22, 1870, copy in PFA.

35. "Church Authority and Power," Sermon for Low Sunday, no date, PFA.

36. "The Saint of Our Day," PFA.

37. "St. Louis Lecture," PFA.

38. ITH to Mrs. King, May 28, 1865, PFA.

39. "Notes on Various Subjects," undated, PFA.

40. ITH, *Aspirations of Nature.* (New York, 1857), pp. 46–47

41. "What Does the Public School Question Mean?" CW 34 (Oct. 1881): 88.

42. "Life is Real," 137.

43. ITH to Richard Simpson, Sept. 23, 1875, PFA.

44. ITH to George Hecker, Feb. 24, 1870, PFA.

45. ITH to Bishop Chatard, April 14, 1873, PFA.

46. ITH to Brownson, Jan. 30, 1870, PFA.

47. *Exposition,* n.p.

48. "Notes In Rome," Jan. 28, 1870.

49. ITH to George Hecker, Jan. 26, 1870, PFA.

50. "Notes in Rome," Feb. 24, 1870, PFA.

51. ITH to Mrs. Cullen, July 24, 1872, PFA.

52. John Henry Newman to ITH, April 10, 1875, PFA.

53. ITH to Fathers, Feb. 11, 1858, PFA.

54. Pope Paul VI, *Evangelization in the Modern World* (Washington, 1975), p. 13.

A Jungian Analysis of
Isaac Thomas Hecker

by Robert W. Baer, C.S.P.

For many years the name Isaac Thomas Hecker brought only a vacant stare from people asked to identify him. The mantle of fame covering his friends and contemporaries, Henry David Thoreau, Ralph Waldo Emerson, Orestes Brownson, Bronson Alcott, did not stretch to include him.

Lately, scholars from various sciences have become curious enough to pursue an inquiry into Hecker's life. They have been rewarded with the discovery of an authentic early American mystic, writer, and lecturer. The spotlight of recognition is too recent for an evaluation of all that has been revealed but there is certainly enough to excite a depth psychologist.

This essay will attempt to look at Hecker from the perspective of analytical psychology as elucidated by Carl G. Jung. The difficulties in trying to analyze someone who has already left the scene of history are enormous and admit of countless possibilities for distortion. Nevertheless with a modest goal, and a symbolical approach such as Jung offers, it is possible to gain some valuable knowledge of the human psyche without further typing or fossilizing it.

The first striking observation from the most casual perusal of Hecker's life is that he never stopped trying to realize his inner potential. Sometimes this was a conscious choice and other times an unconscious fate. This process of Self-realization is what Jung called the the process of individuation and his psychology offers a unique perspective to understand it.

Another prominent aspect of Hecker's life is that his psychic energy seemed bunched around two polarities, either the point of deepest introversion or that of extreme extraversion. There is no question that most of the time he lived in the deepest recesses of his psyche and valued the direction he received from within, more than any other. Much of what Hecker revealed about his inner life: his sense of utter desolation; the conflict of his inner and outer worlds; his religious devotion to his unconscious; his respect for the direction given him in dreams; his attitudes towards the feminine; the tension between nature and spirit; have remarkable parallels in Jung's later discoveries and writings.

Insofar as individuation is a process which aims at realizing the greater personality, the wholeness of the individual not yet realized, it necessarily involves a relationship between the inner and outer worlds. Jung understood individuation and collectivity to be the two opposing poles of one archetype and described their relationship in this way:

> Individuation cuts one off from personal conformity and hence from collectivity. That is the guilt which the individuant leaves behind him for the world, that is the guilt he must endeavor to redeem. He must offer a ransom of himself, that is, he must bring forth values which are an equivalent substitute for his absence in the collective personal sphere. Every further step in individuation creates new guilt and necessitates new expiation. . . . Individuation is exclusive adaptation to inner reality and hence an allegedly "mystical" process. The expiation is adaptation to the outer world.[1]

We will look at the Janus face of this archetype of individuation by studying the alternating current of psychic energy revealed in Hecker's life chiefly at three crucial periods. The first period was the time of his early Diary. This unpublished document of some one hundred and sixty pages offers the most intimate entry to Isaac Hecker's inner life and processes. It will receive the most attention. The second period of importance was that of Hecker's expulsion from the Redemptorists and his founding of the Paulist Fathers. Finally we shall look at the long years of his illness which seemed to begin with Vatican Council I and continued until his death in 1888.

At times our psychic energy flows in greater abundance towards the outer world, drawing us to immersion in the external collective with a possible danger of losing our unique personality to collective aims and purposes. Without risking such a danger there would be no sculpturing of a real person, who is, after all, a composite of matter and spirit in historical context. At other times psychic energy draws us to its source, namely the inner psychic world, which is also a collective but which contains, as well, the directing center for the whole psychic development, the Self, as Jung calls it. The risk of this direction of psychic flow is that our ego will become possessed by the numinous power of the inner archetypes and isolated from outer reality. Without risking this danger we would be cut off from the source of life. The aim of individuation seems to be a mid-point between the conscious and unconscious aspects of the psyche where the unique whole-ness of the personality resides.

Jung asks:

> What is it, in the end, that induces a man to go his own way and to rise out of unconscious identity with the mass as out of a swathing mist? . . . It is what is commonly called voca-tion: an irrational factor that destines a man to emancipate himself from the herd and from its well-worn paths. . . . Vocation acts like a law of God, from this there is no escape. Anyone with a vocation hears the voice of the inner man: he is called.[2]

Isaac Hecker was one of those persons who heard the inner voice and struggled for a lifetime to respond to it.

HECKER'S EARLY YEARS

The first and most important collective which cradled Hecker's early development was his family. Isaac Hecker not only bore a physical resemblance to his mother, Caroline, but was closely attached to her. She inculcated Christian values with her parenting and yet did not demand that her children follow a particular church denomination.

Isaac's father, John Hecker Sr., appears to have had no interest in religion and little input into the family life, but he did provide for it well until Isaac was about three years old. Although Isaac Hecker's letters to family members and friends were numerous, there is only one addressed to his father. The tone of that letter reveals the huge gulf that separated father and son.

> I know of nothing that gives me more pain than when I think
> of the habit that has governed you for so many years past.
> Surely if you do not conquer it you cannot expect to see
> heaven. . . . You can overcome it by prayer.[3]

No one ever mentions the nature of the father's bad habit but it seems to have been the major factor in the bankruptcy of his once successful brass foundry. This forced Isaac to leave school in his early teens. The three brothers then had to shoulder financial responsibility for the family.

John Hecker Jr., born July 25, 1812, soon became the acknowledged head of the family, replacing his father. He had studied the baking business under the tutelage of a maternal uncle. As soon as he was twenty-one, he opened a shop of his own. All three brothers worked to make the bakery a success. By 1843 the Hecker Brothers, operating in partnership, had four flourishing bakery shops and their own mill, called the Croton Flour Mill. George Hecker, born Jan. 5, 1818, was the brother closest to Isaac in age and affection. He and Isaac, born Dec. 18, 1819, were soul-mates from the time they shared the same bedroom until their deaths, a matter of a few months apart in 1888. They sought each other's spiritual and moral insight and George Hecker always supplied his younger brother with all the financial backing he ever needed. Isaac's only sister, Elizabeth, was not prominent on the family scene and little mention is made of her except that she died an untimely death in 1845, while he was studying in Europe.

It is symbolically significant that the Hecker brothers chose to relate to society from the very beginning in a nourishing capacity, that of providing daily bread. This more maternal occupation clashed sharply with the hard masculine trade of metalworker which was the profession of their father and grandfather. It reflected the maternal influence in their family as did their strong social and religious concern. It was only around the onset of Isaac Hecker's vocational experiences at age twenty-two, that religious interest manifested itself among the brothers.

Before that time, the many hours demanded by their bakery were prolonged to include much effort for social reform. New York was a city of ferment during Hecker's adolescent years. New factories were creating a class of wealthy industrialists at the expense of immigrant laborers who were exploited in every way.[4] The brothers felt that their efforts for improvement of conditions would be most effective through the medium of a political party. After the elections of 1837 their party was defeated and eventually disappeared but the lifelong dividend which Isaac received from his political efforts was making the friendship of Orestes Brownson.

Orestes Brownson was basically a fellow seeker, who shared Isaac Hecker's questing nature. When they met for the first time Hecker was only twenty-two and Orestes thirty-eight years old. Neither had much formal education but Brownson had been studying philosophy seriously for ten years and had educated himself very well. His labyrinthine path before meeting Hecker gave him a wealth of experience to offer his young friend at a crucial time. Isaac was to refer to him as brother, father-advisor, and friend.

It seems quite apparent that one of the sources of attraction between the two men were their opposing typologies. Orestes Brownson was clearly a thinking type with inferior feeling, very poor eros development and most probably an extravert. Some knowledgeable friend is said to have remarked, "For Orestes the whole world is a pulpit." Hecker could be described as an introvert with intuition as his superior function and a well-developed eros. Brownson performed the father function leading his young friend into the world of logos and spirit, helping him to discriminate his value system, and encouraging him to self-realization. Brownson remained a protective guide when the storms of the unconscious had dimmed the horizon of Hecker's consciousness. Brownson was a strong enough figure to compensate for the soft presence of authority in Hecker's life also. He was assertive, polemical, intellectual, and discriminatingly definitive. Isaac Hecker commented later in life, "Woe to the man who measured strength with Dr. Brownson and had not the pluck and nerve to withstand him."[5] Young Hecker managed to avail himself of Brownson's strengths without building a dependence on him which would have obstructed his own individuation.

In the early stages of their friendship, Orestes Brownson was a Godsend to a perplexed Hecker family and their youngest son. Now in the middle of his twenty-second year, Isaac Hecker had been leading the life of an ordinary young man of the time, more active than most. Then suddenly his psychic energy reversed its direction drawing him toward extreme introversion in one surge. He had some dreams, which he never recorded, and a vision which occurred while he was seated on the side of his bed. Here is an account of the vision recorded in his Diary on May 18, 1843:

> About ten months ago, or perhaps seven or eight I saw (I cannot say I dreamed, for it was quite different from dreaming as I thought I was seated on the side of my bed) a beautiful, angelic, pure being, and myself standing alongside of her, feeling a most heavenly pure joy. And it was as if our bodies were luminous, and they gave forth a moonlike light which I felt sprung from the joy that we experienced. We were unclothed, pure, and unconscious of anything but pure love and joy, and I felt as if we had always lived together, and that our motions, actions, feelings and thoughts came from one center. And when I looked toward her I saw no bold outline of form, but an angelic something I cannot describe, but in angelic shape and image. It was this picture that has left such an indelible impression upon my mind, and for some time afterwards I continued to feel the same influence, and do now at times, so that the actual around me has lost its hold on me. In my state previous to this vision I should have been married ere this, for there are those I have since seen who would have met the demands of my mind. But now this vision continually hovers o'er me and prevents me by its beauty from accepting any else. For I am charmed by its influence and I am conscious that if I should accept anything else I should lose the life which would be the only existence wherein I could say I live.

Within a year of this vision Isaac Hecker definitely entertained ideas of himself as a mystic. Indeed, the nature of this vision and its powerful and long-lasting effect upon him could put it in the category of the initial phase of the mystical life, that of the "Awakening of the Self to Consciousness of Divine Reality."[6]

It is important here to remind the reader that this short study of Isaac Hecker is done from the perspective of analytical psychology and not religion. Since Jung dealt often with Christian symbolism he was attacked by theologians from all religions who confused or forgot this distinction.

Dr. M. L. von Franz bridges the difficulty in this way:

> Every human being has at bottom of his psyche a divine spark, a part of the Divinity which Jung calls the Self. But then all the theologians jumped down his throat. Critics on the theological side ... always say: You turn religion into something which is only psychological. But if we have in our psyche the image of God as an active center then we should honor the psyche as the highest thing on earth.[7]

One of the first observations about Hecker's vision is that it was very numinous and powerful. It takes a greater amount of psychic energy for the unconscious to intrude on waking consciousness than to produce a dream symbol. The contents of Hecker's vision are not personal but belong to a deeper level of the unconscious. For Jung, the personal unconscious consists of lost memories, painful ideas that are repressed, subliminal perceptions, and contents not yet ready for consciousness. The deeper layer of the unconscious which he called the "collective unconscious" contains the primordial images common to humanity everywhere, and designated as "archetypes."[8]

Both Old and New Testaments are replete with stories of angels, where they usually act as messengers of God. Then there are also the fallen angels or devils, such as Lucifer, who oppose the power of God and represent the dark side of the god-image. Jung says that, "If angels are anything at all, they are personified transmitters of unconscious contents that are seeking expression."[9] They bring illumination and lead toward new consciousness.

This angel in Hecker's vision appears positive and by giving him the feeling that they had always been living together, indicated that she was a messenger from the Self. The Self is a psychological construct which Jung formulated to represent the transcendent center of tension between the conscious and unconscious psyche. The beginnings of our whole psychic life seem to be inextricably rooted in this point, and all our highest and ultimate purposes seem to be striving towards realizing it. It might equally well be called the "God within us." The Self is our life's goal, and the most complete expression of individuality; the full flowering not only of the single individual, but of the group, in which each adds his portion to the whole. Jung said that while such a postulate cannot be proved, it is necessary psychologically to explain the psychic processes which occur empirically.[10]

The angel who draws Hecker irresistibly towards his center is distinguished by him as being feminine because of her form. The moonlike light enfolding their naked bodies, in the vision, speaks of a feminine consciousness also. It appears that she brings a consciousness appropriate for a better understanding of the unconscious. On the one hand she can be described as a guide to higher spiritual awareness, such as Beatrice was to Dante, and on the other hand she represents the archetype which Jung calls the Anima in masculine psychology. The Anima is a personification of all feminine psychological tendencies in a man's psyche. It manifests itself by moods, feelings for nature and prophetic hunches as well as depicting his relationship to the unconscious.[11] The Anima represents the principle of eros in man and is the source of psychic life. Hecker experienced this reality directly saying, "If I should accept anything else I should lose the life which would be the only existence wherein I could say I live."

To have an angel appear as one's Anima would indicate a very spiritualized attitude towards the feminine, such as Roman Catholics have in their devotion to the Virgin Mary. Such a symbol of the feminine in a man would make it difficult for him to integrate the personal feminine qualities which the archetype contains. On the positive side such an Anima prevents a man from projecting it entirely on an actual woman. The writer feels that Isaac Hecker's immediate commitment to celibacy as an appropriate response to the charm of the angelic Anima was due to the fact that he had already developed a very spiritualized attitude toward the feminine in his life, most probably through too great an attachment to his mother.

The feelings produced by the vision were ecstasy and joy, drawing him more powerfully to follow his inner woman. When someone is swept away in exultation we often say that the person was beside himself with joy. Interestingly, the angel with whom he identified his core Self was standing beside him during the vision. Hecker soon realized, however, that the path by which his angelic guide would lead him toward the depths of the Self was going to be a path of great suffering. His joy rather quickly gave way to depression, doubt, feelings of isolation, and general confusion. This happens because the conscious mind is not ready to assimilate these contents of the collective unconscious and their energy flows off into the affective and instinctual sphere. The result is outbursts of affect, irritation, bad moods, and sexual excitement which result in a thorough disorientation of consciousness.[12]

This was an accurate description of the state Isaac Hecker was experiencing after his angelic visitation in the early fall of 1842. A few months later he visited Orestes Brownson in Chelsea, Massachusetts and wrote his brothers a letter, trying for the first time to explain his strange behavior to them.

> I say sincerely, that I have lost all but this one thing, and how shall I speak it? My mind has lost all disposition to business. My hopes, life, existence, all are in another direction. No one knows how I tried to exert myself to work. . . .
> To keep company with females, which you know what I mean, I have no desire. In the sense of marrying, I have no thought. Company for such an end I feel an aversion for. . . .
> This, I am conscious, is no light thought. It lies deeper than myself, and there is not the power in me to control it. I write this not with easiness. It is done in tears, and I have opened my mind as I have not done before. How this will end I know not, but can not but trust God. It is not my will but my destiny, which will not be one of ease and pleasure, but . . . a perpetual sacrifice of my past hopes, though of a Communion I have never felt.[13]

The secrecy which Hecker felt he needed to protect his unique experiences produced severe tension in him. He developed a nervous depression. His appetite was affected and he became physically ill. In their desperation and concern, the Hecker family turned to Orestes Brownson for assistance.

Brownson suggested that Hecker try a Transcendentalist community called Brook Farm, located on the outskirts of Boston, Massachusetts. Brownson had definite Transcendentalist leanings at the time and was a personal friend of the founders of that utopian community, George and Sarah Ripley. The Transcendentalist movement has been seen by historians as a religious revival protesting against dying religious forms. Transcendentalists believed that people have an inward spiritual nature, an intuitive knowledge of God and a natural human dignity. They therefore envisioned the reform of humanity coming through individual awakening and regeneration.[14] By agreeing with Hecker's belief in the potential of the human spirit for complete harmony with the transcendental order, they also offered a support for his mystical tendencies. Hecker grasped at this possibility with uncertainty but hopefulness. A few weeks before entering the Brook Farm community, he wrote his family,

> The life that was in me had no one to commune with and I felt it was consuming me. I tried to express it in different ways, obscurely, but it appeared singular, and no one understood me. This was the cause of my wishing to go off, hoping I would either get clear of it, or something might turn up, I knew not what.[15]

Reviewing Hecker's life from the time of his first vision in the late fall of 1842 until the eve of his departure for Brook Farm in January 1843, one could say that he had experienced an unusual breakthrough of archetypal contents into his consciousness. This invasion was accompanied by an illness which could later be understood as a creative illness because its purpose was to broaden his conscious awareness. Hecker's nervous excitability, depression, and confusion were characteristics of an *abaissement du niveau mental.* Pierre Janet used this term to mean a lowering of consciousness because the flow of energy is directed toward the unconscious. This movement of psychic energy drew Hecker away from the external collectives of family, business, and society to his inner world.

THE EARLY DIARIES

It was not a coincidence that Isaac Hecker began a personal diary at the time of his entrance into the Brook Farm community. The transcendentalists employed intellectual tools such as journals and writing in their new religion. Although almost totally devoid of dream material, Hecker's Diary provides much data to help us understand him from a psychological point of view. His entries reveal the various affects, impulses, thoughts, and actions which were his responses to his encounter with the invading "spirit."

Jung had become interested in such manifestations of the spirit very early in his medical career. His doctoral thesis dealt with occult phenomena and there he posited for the first time the hypothesis to which he devoted a lifetime of exploration. He suggested that the spirits which manifested themselves in a medium during a séance were autonomous, "splinter personalities" which presaged a more comprehensive personality existing in the unconscious and attempting 'o break through into consciousness.[16] During his lifetime Jung tried to find a method of bringing these unconscious elements into consciousness and associating them to the ego so that the "greater personality" could be realized. Jung believed that such a "greater personality" resides in every person. For most people it is left to develop naturally, occurring more or less autonomously without the participation of the person's consciousness. The pitfalls of such a natural path are numerous and few there are who avoid them. Jung developed an approach to the unconscious, based on empirical research, which assists the process of individuation, or realization of the Self, through the interpretation of dreams and active imagination. It can be considered an artificial means but it enables a person to have an active input in shaping the process. This also seems to accelerate psychic development.

Jung speaks of three stages to the process of life or individuation.[17] The first stage he describes as having for its goal the development of a strong ego-complex. This is achieved, with the support of the Self, by a person's mastering his adaptation to the outer world. Such a development is manifested when the person has dealt adequately with the problems of human relationships presented by sexuality, marriage, profession, and children. The second stage Jung saw commencing about ages 35–40. He found it often introduced by a crisis, because the attitudes which made for successful adaptation to the outer world are not appropriate for the goals of the second stage which consist in the development of culture[18] and the conscious re-rooting of the ego in the Self. This latter is required because often there has been an exaggerated one-sided focus of consciousness in adapting to the outer world and this has caused a split or sharp separation of the ego from its source, the Self. Now there must be an adaptation to the inner world, to the unconscious, which requires a person to differentiate between the personal and collective components in the unconscious. Jung stated that it is important for an approach to wholeness of personality that what has been ignored, or pointedly rejected by consciousness in the first stage is gathered up and related to it in this second stage. This is the stage in which psychic opposites can be distinguished and brought together because consciousness has been sufficiently developed. The goal of the first stage was the expansion of life while that of the second stage is the acceptance of the diminution of our physical powers and death. If one views death properly it should be seen not as an end so much as a completion of our attempts at developing a whole personality, one in which the ego became a consciously cooperative servant of the Self in its work of incarnating the personality. The third stage (extreme old age) Jung likens to the first stage in that they are characterized by one common bond, "submersion in unconscious psychic happenings."[19] He directed his research and energies to understanding the second stage.

Isaac Hecker's initial crisis of the "spirit" presents some anomalies to the usual process which Jung observed. Hecker was only twenty-two years old and far from having mastered the usual problems presented by outer adaptation. He had neither married nor established himself socially. He was not really a successful businessman and had no developed persona at this age. He acknowledged to his brothers something which he felt they already knew and indulged, namely, that he never was able to devote himself as fully to the business as they had done. This was not because of a lack of desire to do so, but because he could not. His energy, therefore, was already being drained off into his unconscious. Jung points out that even seemingly spontaneous and radical conversions are not without their antecedents of preparation in the psyche. He cites the conversion of St. Paul as an example, where there was extreme psychic tension manifested in his persecution of the Christians, before his dramatic and apparently spontaneous conversion experience.[20]

When the call to individuation came to Hecker, it appeared as a full blown crisis and radically altered his life thereafter. Jolande Jacobi points out that the greater the areas of experience encompassed by the transformation, the more sudden it will be.[21] Years later, when Hecker had made his acquaintance with the Christian mystics, he realized that his inner experiences were similar to theirs. He then testified that he had passed from a state of little interest in religion through the initial three stages of mystical transformation in the first two years following his early vision. This was most unusual even for the mystics.

Meanwhile, for several months after his initiating vision Hecker struggled and suffered in silence with his inner daimon. On January 10, 1843, he began his Diary with the following assessment of his interior condition:

> Is life dear to me? No. Are my friends dear to me? I could suffer and die for them if needs be, but yet have none of the old attachment I had for them. I would clasp all to my heart, love all for their humanity, but not as relatives or individuals. I feel as if life is too much for me. It is indescribably painful for me to live, and rather than go through the ordeal of living I would prefer leaving this life. . . . My being is full of life but to whom shall I speak? . . . Who shall I cry to for help but he that has given me life and planted in me this spirit. Unto thee, then, do I cry from the depths of my soul for lights to suffer so. Give me rather death in my present form. . . .

The powerful flow of his libido moves toward the unconscious. His plaintive cry sounds like that of a man uprooted from his native earth and sucked into the vortex of a cyclone. One can feel his split between consciousness and unconsciousness and the helplessness of his ego in the face of the spirit. This gives a real picture of the effect of impersonal archetypal forces on consciousness when they are constellated.

Jung would describe the flow of the libido to the unconscious as regression and say that it springs from the vital need to satisfy the demands of individuation. "Man is not a machine in the sense that he can consistently maintain the same output of work. He can meet the demands of outer necessity in an ideal way only if he is also adapted to his own inner world, that is, if he is in harmony with himself."[22]

When the Self appears through symbols in dreams or visions then we can say that the process of individuation is constellated. The very real danger at this point is that Isaac Hecker will be swallowed by the unconscious forces, and abandon the real world and its activities completely. At one point in his life, Jung also felt this tremendous attraction of the unconscious contents of his psyche and reflected later that it was only because he remained faithful to his daily family and professional duties that he was able to ride out the storm safely.

In the following Diary entry, Hecker reports the radical effect of this archetypal spirit.

> I would not take it on myself to say that I have been born again, but I know that I have passed from death to life. Things below have no hold upon me further than they lead to things above. It is not a moral restraint that I have over myself, but it is a change, a conversion of my whole being, that I have no need of restraint. (Jan. 11, 1843)

He describes what has happened to him as something so radical that it could be likened to a rebirth. He avoids the religious phrase "born again" because it reminded him of the over-emotional Protestant sects for which he had an aversion. In a later entry he expresses the change in this way:

> Why is my past to my present like another person? Why have I lost my old memory? Why can I not study? Who is it that

> my conversation is held with when I am in a half waking
> state, as I often find myself? Why is it that I feel an influence
> drawing me out of the life of this world and away from those
> around me? (Feb. 3, 1843)

Although Hecker had experienced a centeredness and inner harmony of the Self through his angel vision, he is hardly prepared
to remain in such a harmony. That was a taste of the goal to
encourage him along the path of individuation which he was
beginning.

Eric Neumann has pointed out that the Self and the ego can
be envisioned as forming an axis which represent their mutual
relationship, as the ego is born from the matrix of the Self. Each
seems to mirror the other in the process of development.[23] At
Hecker's present stage the unitary experience of his center reflects back the diversity of his consciousness. Hecker first needs
to work on his Shadow problem.

The Shadow is a content of the personal unconscious closest
to consciousness, which represents personal inferiorities that
manifest themselves in their emotional nature. They have a kind
of autonomy or possessive quality and occur where adaptation is
weakest. They are consequently often projected on others. The
withdrawal of these projections and the integration of these
Shadow qualities is a very painful process and presents a moral
problem that challenges the whole ego-personality according to
Jung.[24] Isaac Hecker is aware of the duality of good and evil in
himself.

> Oh! I am conscious that there is something, nay some one,
> who does protect me from falling, enticed by evil desires, that
> keeps me from their power or action. . . . (April 24, 1843)

Although he frequently complained of his inability to find an
advisor, a kindred soul, someone who understood him or with
whom he could converse on his own level of inner experience,
Hecker did have the invaluable assistance of his unconscious. He,
in turn, had a very positive attitude towards the guidance which
he received in his dreams.

> Last night I had a dream which was all-important to my
> present circumstances and doubtless to my future happiness.
> How can I doubt these things? Say what may be said, still,
> for all, these have to me a reality, a practical good bearing on
> my life. They are impressive instructors whose teachings are
> given in such a real manner that they influence, would I or
> not. Real pictures of the future, as actual, nay more so than
> my present activity. If I should not follow them I am alto-
> gether to blame. I cannot have such advisers upon earth,
> none could impress me so strongly with such peculiar effect,
> and at the precise time most needed. Is the Lord instructing
> me for anything? (April 24, 1843)

Hecker reveals the prophetic aspect of his initial dreams, several
months before, as having been fulfilled. This increases his trust in
the inner force.

> I had, six months ago, three or more dreams which had a
> very great effect upon my character; They changed it. They
> were the embodiment of my present in a great degree. (April
> 24, 1843)

He understands some of his dreams as having a compensatory
and instructive purpose. In the same Diary entry he notes:

> Last evening's (dream) was a warning embodiment of a false
> activity and its consequence which will preserve me, under
> God's assistance, from falling. Oh! I feel much better from its
> influence.

Hecker's attitude toward his dreams can best be recapitulat-
ed in a statement he wrote toward the end of 1843.

> I lie down in my bed with the same feeling as when I wake in
> the morning. In one I anticipate as much as in the other. The
> events, emotions, and thoughts in my sleep are to me as
> much of my real life as my day events. Waking and sleeping
> are two forms of existence. The latter is full of interest to me
> and expectation. The two states mutually act upon each
> other. (Nov. 17, 1843)

He seems not to have been troubled in discovering meaningful interpretations of his dreams, but unfortunately he never shares with us the details. As a matter of fact, there are only snippets of dreams which he records in his Diary and even these generally lack any associative material. For example:

> On Friday night I saw a red, fiery, glaring-eyed, copper-colored singular-dressed fiend. In stretching to grasp and grapple with it I awoke, sitting up in bed with my arms extended. (May 8, 1843)

One suspects that the highly spiritualized form his life was taking at the time, along with his ascetic practices, had provoked an opposing symbol from the unconscious depths in the form of a sensual fiend. The qualities of red, and fiery, along with copper (the metal of Venus) suggest sensuality. The glaring-eye is well known as the "evil eye" in primitive societies which try to guard against it by the use of mirrors or grotesque masks to reflect the evil back on itself. Hecker's dream ego is engaged actively with the evil one, signifying his attempt on the conscious level to grapple with the destructive aspects of the unconscious components. Hecker is able to see his unconscious both as the source of the highest good and also as containing the darkest evil. Jung agrees. "The unconscious is not just evil by nature, but it is also the source of the highest good; not only dark but also light, not only bestial, semi-human, and demonic but superhuman, spiritual, and in the classical sense of the word, divine."[25]

Under the same entry he records a dream the following night.

> On Saturday night I awoke saying, The world is like a flower bush which bears beautiful flowers; he that attempts to pluck one pricks his finger with a thorn.

To envision the world as a thorny flower bush is to see it as a unity composed of opposites. The beautiful flowers would represent the positive rewards for the feeling function, counterbalanced by the thorns which would represent the painful feeling side. He seems to be experiencing the world as a composite of joy and suffering, pleasure and pain, masculine and feminine.

Each time that Hecker is drawn deeper into his Self he is also touched by the instinctual need to relate to the outer world of people. Dr. von Franz said, "There exists no individuation process in any one individual that does not at the same time produce this relatedness to one's fellowmen."[26] The guilt Hecker felt for having left the collective is manifest in his remark:

> My brothers are hard at work at home. I am here doing nothing. I am doing nothing. (June 24, 1843)

He felt the tension between two opposing impulses without a means of escape. He felt trapped, stuck, imprisoned. He was under the power of an autonomous complex and, as Jung reminded us, when such a complex is constellated, we should not say that we have a complex but rather that the complex has us.

> I ask not for fame, riches, external conditions of delight or splendor. No, the meanest of all would be heaven to me if this inward impulse had action, lived out. But no, I am imprisoned in spirit. What imprisons? What is imprisoned? Who can tell? (June 26, 1843)

This spirit which had Hecker captive is a content of the collective unconscious, which when it becomes associated with the ego is felt as strange, uncanny and at the same time fascinating. The conscious mind falls under its influence, perceiving it as either pathological or else alienating one from normal life. Jung explained that the reason for the alienation is that something which ought to remain unconscious is added to the individual's consciousness. He pointed out that the irruption of these alien contents is a characteristic symptom marking the onset of some mental diseases. By way of therapy, if these contents can be removed from consciousness again, the patient will feel relieved and more normal.[27]

Toward the end of June 1843, Hecker decided that the Brook Farm community was not the place in which he would find his inner fulfillment. He admits to having gained a great deal from his stay, including a considerable culture, increased knowledge, and some loving friendships, but he feels the restlessness of his inner spirit driving him on.

> I cannot accept this place; it is not self-denying enough, sacrificing enough for me: it does not attempt enough for me; it is too much like society. It is not based on the universal love principle. It is not Christlike enough for me. (July 17, 1843)

Hecker had already, for some time, been entertaining the idea of trying another experimental community, called Fruitlands, at Harvard, Massachusetts. It had been founded by Bronson Alcott and Charles Lane along Trancendentalist lines but with a more religious and ascetic rationale. It stressed total dedication to Christ and the creation of a New Eden in this world. The founders felt that there was a living spirit within each soul and that people could enter the kingdom of peace through self-denial and self-abandonment.

Within one week Isaac Hecker realized that Fruitlands also was not satisfying to his spirit.

> I cannot understand what it is that leads me, or what I am after. . . . Can I say it: I believe it should be said; Here I cannot end. They are too near me; they are not high enough to awaken in me a sense of their high superiority which would keep me here to be bettered, to be elevated. (July 17, 1843)

After a two-week trial period Hecker left for home. He had written his family to see if their attitudes regarding the business and their life together had become more spiritualized and if they could accommodate his different life style. He received sufficient reassurance and was calm, although concerned, about his return.

Despite his inner turmoil Hecker showed a great reverence and amazement at the mystery and beauty of the human soul.

> What a charm, what a curiosity, what a picture is the phenomenon of the soul! Every new thought, feeling, or act springs from the depths of the soul, the unknown, the nearest

> to God if not him. . . . Every human being strikes me as a
> wonderful becoming, as if a god were struggling for birth in
> him. He is an imprisoned god. Like the young bird, fearful of
> venturing to fly, man appears to me not as a body but as a
> spirit-being, unconsciously giving utterance to God. Spirits
> doing, acting, suffering, and when I see a man labor, it is not
> as a body I see him, but as an angel, an immortal spirit, the
> infinite breath of God. (July 17, 1843)

The Gnostics also propounded the myth of a hidden God who
needed release. They maintained that in the course of creation,
the Wisdom of God descended into matter, and she became
imprisoned in matter. The hidden God then needed to be released and redeemed. Psychologically speaking, the Divine Wisdom would represent the Self which is hidden in the early stages
of psychological development in identification with the individual ego. The task of psychological maturity is to redeem God
through the work of developing human consciousness, whose
center is the ego. Alchemy also had this same theme of the divine
spirit hidden in matter. The whole alchemical opus was an
attempt to release and redeem a supreme value, a divine essence,
from imprisonment in base matter, the prima materia.[28]

Hecker's enraptured appreciation for the human soul implied a valuation of his very spiritualized Anima. On the other
side, the writer senses a devaluation of the human body if not in
theory, at least in action. While at Fruitlands, the young mystic
further intensified his already severe fasting and bodily mortification. There is a danger here of a passion for the spirit consuming
him at the expense of life. As Jung cautioned, "Just as there is a
passion that strives for blind unrestricted life, so there is a
passion that would like to sacrifice all life to the spirit because of
its superior creative power. Spirit that drags man away from life,
seeking fulfillment only in itself is a false spirit."[29]

Adaptation to the inner life brings with it a terrible feeling of
isolation, because it is such a unique experience to the person. He
naturally seeks some other advisor, in the form of a family
member or friend to give advice and assurance to help him
understand himself. But this is impossible because what is demanded is Self-understanding through one's own soul. The closer

one comes by his circumambulation of the Self to his own divine center, the more radically alone he feels.

> I can find no one who is one with me in my thought or experience, none who is congenial. My nature craves something different from what I have had. (July 31, 1843)

Hecker's experience recorded in the same Diary entry seems to confirm that the deeper one is drawn into the depths of the unconscious, the more that he paradoxically finds his linking with all of humanity. Dr. von Franz refers to a dual process of individuation, whose first stage is the gathering of the multiple aspects of the psyche into one personality. "The second stage, however, has reference to a special process that always accompanies individuation in the single person: namely, the development of relatedness to certain fellow human beings and to mankind as a whole, a relatedness that proceeds not from the ego but from a transcendental inner center, the Self."[30]

> I have been much impressed of late with the very great effect the national and family progenitors have on the characters of their offspring.... Man is in a much greater degree the creature of the past than he gives himself credit for. He reproduces daily the sentiments and thoughts of the dim and almost obscure before. There are certain ideas and aspirations that have not had their fulfillment but which run through all men from the beginning until now and are continually reproduced ... each man is a type, a pattern of the whole human race. (July 31, 1843)

Jung agrees with Hecker and gives a psychological explanation based on his empirical studies. When psychic energy regresses, going past even the period of our early childhood and enters into the legacy of our ancestral life, the mythological images common to mankind are awakened. These are what he calls the archetypes. Suddenly an amazing interior spiritual world reveals itself and manifests contents which contrast most sharply with all our former ideas.[31] This world was what Jung called the world of the collective unconscious and for him proved that the individual consciousness is anything but a *tabula rasa*. For Jung the collective unconscious comprises the psychic life of our ancestors right back to the earliest beginnings.

Hecker returned to his family in New York City on August 15, 1843. By common agreement he was to work with his brothers in the baking business, only during the mornings. He would have the remainder of the day for his personal interests. This was his life for the next eight months. He socialized with some of his former friends, spent much time in prayer, study, and letter writing.

Then in early March of 1844, Hecker notes that his life is becoming more practical by which he means that he is focusing his mind on analyzing his present life situation for possible directions for action. He observes:

> I am neither living in the business nor am I making much progress in my studies. In this case I do not benefit others, nor do I see that I am much benefitted. This should change. One of the two must cease as an object.... One great difficulty seems to be this: I cannot place any definite purpose before my mind and bend all my energies to its accomplishment. (March 8, 1844)

It comes as a shock when he announces in a Diary entry, two days later, that he has made his decision to give up his life and his time to study for the field of the Church. It seems to have been prompted by an unconscious need to serve his fellow man after his long months of introversion and withdrawal. Then he adds a further surprise:

> Which Church? The Roman or the Anglican? To which it is my duty to unite myself I am not fully settled upon. This I will have to leave to a future decision. Whether to prepare myself to enter in a college, or to put myself under the direction of a well-qualified clergyman who will direct my studies ... is not fully settled in my mind, but the latter method seems to me the best way. (March 10, 1844)

While searching possibilities for training closer to home, Hecker nevertheless expressed a need for traveling to establish the breadth of thought and feeling that was possessing him. He felt a fondness for the Boston area which he had come to know and appreciate and made arrangements to study Latin and Greek with George Bradford in Concord, Massachusetts. He boarded at the home of the famous American naturalist and writer, Henry David Thoreau. The two became good friends.

A mere two weeks after beginning his studies with great enthusiasm Hecker faced a problem which would reappear later when he was preparing for the priesthood. He gave this graphic explanation of it:

> I cannot get clear of the conviction that I am now quenching the flow of life from within, and that I should give up my whole time to contemplation instead of this self-active study of the intellect. The delight and enjoyment within is so much greater than the happiness and pleasure without, that constantly I am drawn from without to the conversation within. It is only at moments that I can study, and those are when I am not inwardly engaged. (May 15, 1844)

During this period of time at Concord, one observes in his Diary notations that Hecker is no longer doubting that it is the Holy Spirit guiding him. He calls it such, and confidently allows it to lead and direct him to the extent that he is able. His discrimination between ego-consciousness and the Spirit within, as the source of his actions, is very refined indeed. All this was achieved without a human guide.

> I have been very willful indeed these two days past. The Spirit has chastised me by its receding from me for a distance and a while. I begin to feel youthful again. The *understanding's* office is to submit to the *superior standing.* Whenever it attempts to officiate in the place of the superior standing, it makes but poor and botch-work of all its attempts. The union of the Spirit with me is transiently taken place but not permanently established, and I am too willful to let it permanently be with me. I can as yet supply only the transient conditions. No one can imagine what the permanent conditions are who has not been permanently united with the Spirit. . . .
> While this is going on there is nothing that I can do but be

perfectly submissive to its own direction and motions. My study will have to be laid aside, for how long a time I cannot say; I hope not forever. (May 19, 1844)

Meanwhile he was disturbed enough by his inability to study that he decided to write his friend Orestes Brownson about his situation and explain himself. On June 6, 1844, Brownson replied with a letter that was typical of his forthright and direct manner:

> There is much in your present state to approve, also much which is dangerous. The dreamy luxury of indulging one's thoughts and ranging at ease through the whole spirit-world is so captivating, and when frequently indulged in acquires such power over us, then, we cease to be free men. . . . Be careful that you do not mistake a mental habit into which you have fallen for the guidance of the All-Wise. . . . Where is the sacrifice in following what the natural tendency and fixed habits of our mind dispose us to? Here is your warfare. You have not won victory till you have become as able to drudge at Latin and Greek as to give up worldly wealth, pleasures, honors and distinctions.[32]

Brownson challenged Hecker with a direction in life which was consuming his own thoughts at that moment, namely whether to join the Catholic church. It was the only part of Brownson's letter which Hecker recorded in his Diary. It obviously touched him deeply and for all its strangeness, seemed to be the impulse from the Spirit for which he had been waiting.

> You doubtless feel a repugnance to joining the Church. But you ought not to be ashamed of Christ, and the Church opens a sphere for you; and you especially, you are not to dream your life away. I have made up my mind, and I shall enter the Church if she will receive me. There is no use in resisting, you cannot be an Anglican, you must be a Catholic or Mystic.[33]

Brownson's admonition touched Hecker in the core of his being. The joyous ecstasies which Hecker reported having during the month of May gave way to very sober June days. He underwent mental anguish and painful scrutiny of soul in wrestling with his problem of conscience. Finally he decided to see Bishop Fenwick in Boston. Brownson arranged the appointment. It went well. Two days later Hecker met with Bishop Fitzpatrick, Fenwick's assistant. Hecker was delighted with both men and the interviews. His doubts about becoming a Catholic were removed.

That Hecker was not a thinking type was revealed in his approach to joining a church. He was not held back because of some logical or philosophical questions which remained unanswered. He was waiting for an indication from his inner Spirit. Brownson, on the other hand, had to have certain objections clarified before he could intellectually assent to the Catholic church. As a result he entered the church several months after Hecker did.

Isaac wrote his family and in a calm, determined fashion told them of his decision. He planned a trip home immediately to discuss it personally with them. Although he knew that his mother would have preferred his joining the much more prestigious Anglican church, he anticipated no difficulties from his tolerant family in pursuing his new course.[34]

ISAAC HECKER AND THE FEMININE

Hecker's Diary is important because it also reveals his youthful attitude towards women and sexuality. As might be anticipated, he valued the feminine highly because of his special positive relationship with his mother and his angelic Anima. In a few direct statements he expressed views about the feminine which are very compatible with analytical psychology. For example:

Man requires a new birth, the birth of the feminine in him.
(July 22, 1843)

About one month later he noted:

I had yesterday afternoon a conversation with an acquaintance, Dr. Vethake, author of two articles in the 'Pathfinder' on 'Femality'. . . . The subject of the differences of sexes has of late been a subject which has occupied my attention very

much. I differ in my opinions and sentiments very widely
from him. He holds that man is to be more of a man and
woman is to be more of a woman, so that the two may form a
whole. Man is Truth, woman is Love; and marriage is the
union of Truth, or Wisdom, and Love (he has studied Swe-
denborg deeply although he does not speak of him). The
delight of marriage consists in the communion of the two
natures. Now I am inclined to think the two sexes should be
in the same individual being; that the same individual should
unite in his own being both sexes. (August 26, 1843)

Isaac Hecker, in the writer's opinion, was one of those
persons who could be said to have had the charism of celibacy,
and who was conscious of it from an early age. Psychologically
speaking, the writer understands celibacy to mean an exclusive
dedication to the demands and development of the feminine
within oneself. Hecker had this call before he knew that he would
become a priest. Although there are intimations of it before his
angel vision, we can say, with confidence, that he possessed it
from the time of his vision onwards. From that time Hecker was
careful as he could be, to guard his heart from feminine companions whom he felt he might love or want to marry. He was not totally successful with his conscious control however.

At Brook Farm women sought out his companionship and
his heart went out in affection to a few. One of his women friends
was Swedish-born Ida Russell, whose father had been American
minister to Sweden. Their relationship was very formal. After
Hecker left the Farm, Ida begged him when writing to her, not to
begin the letter, "Dear and Respected Miss Russell."

Hecker was much more personal with Ora Gannett whom
Nathaniel Hawthorne described as, "a bright, vivacious, dark-
haired, rich-complexioned damsel." Hecker described her in his
Diary as, "one of the loveliest, most love-natured beings that has
met my heart. There is more heart in her bosom, more heaven in
her eyes than I have felt or seen in any other person. She is not
lovely but love itself."[35] This effusive feeling never blossomed into
romance because as she wrote him, "You are a brother to me."[36]

Isaac speaks with greatest fondness about an Almira Barlow
at Brook Farm. According to Dr. Holden, Mrs. Almira Barlow
was a charming and beautiful woman who had separated from

her husband after he refused to settle down in any one place. Tiring of a nomadic existence, she and her three sons went to Brook Farm and lived in the same building in which Hecker had his room. She was popular with the men, but dubbed as a "flirt" by the women.[37] Although other men at Brook Farm were interested in her, she had eyes only for Hecker, who was given friendly advice to keep his distance from this woman twelve years his senior. Almira was in love with him, and on one occasion even blurted her feelings out to him, just after his return from a trip to New York. Hecker started to record the conversation in his Diary but then abruptly stopped and tried to scratch out her name. In his Diary, Hecker referred to her as, "one who had come nearer to my heart than any other human being"; as "one who to me is too much to speak of; one who would give up all for me." But she had come into his life too late. After Hecker left Brook Farm they corresponded regularly for a time but she was not satisfied with the growing indifferent and preoccupied tone of his letters. She finally stopped writing.

As Hecker was leaving his friends in New England and returning home, he expressed in his Diary his deep sadness at having to separate. He also added a description about his inner experience with women which helps to explain his relationships while at Brook Farm.

> For instance, as I am now I have less union and sympathy with her and those whom I have met much nearer heretofore. It appears their atmosphere is denser, their life more natural, more in the flesh and instead of meeting them on my highest plane, I can only do so by coming down into my flesh, into my body, which it appears to me I am almost unconscious of in that sense. There is not that sense of heaviness, dullness, fleshiness in me. I feel no natural desires, no impure thoughts nor wanderings of fancy. Still, I feel more intensely and am filled to overflowing with love and desire for union, but there is no one to meet me where I am, and I cannot meet them where they are. (July 31, 1843)

This statement shows that Hecker was pulled into an ethereal one-sidedness by the archetype of spirit and cut off from the awareness of a grounding in his body. This will naturally affect

all his bodily relationships, including those with the opposite sex.
Several months later, while acknowledging that he is feeling
better and enjoying more continuous and higher communion
with the Spirit, he also says that he is so sensitive in terms of his
bodily condition that he cannot bear to have anyone even touch
him. His body is therefore, in effect, taken out of this world of
contact.

A man's relationship to the feminine can be understood by a
study of his Anima, the archetype which represents the psychic
contra-sexual component in his unconscious. "It represents the
image of the opposite sex that we carry in us as individuals and
also as members of the species."[38] The Anima can be discovered
within oneself in dream images, or in visions and fantasies where
she takes on a personified form of a feminine being. The first
bearer of the soul-image or Anima, says Jung, is always the
mother. Later it is carried by those women who touch a man's
feelings, whether in a positive or negative sense. The fact that the
Anima appears first in unconscious fashion means that it will be
projected on someone in the outer environment. And so another
way in which we can study a man's Anima is from considering
the women who are significant in his life. In Hecker's case he
seemed to be projecting his "angel" Anima on Ida Russell and
Ora Gannett of Brook Farm, by idealizing and spiritualizing
them. An archetype such as the Anima will never fully coincide
with the concrete reality of an individual woman. This is particularly true when the Anima is such an abstract and ethereal one as
an angel. The individual is the exact opposite of the archetypal.

In the case of Hecker's love for Almira Barlow, it seems this
is the projection of the dark side of his Anima. As Jolande Jacobi
points out, the Anima has two basic forms, the light or dark,
upper or lower, positive or negative, as do all archetypes. In
reference to Hecker it can be said that the higher form of his
Anima was represented by the angel in his vision and the lower
form was represented by Almira. She was a woman who wanted
roots on earth. She had a family and enjoyed her sexual attraction to men.

There is a more pervasive feminine aspect to Isaac Hecker's
personality, however, that needs capturing. Two brief comments
put the writer on the trail of a more satisfactory explanation. One

statement was made by a close friend of Mrs. Hecker, a certain Georgianna Bruce Kirby, who described Hecker as someone who was inclined to be a mystic and had been, "nearly crazed by the direct rays of the moon."[39] Had this declaration stood alone, it would probably have cast more suspicion upon its author than on Hecker. We have, on the contrary, an interesting parallel by Hecker himself which comes close to verifying this extreme effect of the moon.

> I am sitting by my table with the window up, the moon shining through it in the room. The evening is beautiful. The light of the moon has a marked effect upon me; it stirs me; I feel eager, wild, audacious, restless and awakened. I am conscious that is plays an important part in the different states of my mind. (May 12, 1843)

This Diary entry provoked the insight that Hecker can be much better understood if we consider him a man who had devleoped a matriarchal rather than a patriarchal consciousness. Eric Neumann's article, "The Moon and Matriarchal Consciousness," explains this distinction very well.[40] Neumann points out that in the historical development of ego-consciousness there are successive stages. The first is the matriarchal which describes the condition of consciousness as dependent in its relation to the unconscious. It is represented in the myth of the Great Mother, but goes beyond that to express a total psychic situation in which the unconscious and feminine are dominant. The next stage is the patriarchal, which is attained when masculine consciousness succeeds in establishing itself firmly in a position opposite to and independent of the unconscious.

Matriarchal consciousness or moon consciousness as Neumann calls it, is not confined to women; it exists also in men. It is particularly to be found in creative people and mystics like Hecker. In reality everyone is dependent on the unconscious as the true source of all creativity, for inspirations and hunches of all kinds, and for the functioning of instincts. All these things Neumann points out are ruled by the moon and require from the person a harmony and adjustment.

At the stage of matriarchal consciousness, the ego's task is to wait for the favorable or unfavorable time, to put itself in harmony and mood with the changing unconscious. Hecker's Diary, even as excerpted in this study, gives several examples of how his ego-consciousness was at first overpowered and then trained by his unconscious to follow its direction without battle. Hecker talks about his life being beyond his grasp and bearing him on will-lessly. He mentions his need to be perfectly submissive to the unconscious and its direction and motions, sacrificing his conscious desire even to study.[41]

The act of understanding is also significantly different in matriarchal and patriarchal consciousness according to Neumann. In patriarchal consciousness, understanding is too frequently an act of the intellect which cuts things apart with the scalpel of analysis. In matriarchal consciousness the understanding is more brooding and contemplative, more ordered to organic growth than logical causation. It is more like a passive sufferance whereby the ego tries to accept the content presented mysteriously from the unconscious, and come into harmony with it. This comparative passivity is not due to any incapacity for action, but rather to an awareness that one is subject to a process which one can only let happen.

Contemplation and passive sufferance are words which describe Hecker's life, not only during the period of his Diary but later as well. His theological writings are anything but products of logic such as a systematic theologian might bring forth. They were much more inspired, religious intuitions based on the signs of the times. They tried to appeal to the whole person in a practical way. Often they contained inconsistencies. His approach was the perfect counterpart to the extreme thinking approach of his friend Brownson.

Hecker closed the first book of his Diary with the comment, "I feel like a child full of joy and pliability, and all ambition seems to have left."[42] One would think that Eric Neumann had him particularly in mind when he wrote:

> Moon-light is the first light to illumine the dark world of the unconscious, whence consciousness is born and to which it remains bound; and all things that are child-like, growing, creative, and feminine remain faithful to their relation to the moon-spirit.[43]

Since wholeness of personality, according to analytical psychology, requires a union of archetypal opposites, the matriarchal and patriarchal need to come together and mutually supplement and fructify one another. Hecker's matriarchal consciousness sought its opposite in his friendship with Brownson and with the Roman Catholic church in its patriarchal aspect.

HECKER AS REDEMPTORIST

On August 2, 1844, Isaac Hecker was received into the Roman Catholic church by Bishop John McCloskey of New York City. Almost two years had passed since Hecker's unconscious psyche had drawn his ego into the cauldron of suffering and renewal; the agony and ecstasy of the transforming process, which Jung named individuation. During this time Hecker had basically given himself over to the needs of inner adaptation. His guilt feelings for having abandoned outer adaptation were manifested, at first, in his self-recriminations about his doing nothing while his brothers were hard at work. They were implied also in his decision to devote his life to religious ministry before even being a member of an organized religion.

Jung adds another complexity to the individuation-collective polarity. He draws attention to the fact that there is a two-fold collective function. Not only is there such a function in relation to society as we have just seen, but there is also such a collective function in relation to the unconscious itself, which considered as the collective psyche, is the psychological representative of society. Jung says that when the persona is extinguished in the unconscious then there arises "individuality as one pole that polarizes the unconscious, which in turn produces the counterpole, the God-concept."[44] He goes on to describe the remainder of the process in this fashion:

> The individual must now consolidate himself by cutting himself off from God and becoming wholly himself. Thereby and at the same time he also separates himself from society. Outwardly he plunges into solitude, but inwardly into hell, distance from God. In consequence, he loads himself with guilt. In order to expiate this guilt, he gives his good to the soul, the soul brings it before God (the polarized uncon-

scious) and God returns a gift (productive reaction of the unconscious) which the soul offers to man and which man gives to mankind.

Some of the entries from Hecker's Diary have shown the elements of this process in action. For example, his acknowledgement that he was "very weak in the sight of the world" and "felt no more potence than a babe,"[46] indicates that his persona has been returned to his unconscious. He was also very sensitive to his distance from God, as when he spoke of being out of his center, or in his flesh or in the outer superficies of life instead of living in union with the spirit. This distance caused him suffering and he felt guilt for not being responsive enough to the spirit.

The writer believes that Hecker intuited the good he could give his soul as submission to its direction, celibacy, fasting, prayer, and all kinds of self-denial. These gifts he presented to his soul, his Anima, which brought them before God, and God, the productive reaction of the unconscious, offered him the gift of a closer communion and at this time the gift of becoming a religious minister to mankind.

Shortly after his decision to convert, Hecker conceived the idea of making a pilgrimage to Europe. He wrote his friend Henry David Thoreau in the hopes that the young sage would join him. He told Thoreau, "We desire to go without purse or staff, depending upon the all-embracing love of God, humanity and the spark of courage imprisoned in us."[47] At this point, Hecker seems to be influenced by what Jung calls the finest of all symbols of the libido, the hero symbol. He says, "Heroes are usually wanderers, and wandering is a symbol of longing, of restless urge which never finds its object, of nostalgia for the lost mother."[48] Hecker was certainly a wanderer. Although this trip never materialized, he was fated to make no less than five ocean crossings to Europe in his lifetime. Four of these journeys brought significant changes to Hecker's life because they had an inner psychic counterpart as well.

These voyages could be considered analagous to the myth of the "night sea journey"[49] which Jung used, to describe the individuation process as a whole or in each of its stages. It describes the regressive flow of energy into the unconscious or maternal matrix where it activates creative forces for the renewal of the conscious situation. Jolande Jacobi says, ". . . submersion of consciousness in the darkness of the unconscious, can be regarded as a return to the mother's womb, as a regression. This should not be looked upon as an incestuous wish-fulfillment, as Freud thought, but as the possibility of rebirth . . . the realm of the unconscious is certainly not a refuse bin; it is a treasure-house of the nourishing and creative forces which dwell in all living things. When brought into contact with consciousness, they become activated and place themselves at its disposal: they are reborn."[50]

One year following his conversion Isaac Hecker was making his first ocean trip as an aspirant to the priesthood in the Redemptorist Order. His theological studies in Belgium, Holland, and England were plagued with difficulty. He felt the inner Spirit directing him to cease his mental activity of studying and dwell in his psychic center in contemplation. To test the authenticity of the Spirit, Hecker's superiors put him in the crucible of suffering through tests of humility and obedience. Although such trials were painful, the strength of his inner call was more powerful. Nothing stopped the flow of that inner life. Often in prayer and meditation he experienced "a celestial joy and peace and a readiness to do all for Jesus Christ."[51] Even after he left his prayer and resumed his daily tasks, he reports that the consciousness of the divine presence never left him. He was living constantly in communion with the God within.[52] From the psychological perspective of individuation we could say that his ego was acting in conformity with the direction of his Self and he was receiving continued enlightenment from the unconscious about his conscious situation.

After years of prayer and informal study, Hecker was ordained in England on Oct. 23, 1849 and began his priestly ministry there. It was not long before a conviction welled up from his creative unconscious that he should return to America and labor for the conversion of his fellow countrymen. His superiors agreeing, the young priest returned to New York City after six years in Europe. As though to repay the collective for his long absence he plunged himself into extraverted activities immediately.

The Redemptorists had been primarily engaged in the work of pastoring to the large German populations living in the United States. With continuing immigration the demands of this work grew, often leaving little time for missions to native Americans. In time this brought a basic dissatisfaction to Hecker and his small band of American priests. They desired a separate English-speaking Redemptorist community for their purpose. Hecker volunteered to explain the idea to the Redemptorist Superior General in Rome and his four companions deputized him to do so.

Hecker quickly made plans to sail for Europe and obtained money for his trip from his brother George. This was to be a continued practice of Hecker's for many of his future activities and travels. George functioned in part as a Shadow figure, retaining contact with the world of business and finance which Hecker could not maintain. He was also a supplier of energy for Isaac, symbolized by the money gifts, as well as confidant and supporter. This latter seemed more like a substitute mother role. George was the only other family member who became a Roman Catholic and in all Hecker's troubles, which were naturally related to the church, he quickly sought out understanding and nurturing from brother George.

Father Mauron, the major superior, saw Hecker's journey as one of insubordination, a simple matter of disobedience on Hecker's part to legitimate authority. He issued Hecker an immediate letter of expulsion from the Redemptorist Order. The young missionary was shocked to his core as he read and reread the proclamation. If his personal source of authority had been only external, namely in exclusive obedience to the Holy Spirit working in the church, he would have been completely decimated by this change of events. But Hecker had experiential knowledge of the Spirit within. He could not deny its presence, power, or authority, to direct his life. A very compact understanding of his working theology of the Holy Spirit as related to authority is contained in a letter of spiritual direction to Mrs. Cullen:

> For we must never forget that the immediate means of Christian perfection is the interior direction of the Holy Spirit, while the test of our being directed by the Holy Spirit

and not by our fancies and prejudices is our filial obedience
to the divine external authority of the Church.[53]

Hecker taught that obedience to the external authority of
the church would be evidenced by faith, prayer, and good works.
Basically, whenever Hecker felt a disagreement with an important authoritative position of the church, he turned inward to see
what his own inner Spirit was saying. Whenever he received
some powerful inspiration from the Spirit within, directing his
life and activities along some new path, possibly at variance with
external authority, he sought guidance and advice from experienced persons in the church to test its authenticity. Then he
made his decision.

This approach has overtones of the psychological path of
individuation, consciously pursued. When a person is in conflict
between two opposite and seemingly contradictory positions, and
there seems no conscious resolution, he maintains his relationship to both polarities and trusts the transcendent function, the
symbol-making factor in the unconscious to provide a *tertium
quid*, a resolution in which both polarities are united on a higher
level.

Other important psychological factors undoubtedly entered
into Hecker's attitude toward external authority. In his family
experience the paternal authority had been missing. His father
might as well have been totally absent. Hecker's mother exercised
a maternal authority that was collegial. We can read in Isaac's
letters that his whole family participated in discussions when he
was experiencing his difficulties at home and at Brook Farm. A
collegial principle seemed to operate in which a decision was
reached after each member had a chance to have an input. The
authority exercised by the brothers, when they were in partnership with the bakeries, was truly collegial and equal, even though
Isaac contributed less effort than his two brothers. Against this
background of a more maternal, that is, more eros or related
style of exercising authority, the monolithic, paternalistic style of
the church authority was quite different and strange to Isaac
Hecker.

In his predicament with the Redemptorists, Hecker again
turned to the Spirit within himself for guidance. He discerned

that his cause was right and that he had been dealt with unfairly. He would stay in Rome and fight the expulsion, relating with the authorities in dialogic fashion. These nine months alone in the city were another period of psychic incubation and soul-searching for Hecker. Out of his introspection came two articles predicting a positive future for the church in America which gained him recognition and favor in Rome. His unconscious also fastened on the idea of a new community of priests for the special needs of the American church. When Pius IX removed the obstacles from his path, Hecker rushed home to work with his four companions in forming the first American community of priests. It bore the stamp of his convictions. Religious vows were replaced by promises, to allow the members greater freedom to respond to their fellow Americans. External controls and governing structures were minimized and obedience to external authority was present but not stressed. To the degree that the individual was faithful to the direction of the inner Spirit, to that degree Hecker believed he would be in conformity with the authority of the church.

The years from the founding of the Paulist Fathers in 1858 until 1869 were extremely active ones for the young community and Hecker, who had been chosen its major superior. During this period Hecker left very little information about his own interior journey. What is available are letters to persons he was guiding in spiritual direction. These reveal his continuing preoccupation with encouraging people to give themselves over to the inner direction of the Spirit. He worked like an analytical psychologist might, supporting the unique process of individuation in each person, very concerned not to usurp the principal director of the soul.

THE LINGERING ILLNESS

In 1870 the Ecumenical Council, called Vatican I, was summoned in Rome. Hecker was invited to attend by Bishop Rosecrans of Columbus, Ohio, as his peritus (expert) theologian. With Hecker's minimalizing attitude toward external authority, it is not surprising that he was aligned with the forces opposing the definition of the doctrine of infallibility, the most important matter on the agenda. His theological difficulty was intertwined with a philosophical problem as summarized in his notes for April 21, 1870. "Who can define a Supreme Authority? Can that which is below reach that which is above it? Is it not a contradiction *in se*?"[54] He also sided with the American Bishops who saw the definition as inopportune for the religious situation in the United States.

The experience of the Council was positive for Hecker in the sense that it was the occasion which convinced him that America had been given a providential mission to renew the religious life of Europe. He felt, also, that the Paulists would be a means of accomplishing that goal by expanding their work to European shores.

The Council was also a source of trauma and inner conflict for Hecker. He was disillusioned by the intrigue, party struggles and politicking that went on, particularly by the Italians, and could not hide his chagrin. But the theological consequences of the definition, as he envisioned them, were a source of deeper upset. He felt the Church had moved backwards, buttressing a European concept of Church and authority that was waning and out of tune with the more democratic aspirations of the ordinary American.

At first Hecker thought that the question of infallibility had been successfully tabled. When he realized the inevitability of its being passed, his health began to decline. By April he was complaining of "habitual exhaustion." Although he had written to his brother George, that it would be unwise to leave the Council in the middle of the debate on infallibility, Isaac Hecker did so.*

Hecker accepted, on faith, the definition of infallibility voted on July 16, 1870 and never spoke against it, but it produced an inner conflict. Eventually he was able to interpret the dogma as having been necessary to settle the problems of authority which were initiated with the Reformation. Its providential purpose, as Hecker uniquely interpreted it, was to clear the path for the authority of the Holy Spirit in the individual soul.

*For an alternate point of view, see Farina, "Isaac Hecker's Vision for the Paulists," below, pp. 201–210.

Hecker's health began to fail him seriously in the latter part of 1871. He suffered from nervous exhaustion and could no longer concentrate or remain in community. Doctors diagnosed his illness as a blood disorder compounded by acute angina pectoris. Any work was impossible and he divided his duties among other Paulists.

Elliott wrote of this illness, which lasted until Hecker's death seventeen years later, as, "a dark chamber of sorrows, though it was sometimes peaceful sorrow," alternating between seasons of, "desolation and seasons of peace."[55]

After spending the winter of 1872–1873 in the southern United States, the doctors decided that Isaac's illness was not terminal. They suggested that he travel to Europe. Hecker was not anxious to do so, but left in 1873 nevertheless. He journeyed to the health spa at Ragatz, Switzerland, financed as always by his faithful brother George. In a somber departure he told his brother Paulists, "Look upon me as a dead man . . . God is trying me severely in soul and body, and I must have the courage to suffer crucifixion."[56]

Two years of search for renewed physical health in Europe were a time of extreme psychic regression for Hecker. His physical pain and psychic conflict were so intolerable, on occasion, that he even desired death. "Death invited, alas, will not come! What a relief from a continuous and prolonged death!"[57]

Through this inner suffering Hecker gained some important insights. One was the awareness that his illness was not merely physical but more psychically induced. He came to see its roots in a conflict between himself and his fellow Paulists over the direction of the Paulist community. "During the years of the formation of the Paulists, all my companions were more and more inclined to increase the discipline, fixed rules, and external authority, than I was. . . . This struggle was one of the chief causes of breaking down my physical health."[58]

Hecker mentions that after he left the community in the hands of his companions it moved markedly in their direction, i.e. toward more elaborate structuring. He, on the other hand, went deeper in his desire for radical dependence on the guidance of the inner Spirit.

While one can readily agree that Hecker's inner conflict had as one of its important sources, the conflict with the Paulist community, that cause alone seems inadequate to explain his long years of suffering, or his other experiences since his return from Vatican I. With a paucity of information about his inner life during this period it would be arrogant and misleading even to attempt a careful psychological analysis. The writer hopes to present, rather, a symbolic understanding of factors operative in Hecker's personality from his earliest years and continuing throughout his life, based on the principles of analytical psychology.

Hecker presented his life in symbolic form in a fable he created while midway in his last European visit. He shared it with his brother George on September 10, 1874.

> Once upon a time a bird was caught in a snare. The more it struggled to free itself, the more it got entangled. Exhausted, it resolved to wait with the vain hope that the fowler, when he came, would set it at liberty. His appearance, however, was not the signal for its restoration to smiling fields and fond companions, but the forerunner of death at his hands. Foolish bird! Why did you go into the snare? Poor thing; it could not find food anywhere, and it was famishing with hunger; the seed was so attractive and he who had baited the trap knew it full well, and that the bird could not resist its appetite. The flower is our Lord. The bait is divine Love. The bird is the soul. O skillful catcher of souls! O irresistible bait of Divine Love! O pitiable victim! but most blessed soul; for in the hands of our Lord the soul only dies to self to be transformed into God.

The bird is a universal symbol for transcendence; the soul; the ability to communicate with gods or to enter into a higher state of consciousness. In Christian mythology, birds are sometimes symbolized as winged souls. In Egyptian mythology the soul, the Ka, leaves the body at death in the shape of a bird. In the Shinto tradition the bird is the creative principle. In Scandinavian mythology the bird stands for the spirit freed from the body.[59]

The writer finds that the bird, self-chosen by Hecker, is a marvelous symbol to represent the tensions and directions of his entire life. On the level of physical reality alone, he experienced a continuous delight in observing birds. His writings show that he was immediately aware of the presence of a bird in his environment. On occasion he even understood their song or presence synchronistically, noting at what particular line of his writing their song had suddenly burst forth. The bird in the form of a dove, is also a symbol of the Holy Spirit to whose guidance Hecker gave over his entire adult life and energies.

Psychologically speaking, it can be said that Hecker gave himself over to the archetype of the spirit; the numinous, collective force of the unconscious which draws one to the heights, where traditionally the gods dwell. Hecker followed eagerly, yearning to remain in permanent communion with the divine at all cost.

The tension and goal of individuation, however, is striving to live all of one's reality and for a human being this includes living in one's body. The opposite pole of the archetype of spirit is the archetype of matter. The attraction of the spirit was so delightful at times, and Hecker so immersed in it, that his relation to his body suffered great neglect, or was deliberately denied the fulfillment of its instinctual needs. The last seventeen years of his continuing physical infirmity could be seen symbolically as the archetype of matter showing its power, compensating his one-sided focus on the spirit.

Hecker frequently affirmed in speech and writing the need for recognizing the importance of body, soul, and spirit while living in this temporal world. But these were words, and whether spoken or written, were also a manifestation of the archetype of spirit. They belong to the world of logos. His whole apostolate of the press is also under the influence of this archetype. In reality, Hecker had a most difficult time trying to integrate the world of matter into his life.

The tension between body and spirit was present beginning with Hecker's early vision. He wrote in his Diary that it was difficult for him to get down into his fleshy body to meet others where they were. He complained that they could not meet him where he was dwelling. While at Brook Farm he rejoiced in clever stratagems to defeat his bodily instincts. His discipline and bodily austerities were severe. These continued and intensified during the time of his priestly training as we have evidence from his letter to his spiritual director. Undoubtedly, they were present in various forms throughout his life.

This conflict within himself, between the archetype of spirit and matter, Hecker met in projected form in other "bodies." The Paulist community was one such body, which as he confessed, caused him severe confict. This group of men were, in his vision, the unique embodiment of the Spirit in communitarian form. His Paulist body of priests would not conform to his spiritualized concept. They moved in a compensatory manner to concretize themselves in discrete forms and structures. They felt the unconscious need to become incarnate in the world of material reality as strongly as their founder seemed to resist becoming so.

Hecker, as an introverted intuitive, had many splendid futuristic insights and inspired prophetic interpretations for the times, but incarnating them was not his forté. The real community builder of the Paulists was his assistant, Father Augustine Hewit, a co-founder of the community, who also acted as Hecker's spiritual director and confidant for long years.

Hecker's last journey to Europe brought him experiences which widened the gulf between himself and all others. On April 17, 1874, he wrote his Paulist assistant, Father Hewit, trying to explain the inner changes which had been working within his soul the previous two years:

> Conceive for a moment that within the inmost center of your soul there should appear a light towards which and on which, your whole attention is fixed and absorbed. That in this light a new insight is given to the soul of all things, spiritually and temporally, with singular peace and tranquillity.
>
> Consider that in this light, all your relations to your past life, your' companions, your relatives, your country, have been altered, independently, and without any voluntary act of your will ... and take into account my natural dispositions, and you can imagine the struggles, trials, and conflicts and my interior.

Such a light coming from the center of one's being can symbolize a manifestation of the divine or represent an encounter with ultimate reality. Such an illumination is not infrequently experienced by the dying and accompanied by great peace.

Light represents consciousness in psychological terms and in this case, a consciousness coming from a very deep unifying level of the collective unconscious. Dr. von Franz says that the collective unconscious appears at first to be a multiplicity of structures which can be observed empirically in mythological motifs common to all human beings. When one makes contact with the deepest area of the unconscious, one finds the psyche acting as a unit. As this center is approached, space and time become more and more relativized. It appears that in this deep unity, the multiplicity of the archetypes is nullified or suspended.[60]

While travelling the length of the Nile during the winter of 1873–1874, Hecker seemed in touch with this deep unifying level of his unconscious. He wrote in his Egyptian notes:

> The Holy Spirit fills the whole earth, acts everywhere and in all things, more directly on the minds and hearts of rational creatures. . . . This all-wise, all powerful action now guides, as He ever has and ever will, all men and events to His complete manifestation and glory.[61]

This unity which Hecker felt and experienced in a more expansive context included the reconciliation of the opposites. He envisioned, "The Church in her doctrines can reconcile the Moslems, the Chinese, etc., without any violence to the primary doctrines which these hold."[62]

Hecker began to think of himself as an International Catholic. The power of this new vision universalized his ideas about the renewal of religion which he published under the title, *An Exposition of the Church in View of the Recent Difficulties and Controversies, and the Present Needs of the Age*. The Roman hierarchy blocked the publication of the work locally, so Hecker sent it to England where he had it published at his own expense.

As Hecker's ideas became more universalized, they also abstracted him more from human relationships. He wrote that his entire past and his feelings for all previous relationships seemed crushed out of him.[63] Again he was experiencing a new level of transformation in the process of individuation. Not only was he further removed from the collective without, but again God tested him by inner trials. He felt the estrangement from the divine within. He wrote:

> There was once a priest who had been very active for God, until at last God gave him a knowledge of the Divine Majesty. After seeing the majesty of God that priest felt very strange and was much humbled, and knew how little a thing he was in comparison with God.[64]

With all this severing of relationships of family, community, and friends and the distancing of God within, it is not surprising that Hecker felt like a disembodied spirit and suffered accordingly. It is hard to conceive such an experience of human loneliness.

Small wonder that Hecker found it difficult to relate to the Paulist body when he was summoned home by Father Hewit in July 1875 to resolve a crisis state in the Paulist community. It was a pivotal decision because Hecker had just about determined that he would sever his ties with the Paulists and spend his remaining years in Europe working for his vision of religious renewal. He decided in favor of return and wrote Hewit:

> The past has not given any grounds for suspicion of my willingness to sacrifice myself for the good of the Community, and as for the present, it is in its hands. Let the Community deliberate and decide, and if it be for immediate return— send me a telegram—it will find me indifferent to my health or what physicians may say.[65]

Hecker returned home to work in limited fashion for the last thirteen years of life. At first he chose to live with his brother George, apart from the community. He feared the ravaging results of a renewed conflict with the Paulists over community directions. Hecker refused to try to impose his ideas on his brothers by virtue of his power. He even made a symbolic compromise with them by collaborating on the building of their new church at 59th Street in New York City, the mother church of the Paulists. The building of this new church came to be the symbol of the difference of their conceptions of church renewal.

One was a concretization in terms of brick and mortar, and Hecker's idea was a Spirit-bonded one. Even in this compromise, Hecker chose to confine his assistance to the form of the building, the spiritually creative side, calling upon three of America's greatest artists to give it soul.

Hecker remained his individuated self until the end. He experienced the estrangement and death of his life-long friend, Orestes Brownson, who in his later years adopted ever more conservative ideas regarding the church. Hecker always esteemed him and was ever grateful for his invaluable friendship, but understanding gave way to incomprehensibility in later years.

After much urging, Hecker returned to the 59th Street parish in New York in 1879, to live with the Paulists. His continuing physical illness made his public appearances more and more rare. Finally, after experiencing the death of his brother George a few months earlier, Hecker died peacefully. His spirit was free at last to soar forth to that permanent union with the divine in the beyond that his being had always sought.

A LIFE OF INDIVIDUATION

Isaac Hecker was an introverted, gentle, warm-hearted man with a highly developed intuition. Many of his finest insights about the needs of the Roman church in his day have been recognized by their realization in our times. Perhaps his prophetic sense of urgency and sanguine personality nudged them along a little more quickly.

Hecker enjoyed an accepting, strong, positive mother and suffered from an extremely weak father. His need for fathering was projected on his friend, Orestes Brownson, and his spiritual directors during his Redemptorist days. For the remainder of his life Hecker was a supreme authority himself, in his Paulist community. This authority he exercised rarely, and always in a brotherly, collegial fashion. He believed in the voluntary principle on every level. Power was locked in his Shadow side.

Through most of his life Hecker's natural *attrait* was towards the inner reality. He lived at the edge of the oasis of life, the unconscious, and dipped in daily for fresh living water to nourish himself. One day, when he was in his early twenties, the

Spirit troubled the waters with His presence, and Isaac's life was quickened. He became single-minded; searching for the kingdom of God within, and calling others to do the same.

The Spirit often leads one first into the desert of loneliness. Isaac had to sever his ties with his family and friends to be free to follow the hero's path. Individuation is the lonely way. Having made this decision, Hecker never deviated from his commitment, although he was tested in the crucible of suffering constantly.

The powerful presence of the Spirit kept drawing Hecker to his unconscious, which then shaped his consciousness in its maternal matrix. His discovery of the mystics while preparing for the Catholic priesthood was a liberating experience because it helped Hecker realize that his experiences were not unknown or totally unfathomable. This is the kind of consolation that mythological amplification brings to an analysand who is troubled by seemingly bizarre dreams or unconscious impulses.

Every time that Hecker was drawn deep into the well of the unconscious, he was naturally isolated from his external relationships. At times he received the compensation of ecstasy and soul-satisfying communion with the divine within. At other times, he suffered separation from the divine as well, a double isolation to transform still further his individuality.

Strangely enough, in the deepest of these submersions, Hecker also made contact with the principle of relatedness and returned to the world with a substitute offering for his absence. These were sometimes abstract, spiritualized offerings such as an improved vision of the needs of the church, which he then communicated in writing or active labor. At other times they were more concrete, as when he became convinced that a new congregation of men was needed for the conversion of America. This was his most embodied offering.

The experience of Hecker seems to confirm Jung's findings, that individuation is an exclusive adaptation to the inner reality, which the external world will accept if a fitting substitution is offered as expiation for one's absence. Each new step in individuation requires a new expiation. Hecker offered successively: a promise to minister to people after his transforming experience of Brook Farm; a dedication to work for non-Catholic America after his priestly ordination; the formation of a congregation of men to work for the evangelization of America after his expulsion from the Redemptorists; a more universalized vision of the church in an article written in Italy after months of desolation and travel in search of physical health; a final unpublished work at the end of his life to compensate for his long years of separation from the Paulists and their activities.

In many fields of endeavor, heroes find their living made buoyant and their dying made smooth by crowds of admirers affirming their human contributions. The heroism of individuation often leaves one scorned for having left the trodden path, misunderstood for having dared to be unique, alone and frightened to extinguish one's ego in the darkness one has seen as a long-time adversary.

Isaac Hecker was a lonely figure in his last years, misunderstood or ignored by many who were called his brothers, afraid of death and yearning for it. Some of this was the mystic's plight. Hecker, like so many mystics, after an experience of the divine, tortured himself to preserve and improve the mystical union. Bluntly expressed, he felt that the body was a hindrance to spiritual transformation. Hecker expressed it more adroitly noting, "When a body gets into the water at a certain depth, it is difficult to keep on the ground with the feet; so when the soul is bathed in a certain spiritual atmosphere, the weight of the body is overbalanced."[66]

Hecker's life was so highly spiritualized that one can readily understand his difficulty to keep his feet on the ground of external reality. He found it difficult to adapt to his body as physical entity or psychic projection. His body became a Shadow aspect of his psyche. He lived out a life of tension crucified between the opposites of spirit and matter, ecstasy and suffering, extreme activity and coma-like passivity. The one constant in his life was his conviction of the presence of the Spirit guiding him from within. Hecker had religion in Jung's sense.

> Religion is a relationship to the highest or most powerful value, be it positive or negative. The relationship is voluntary as well as involuntary, that is to say you can accept, consciously, the value by which you are possessed unconsciously.

That psychological fact which yields the greatest power in your system functions as a god, since it is always the overwhelming psychic factor that we called God.[67]

Isaac Hecker would have understood Jung's seemingly cryptic answer to the question, "Do you now believe in God?" Jung replied, "Now? Difficult to answer. I know. I don't need to believe. I know."[68]

NOTES

1. C. G. Jung, *Collected Works*, Bollingen Series XX. (Princeton: Princeton University Press, 1970–76) Vol. 18, p. 451.

2. Jung, *Works* 17, p. 175.

3. ITH to his father, 1847 or 1848, PFA.

4. Vincent F. Holden, C.S.P., *The Yankee Paul* (Milwaukee: Bruce, 1958), p. 11.

5. ITH, "Dr. Brownson in Boston," CW 45 (July 1887): 469.

6. Evelyn Underhill, *Mysticism* (New York: Dutton, 1961), p. 169.

7. M. L. von Franz, *Alchemical Active Imagination* (Spring: Texas, 1979) p. 53.

8. Jung, *Works* 7., p. 65.

9. Jung, *Works* 13, p. 82.

10. Jung, *Works* 7, p. 238.

11. C. G. Jung, *Man and His Symbols* (Doubleday: New York, 1964), p. 177.

12. Jung, *Works* 13, p. 82.

13. ITH to his brothers, December 26, 1842, PFA.

14. Susan J. Perschbacher, "Journey of Faith" (Ph.D. Dissertation, University of Chicago, March 1981), p. 54.

15. ITH to his family, December 28, 1842, PFA.

16. Jung, *Works* 1, p. 79.

17. Jung, *Works* 8, p. 391.

18. Jung, *Works* 10, p. 132.

19. Jung, *Works* 8, p. 403.

20. Jung, *Works* 8, p. 307.

21. Jolande Jacobi, *The Way of Individuation* (New York: Harcourt, Brace & World, 1967), p. 24.

22. Jung, *Works* 8, p. 39.

23. Eric Neumann, *The Child* (New York: Putnam's Sons, 1973), p. 20.

24. Jung, *Works* 9 ii, pp. 8–9.

25. Jung, *Works* 16, p. 192.

26. Von Franz, *Projection and Re-Collection in Jungian Psychology* (London: Open Court, 1980), p. 177.

27. Jung, *Works* 8, p. 311.

28. Jung, *Works* 12, pp. 304–306.

29. Jung, *Works* 8, p. 337.

30. Von Franz, op. cit., p. 174.

31. Jung, *Works* 7, p. 77.

32. O. A. Brownson to ITH, June 6, 1844, PFA.

33. Ibid.

34. Holden, op, cit., p. 94.

35. Ibid., p. 431.

36. Ora Gannett to ITH, July 28, 1844, PFA.

37. Holden, op. cit., p. 50.

38. Jolande Jacobi, *The Psychology of C. G. Jung* (London: Routledge & Kegan Paul Ltd., 1968), p. 114.

39. John Farina, *An American Experience of God: The Spirituality of Isaac Hecker* (New York: Paulist, 1981), p. 48.

40. Erich Neumann, *The Moon and Matriarchal Consciousness* (Zurich: Spring, 1973), pp. 40–60.

41. ITH, Diary, May 19, 1844, PFA.

42. Ibid., May 23, 1844.

43. Neumann, op. cit., p. 60.

44. Jung, *Works* 18, p. 453.

45. Ibid.

46. ITH Diary, May 23, 1844, PFA.

47. ITH to H. Thoreau, July 31, 1844, PFA.

48. Jung, *Works* 5, p. 205.

49. Jung, *Works* 5, p. 210.

50. Jacobi, op. cit., p. 70.

51. Holden, op. cit., p. 144

52. ITH to Mon. T. R. Père, May 30, 1848, PFA.

53. ITH to Mrs. Cullen, July 24, 1872, PFA.

54. ITH, Notes, April 21, 1870, PFA.

55. Walter Elliott, *The Life of Father Hecker* (New York: Columbus, 1894), p. 371.

56. Ibid., p. 370.

57. ITH, "Notes on Interior States While Abroad," p. 5, PFA.

58. Ibid., p. 21.

59. J.C. Cooper, *An Illustrated Encyclopaedia of Traditional Symbols* (London: Thames and Hudson, 1978), pp. 20–21.

60. Von Franz, op. cit., pp. 84–85.

61. ITH, "Notes on Interior States," p. 3, PFA.

62. Ibid.

63. ITH to Augustine Hewit, April 7, 1874, PFA.

64. Elliott, op. cit., p. 380.

65. ITH to Hewit, July 30, 1875, PFA.

66. ITH, "Notes on Interior States," March 4, 1875, PFA.

67. Jung, *Works* 11, p. 81.

68. William McGuire and R.F.C. Hull, editors, *C.G. Jung Speaks* (Princeton University Press 1977), p. 428.

Isaac Hecker's Vision for the Paulists: Hopes and Realities

by John Farina

In 1858 four young men, all converts to Catholicism, announced the formation of the first indigenous religious men's community in North America, the Missionary Society of St. Paul the Apostle. The leadership of the little band was entrusted to Isaac Hecker. His ideas shaped the early community: his missiology, his belief in the values of American civilization, and his mystical perception of the synthesis of modern thought and Catholic tradition. Despite this, part of his vision was never fully represented by the Congregation. From the start, he compromised his ideas in an effort to accommodate the concerns of other Community members and, especially, other Catholics. The Paulists, then, were an amalgam of Hecker's missionary vision and the institutional realities of nineteenth-century American Catholicism. At times in his life he was comfortable with this. At others, he was rattled and shaken by its weaknesses and imperfections.

In what follows, I would like to illustrate this by examining the relationship between Hecker's hopes for the Paulists and the historical realities at different points during the Community's development: (1) the Redemptorist period prior to the writing of the Programme of Rule; (2) July 1858 at the drafting and issuance of the Programme; and (3) the 1870s and early 1880s when the tensions between Hecker's ideas and the actual course of the Community's development were most pronounced.

This examination will shed light on the early history of the Community and on the personality of its founder and will clarify the reasons why the Paulists had trouble fulfilling Hecker's vision for them. In addition, it will show that the tension between Hecker's vision for the Paulists and the historical realities was not merely a struggle between one man's dreams and the imperfections of life. Rather it was a struggle between two conceptions of the Christian life that vied with one another during the second half of the nineteenth century.[1]

THE PERIOD PRIOR TO THE PROGRAMME OF RULE

Redemptorist Days

In order to understand Hecker's vision for the Paulists, one must understand the formation of that vision during the 1850s when he, Augustine Hewit, George Deshon, Francis Baker, and Clarence Walworth labored as Redemptorist missionaries in the United States.[2] The story begins in 1848 when Hecker, still a Redemptorist brother, and Walworth, a newly-ordained priest, met Bernard Hafkenscheid, the vice-provincial for the United States Province, which at that time was part of the Belgian province of the Transalpine Redemptorists. The Liguorian missionary, one of the most dynamic and progressive members of the Congregation, had plans for missions in the U.S. and was looking for workers who knew the American language and culture well enough to conduct effective programs. Up until this time, Hecker had developed only a strong desire to return to America as a Redemptorist missionary and share with his fellow countrymen the treasures of Catholicism that had so delighted him. How he would fulfill that desire remained unknown until he met Fr. Bernard whose plans matched his own inclinations.

In 1851 Hecker traveled with Fr. Bernard and Walworth to New York to begin their work. There they added to their band Augustine Hewit, like Walworth and Hecker a convert from Protestantism, and an Irish-born priest, John Duffy. For the next three years the troop carried on highly successful missions in the Northeast and South. The positive and at times even dramatic response that their efforts brought encouraged the American fathers to plan for what promised to be a bright future as Liguorian missionaries. To their number were soon added yet two more American-born converts, George Deshon and Francis Baker.

1854 proved to be a crucial year for the missionaries. Pius

IX, attempting to remedy problems in the Congregation that lingered on from the conflicts between the Cisalpine and Transalpine sectors, reorganized the Redemptorists placing a German Rector General in Rome in charge of the Transalpine Community. The attempts of the Rector General Rudolf Smetana and his successor Nicholas Mauron to consolidate the Congregation under a carefully-structured, highly-regulated form conflicted with the progressive missionary ideas of Fr. Bernard, who was not reappointed to his post as vice-provincial but transferred to work in Ireland. In his place George Ruland was named American Provincial who, under the new organization, was responsible directly to Rector General Mauron in Rome.

The American fathers perceived quickly that the cause of missions, in the style they had become accustomed to, was not a priority with the new administration. They had begun planning for an English-speaking house that would function as their base of operations. They were convinced that this was necessary to aid their own labors and to provide a setting in the Community that would attract Americans to the Congregation. The predominant German culture of the Redemptorist houses in America was seen as a hindrance to vocations.

To the Redemptorist hierarchy, talk of an English-speaking house and missions to non-Catholics conducted by American fathers sounded like a dangerous blending of nationalism and religion.[3] Their fears were fanned by the new outbreaks of Nativism that marred the 1840s and '50s. The Nativists' slogans of "America for Americans" and their imprecations against "foreign" influence seemed very much like the American fathers' insistence on missions for Americans, by Americans, and on a distinct house established along the lines of language and national culture. For the European Liguorians who were witnessing the fury of nationalistic, anti-clerical movements in France, Belgium, Germany, and Italy at mid-century, any mixture of nationalism and religion was perceived as a disastrous mistake.

To add to the Redemptorist hierarchy's troubles, the American province, true to its frontier nature, had been a rather wild and woolly place where numerous irregularities were a frequent part of religious life. Compounding this was the tendency, which Ruland complained about to the Rector General, of dumping troublesome fathers in America.[4] One such fellow was Gabriel Rumpler, master of the Redemptorist novitiate in Baltimore in the 1850s. Despite his past valuable service as consultor to the American Provincial, Fr. Rumpler unfortunately had by 1854 become rather alarmingly insane. As novice master he literally terrorized his young charges forcing them to march across the thawing ice of a river, insisting on constant acts of mortification, boxing the ears of acolytes at Mass, tearing out and stomping on leaves of the missal, and preaching sermons declaring that he was the most learned man in the world. The effect on the novices understandably was devastating. One committed suicide, another tried unsuccessfully, and at least one other himself became insane. Through all this the Provincial George Ruland seemed rather powerless, unwilling or unable to deal with the problem. The American fathers, shocked by the situation at the novitiate that threatened to vitiate any of their efforts to encourage American vocations, acted to remedy matters. Walworth left the mission band in June 1855, and, with his superior's consent, lured the raving Rumpler to the nearby Mt. Hope insane asylum in Baltimore with the bait that a carriage was waiting to take him to Rome to be canonized. Hecker later got involved and, against the wishes of Hewit, who was at the time a consultor to the Provincial, received permission to bring Rumpler to New York under the care of Dr. Watson who, Hecker claimed, was capable of working wonders with the mentally disturbed. What the mysterious doctor actually did to his patient in the days of water-cures, animal-magnetism, ozone paper, and panacea tonics, is unknown. Fr. Rumpler, after showing some improvement, died not long after.[5]

The combination of internal troubles and resistance to the American fathers' ideas on missions was enough to prod the American Redemptorists into action. When it appeared that the mission band would be broken up to man new foundations in St. Thomas and Quebec, the American fathers determined that they would send Hecker to Rome to plead their case for an English-speaking house to the Rector General. The story of Hecker's trip to Rome, his expulsion from the Redemptorists, and his appeal to the Holy See that resulted in the annulment of his and his American confreres' vows, is too detailed to tell at length here.

There are, however, two points that need to be made when evaluating the important events that took place during Hecker's time in Rome that shaped his conception of the new Community that was to emerge from his struggle.

The first point to be noted is that although the Americans were hoping for the best, they were very much ready for a struggle in Rome.[6] They knew full well (and this is not at all clear in Holden's account) that the Rector General was not in favor of the English-speaking house. They also knew that the circular that Mauron had issued on June 12, 1857 could be interpreted in a way that would preclude trips to Rome that were not specifically authorized by him.[7] This authorization they did not seek; and I think it is clear why: they feared they would not receive it. Instead they appealed to the Constitutions of the Congregation that gave members the right to appear in person before the Rector General in extraordinary situations of grave importance. Standing on this constitutional right, Hecker in the name of his colleagues would argue for their agenda. Anticipating a cool response from the Rector General, the American fathers prepared an alternative beforehand: they would appeal their case to the Holy Father. Thus they assembled letters of recommendation from American bishops and letters of introduction to influential people in Rome. Hecker himself anticipated trouble. He wrote to his brother George comparing his risky trip to the peril of soldiers in battle who risk their lives for the glory of their country. Why, he asked, should not he be willing to risk his for the glory of God? Immediately after his expulsion he wrote to George that the turn of events had not been "altogether unexpected" and discussed, despite his disappointment, rather calmly his plans to get a room conveniently located and settle down to the work involved in making an appeal.[8]

The conflict between Hecker and the Rector General Mauron was a classic clash of cultures, which was couched in theological terms. The American appealed to the authority of law as written in the Redemptorist Constitution; the German Redemptorist to the personal authority that he as Rector General held over his subjects. That the Americans would set that aside was clear proof to him of their rebelliousness. The American, on the other hand, felt that both he and the General stood under a higher law—that of the Constitution, which guaranteed them redress of their grievances. Rational debate, not the fiat of a superior, would determine the matter. The American was in Rome to openly crusade for an approach to missions that was tailored specifically to Americans. Mauron, conversely, was opposed to the plan precisely because it made questions of national culture an issue. He was the architect of an effort to regularize the practice of his Congregation and to bring it under the unified control of his office at Villa Caserta. Hecker wanted, in typically American fashion, to experiment with a new idea that his experience had shown to be accurate. Mauron stood for a long tradition of religious obedience in its most rigorous Germanic form. He wished to project a picture of Catholicism as a unified, unchanging system in contrast to the disunity that had always earmarked Protestantism. He was grounded in the theological theorem that said the Church is one and catholic, and he was not about to countenance change at the insistence of cultural, secular factors. Writing to John B. Purcell, Archbishop of Cincinnati, Mauron told it plainly. Hecker's act was "a scandalous violation of the religious vows and of all *regular* [italics mine] discipline."[9] That regularity was, in the General's view, the single most important factor in the success of the Redemptorists in America until now. Hecker writing just one day later to his brother George was gnashing his teeth at just the kind of passive view of Christian virtue that the General extolled.

> The faithful depend on the priests for the advancement of religion, the priests on the bishops, the bishops on the cardinals, and the cardinals on the Pope, and the Pope on Almighty God—and all this is only an excuse for flunkyism.[10]

The second point that should be emphasized when looking at this period is that Rome adjudicated the conflict between the Rector General and Hecker precisely on the basis of its being a cultural conflict and avoided the theological questions it raised. (This was just the opposite of how Rome responded to the Americanist controversy later.) Hecker and the American fathers to their credit were able to enlist the support of numerous American bishops—John Hughes, John B. Purcell, and John

Barry among them. As one of Hecker's friends from Baltimore, George H. Miles, said of the American fathers: "To me and to the multitudes you were never Redemptorists—never Liguorians—but Hecker, Walworth, Hewit."[11] The sympathies of the laypeople were with the Americans who had become celebrities as a result of their highly-successful missions. Not even the bishops would side with a German General far off in Rome who seemed so out of touch with life in the U.S. and the religious needs of the people. To the support of the prelates and laypeople were added the recommendations of the editors of two influential periodicals: James A. McMaster, editor of the *Freeman's Journal* and Orestes A. Brownson, editor of his famous *Review*. With this type of backing it is not surprising that Propaganda sided strongly with the Americans.[12]

Piux IX in a masterful move of diplomacy took a course that allowed both parties to save face and to carry on their legitimate works. Not wishing to humiliate the Rector General of an established Congregation that he himself only recently attempted to aid through a major reorganization, Pius IX chose to ignore the issue of whether or not Hecker's expulsion was valid. Instead Hecker and his fellows were granted dispensation from their Redemptorist vows on the basis of a petition that Walworth, Hewit, Deshon, and Baker had made to which Hecker finally agreed after originally contending that the matter of the dismissal must first be settled. The Pope's decision, as Hecker was rightly led to believe by Propaganda, stemmed from the "conviction that Americans and Germans are too different and opposite to live together." As Pio Nono himself told Hecker in a private audience: "The best solution then was to divide them as the Lord had divided Abraham and Lot."[13]

As is the case with skillful diplomacy, each party seemed satisfied with the results, and even assured that they had gotten the better part of it. Mauron wrote to Cardinal Alessandro Barnabò, Prefect of Propaganda, telling him that the decision was "most welcome." In a letter to George Ruland, he exulted in the decision, sure that he had been vindicated and that the Congregation had escaped harm. Hecker, on the other hand, was convinced that he had obtained all that the Americans had desired.[14] Armed with the decree of annulment, a verbal encouragement from the Pope to start a new institute, a rescript from the Pope granting special dispensations and faculties to the American fathers, and a letter from Cardinal Barnabò stating that he was free from ecclesiastical censure and "well beloved" of Propaganda, Hecker was in fact in good shape. But the question of the validity of the expulsion still cropped up. Hecker concluded that since he was released from his vows with the others, this implied that they were still in effect and the expulsion, therefore, was invalid. The Redemptorists challenged this, however, maintaining that the Pope had refused to declare the expulsion invalid.[15]

March–October 1858

During the struggle at Rome, it had become evident to the American fathers that they must develop alternatives for their plan for an English-speaking Redemptorist house. They considered establishing a relation with the Cisalpine Redemptorists; and Hecker himself visited Naples and gave an enthusiastic report of the Neapolitan Congregation that had in his view kept alive the spirit of St. Alphonsus. Practical difficulties made this an improbable alternative, especially for the Pope, who was not interested in adding fuel to the fires of rivalry that had long raged between the two groups of Redemptorists. Hecker and his friends also considered, when the possibility of remaining Redemptorists evaporated, placing themselves directly under the control of Propaganda Fidei and continuing their missions under its guidance. Again Rome judged this move imprudent because it could be construed by U.S. bishops as an affront to their own authority. It soon became clear to Hecker and the American fathers that the best course would be to establish themselves as a new religious institute under the care of a local bishop.

This he received approval for orally from Pius IX and Cardinal Barnabò. He moved ahead quickly and under the tutelage of the Prefect of Propaganda formulated a plan, which he described to his American colleagues during March 1858. Hecker believed that the five should find themselves secluded quarters away from the bustle of the city and the press of parish duties and there pray and reflect together on the future direction of the Community.[16] This the other missionaries readily agreed with, since they had not thoroughly considered the details of founding a new institute prior to Hecker's departure and had had a difficult time communicating with him and with one another during the trying of the case due to the great distances involved and the censure of the Redemptorist superiors who attempted to cut off all discussion of the case.[17]

The American fathers and their confreres in Rome, however, had discussed briefly the possibility of founding a new institute and had discovered some disagreements among themselves. On the one side was Hecker who believed that he was in Rome not merely to straighten out his own difficulties with the Redemptorist hierarchy but to represent the needs of the American church to Rome, and indeed to all of Europe, and to win sympathy for his cause to convert Americans to Catholicism and adapt the best parts of American culture to Catholicism.[18] This case he made clearly in the two-part article published in *Civiltà Cattolica,* "Present and Future Prospects of the Catholic Faith in the United States." Privately, he had confessed to his brother George that American Catholics must be led by fellow Americans who understood and sympathized with their nation's ways. Europeans, he was sure, "will not and do not trust us Americans." The Irish and German hierarchs, who made up the majority of the U.S. leadership, would mend their bridges and unite in a common cause to keep the Americans out of power. "I go in for emancipation from foreigners," he told his brother in one of his feisty, delightfully Yankee moments. By drawing the struggle between him and the General on such a broad scope, he felt his chances for victory would be improved.[19]

In regard to the function and structure of the new Institute, he believed that it should adapt itself to the special needs of its homeland. He had in mind missions to non-Catholics, to which he felt providentially called—a point with which Cardinal Barnabò and his secretary Archbishop Cajetan Bedini agreed.[20] He also advocated being free from the Redemptorist Rule, which in his mind was designed for "another age and people than ours."[21] The new Institute should adapt American models of polity in regard to the election of superiors and the suffrage of all members. It also should have a certain open-ended quality that would render it "free to develop itself according to the fresh wants which may spring up." Such an institute would, in addition to its other benefits, attract young men with religious vocations.[22]

On the other side of the debate were the American fathers Deshon and Baker, led by Walworth. (Hewit was in the middle.) They believed, first off, that it was a serious mistake to bring the larger questions of the church in America into the picture—especially since Hecker's ideas on that subject were controversial. George Deshon, who had just learned enough Italian grammar to get through *Civiltà Cattolica* with the help of a lexicon, told Hecker: "I tremble at your boldness in hazarding views and opinions which are likely to prove obnoxious to the prevailing current of the Italian mind." Walworth shared this opinion and was quick to add that "the rest of us do not altogether sympathize with you."[23]

Walworth and the others insisted that he stick to the central point of the memorandum of the American fathers to Rome—the continuation of their missions. They advocated taking their present work and manner of religious life as the models for the future: "We have no thought or intention of entering upon any new way of life." If Rome granted them freedom from their vows as Redemptorists, they would simply function as missionaries under the U.S. bishops. Only slight modification of the original Redemptorist Rule would be needed so that they might elect their own superior. The first two parts of the Rule that dealt with the practice of religious life and missionary labors, respectively, were "beautiful" and quite well suited to the fathers, Walworth thought.[24]

Hecker was enthusiastic but not foolish. He knew he would have no chance of successfully resolving the situation apart from his American colleagues. He also sincerely wished to remain united with them and could easily appreciate their fears about starting the kind of bold new adventure he dreamed of. Although willing to move ahead on an unchartered course, he was not unaware of the perils and wrote to his fellows on January 23 that he would gladly adopt their position of taking the missions and their present mode of life as the model. He summed up their differences accurately and pledged to do all he could to accommodate their concerns.[25] At this point Hecker was compromising, to be sure. But he felt certain that it was in his best interests and those of the American church to do so, primarily because he was convinced that the founding of a new missionary institute in the shape advocated by Walworth also would enable him to conduct the work of missions to non-Catholics. He realized that Rome would more readily approve such a design than it would a more novel one and he also knew that Propaganda in the person of the warm and affable Barnabò favored his plans but wished him to move cautiously ahead with them.

There was, however, one point that Hecker did not wish to compromise. He insisted that the new Community be free for mission work. Repeatedly he made this point in letters to his brother George and the American fathers. On March 17, 1858, he wrote to his confreres expressing his "matured and confirmed" views.

> We must be entirely free to devote ourselves to our Mission-
> ary labors, upon this point we must insist, though it com-
> pelled us to locate in the region of the Rocky Mountains.

Having been caught in the conflict within the Redemptorists between missions and parish work, he resolutely sought to avoid that conflict in the future:

> We are free, thank heaven!, and let us avoid the trap in which
> the German Redemptorists have been fatally caught.

He was very sure of the consequences of failing in this regard: "Any offer of a location which involves parish duties, however favorable, would prove the grave of our little bands and the death of our hopes."[26] Both Barnabò and Bedini agreed. If a local bishop tried to interfere, they counseled Hecker to "tell him frankly beforehand you will not be his blind instruments."[27]

Hecker had persistent misgivings about what might happen when he met with the American fathers to plan their future. En route home, he wrote to George urging him to use his influence with the fathers, who were staying in his home on Rutgers Street, to dissuade them from making any decisions before he arrived.[28] The idea of taking a parish was in the air, and according to Hewit, it was Clarence Walworth who was strongest in favor of it.[29] On May 10, Hecker arrived in New York from Rome. The fathers had been conducting missions while the case was pending as Redemptorists and, after the annulment, as secular priests under the aegis of James Bayley, bishop of Newark. They had agreed to suspend all activity after the completion of the mission at St. Bridget's in New York and address themselves to the questions of the goals and structure of their new Community.

They held their conference at George Hecker's home on Rutgers Street. On the question of location, the young American missionaries had been offered a home for their new band by the bishops of Newark, Cleveland, and the Archbishop of New York. Hughes won out, and the fathers who had long been based in New York gained the advantage of staying in what doubtless was the most influential city of the nation. There they had the assistance of many wealthy and influential friends not the least of whom was George Hecker, whose financial aid had gone a long way in helping Isaac to win his way at Rome. They also had access to the media in the person of James McMaster, their former fellow novice. Isaac had favored New York, and prior to his return had even engaged the ever-faithful George to approach Hughes and suggest that the new Institute be housed in his diocese near the New Park.[30]

But the price paid for New York was a dear one: Hughes apparently had had no intention of losing their services for the care of souls in his diocese. Given Hecker's strong feelings on this subject, his silence on the compromise is strange. Writing toward the end of the year to Propaganda for permission to receive novices, he says merely that "the Bishops in the United States make the charge of parishes, on account of the small numbers of priests, a *sine qua non* of all religious communities." But this itself is odd, since the bishop of Cleveland specifically had offered the Paulists a house and land, free from a congregation. Also, as seen, Barnabò was in favor of sticking exclusively to missions. But in the above-mentioned letter to Propaganda, Hecker went on to state a reason for taking parishes that may have helped resign him to the compromise. "The income from parishes," he wrote to Barnabò, "is the principal source of their [religious communities'] support."[31] Taking a parish was viewed as a necessary step for the subsistence of the new Institute. To this reason was added the strong preference for a parish base on the part of Walworth, who, more than any of the fathers, reflected the concerns of the American bishops. Hecker knew, despite his preference, that he would have to work closely with the American bishops and that a more conventional format would be more widely accepted. The Cleveland option doubtless was rejected because a house in the Mid-West was too remote for men who had become accustomed to being national figures. Hecker's insistence on the Rocky Mountains as preferable to parish duties gave way when put to the test. If they were to work in New York, then parish duties would have to be part of the package. They accepted this with amazingly little fuss, given their awareness of the potential troubles entailed.

In fact those troubles soon appeared and soon began doing just what Hecker feared—sapping energy from the missions. In typical nineteenth-century form the Paulists raced ahead with ambitious plans for a church and convent at Fifty-Ninth Street and Ninth Avenue, which cost $20,000. Efforts to raise this money occupied more and more of their attention. Their active mission schedule was laid out with an eye for fundraising. Hecker and Deshon formed one band, Hewit and Baker another. The two bands fanned out across parishes from Quebec to Savannah. Their correspondence shows how concerned they were about money; in fact during 1859 they talked less about the spiritual impact of their missions than the size of the collections.[32] Parish work drained not only their attention but their manpower as well. With the opening of the parish in September 1859, two fathers had to be taken off the mission band to serve the church.

The Rutgers Street conference was disrupted by another affair, one which, at the time, seemed more crucial to the young missionaries than did the matter of taking on a parish. Clarence Walworth, the golden-tongued prince of a man, had disagreed so strongly with Hecker, Hewit, and Deshon on the form of Rule for the new Community that he was threatening to leave the group. The prospect of losing him filled Hewit, Deshon, and Baker with the deepest grief, and for good reason. By all accounts, Walworth was the best preacher among them; he was so good, in fact, that many rated him among the best in the country. He had a degree from Union College, was a member of the New York State Bar, and was the son of the Chancellor of New York State. During their Redemptorist days, he was the superior of the mission band. Deshon in attempting to dissuade him from leaving told him that he could more easily bear the death of his own father than the loss of Walworth to the group. Hewit also pleaded with him, assuring him that he had "always regarded you as possessing in a peculiar manner the spirit of St. Alphonsus . . . and as the chief instrument in the hands of divine Providence for transplanting and continuing the missions in this country."[33]

Doubtless Walworth was committed to continuing the missions and doing so in the spirit of Alphonsus, which Hewit attributed to him. It was this concern that had caused him to break the lance with Hecker earlier and now with the others when, during their early sessions, it became clear that Hecker's insistence on giving a fresh form to the Community would mean no perpetual vows, but only solemn promises of commitment, which were described as the voluntary principle. The revelations of these feelings shocked Walworth and filled him with a certain distrust of his confreres' ideas. As he saw it, perpetual vows were placed by Canon Law "in the very definition of the Religious life." Furthermore, he felt that they had presented themselves to the bishops and to Rome as religious and to change now would be unfair to those who had supported them. In an attempt at compromise, the others offered to take annual vows. Walworth accepted the idea, then refused. They also offered to submit the question to a bishop or to Propaganda, but again he refused. He simply could not tolerate the possibility that they might end up without vows, nor could he shake the suspicion that "the spirit of chance and innovation" which began by chopping the vows would quickly discard the rest of the practices of religious life. Without those spiritual and moral disciplines, he was sure the missions could not be sustained.[34]

The brief efforts at rapprochement failed during the third

week of June, when Hewit, in the name of the others, sent Walworth a note that pressed him to decide immediately. He decided against joining and went off to a parish in Troy, New York, parting cordially without "any breach of charity."[35]

Whatever the Walworth affair indicates about the personality of the dissenting missionary, it also makes plain some things about the early Paulists.[36] First, even if Walworth's pride was wounded by Hecker's election as superior, it would be wrong to infer from that that his concern over the nature of the Rule was insincere or unimportant. The late 1850s was an age in which the church in America was struggling to impose some sense of order on the vast and confusing array of Catholic life and practice that characterized the province of America. The innovation and variety that were part of the American cultural experience found their way into the life of faith and were the constant bane of nineteenth-century bishops like John Hughes and the subjects of numerous decrees from the Plenary Councils of Baltimore. For the traditional religious, the Rule was the instrument that imposed unity and order. One only need look to the letters of the devout Redemptorists in America who, at the urging of the Provincial, wrote to the General Rector protesting their loyalty and their disapproval of Hecker and his friends. Father Thomas Anwander, for example, wrote to Mauron in May 1858: "The Holy Rule shall now be our protection afresh"—now that the American rebels had been purged.[37]

Walworth, though he had supported the break with the Redemptorists, had never dreamed of a break with the Rule of St. Alphonsus. His lawyer's mind, in true American fashion, had appealed to the authority of the Rule in justifying the break with the hierarchy. But now when it appeared that his confreres would actually dare to change the Rule itself, that was too much innovation; it was casting off the law and opening the way for anarchy in the private life of devotion and in the corporate life of the Community.

Hecker felt very differently about this. He, more than any of his fellows, had suffered at the hands of what he saw as corrupt authority. In particular, the revelation at one point in his case that the General had made spurious, *ad hominem* attacks on his character caused him to be wary of ever placing himself so fully under another's authority again.[38] Hewit also, who as Redemptorist Consultor had gotten an inside picture of the effects of incompetent authority on the lives of others, was unwilling to rush into perpetual vows. Deshon and Baker also followed Hecker's lead. For Hecker, launching out without vows was no problem, since there were precedents in Catholic history such as Alphonsus and his early band who had started without vows. Innovation was seldom viewed by Hecker with trepidation, and he did not fear controversy. The affair at Rome had taken his solid Yankee character and made it all the more resolute. Early in 1859, he wrote to a friend that "defeat" had become a meaningless word for him. "Conquer" was his motto; "bounce back" was his strategy. He loved comparing himself to the then novel Indian rubber ball: "The harder you hit it, the harder it do bounce back."[39]

The second thing the Walworth affair illustrates about the early Paulists was the haste with which they moved. In ten months they had gone from Redemptorists seeking an English-speaking house to Paulists with a completed programme of Rule for the new Institute despite formidable opposition! Upon Hecker's return in May 1858, they began planning not only the new Community, but numerous missions and the building of a church and convent with the major fundraising effort it entailed. They could not wait more than a few weeks, which to them must have seemed a very long time, for Walworth to make up his mind so that they could get on with it. Confident to a degree that the late twentieth-century observer can only regard as awesomely optimistic or incredibly naïve, Hecker and company believed that nothing was impossible.

But the fearless headway that Hecker and his friends made was not without its costs to the future of the Community. Walworth was lost for the first two years of the Community's existence when his presence would have been most desirable. (He joined the Community in 1860 and stayed for four fruitful years before leaving a second and final time, convinced that he was not called to be a Paulist.) With the loss of Walworth came the temporary diminution of the confidence of at least two American

bishops who had been among the new Institute's best friends—
James Bayley and John McCloskey. Also their haste brought
them the critical ire of Propaganda and of John Hughes, their
bishop. Although Hughes basically remained positive, he was
critical of the pace at which the missionaries moved. While
always wishing them well, Barnabò similarly complained to
Hecker in October 1858 that he was moving too fast.[40]

THE PROGRAMME OF RULE, JUNE 1858

Given the process that brought it about, it is not surprising
that the Programme of Rule of the Missionary Society of St. Paul
the Apostle, presented to John Hughes for approval in July 1858,
reflected only in part Hecker's vision for a new missionary
community. This will become evident from a brief discussion of
what the Programme did and did not include.

The Programme was designed as a temporary instrument to
gain the approval of the fledgling Community by the archbishop.
It was a "programme," that is a preliminary, to the actual Rule,
which the Paulists realized could not be submitted to Rome for
approval until some time had passed during which they could
demonstrate their merit and effectiveness. (The fast-thinking
Americans doubtless never thought that it would be eighty-two
years before the Rule was finally approved!) They believed that
the experience of a few years would be needed to learn how best
to shape the Institute to meet the needs of their situation. Also,
Hecker was aware that some of his ideas were open to criticism
from traditionalists who found his friendship with the principles
of the American Revolution incompatible with Catholicism. He
told George to warn McMaster not to print things about the new
Community that would give "any handle for any suspicions of
any Americanisms."[41]

As he had agreed to deemphasize his novel ideas during the
struggle with the General, he now was easily persuaded to do the
same in the preliminary Rule. Accordingly, the Programme
resembles the original Redemptorist Rule that Walworth had
suggested as a model. Three sections deal with disciplines for the
religious life, missionary work, and the form of government for

the Institute. Section One is the longest, running about two-thirds of the document. It states the first purpose of the Congregation as the promotion of the members' sanctification by leading a life "in all essential respects similar to that which is observed in a religious Congregation."[42] It delineates the practice of the virtues of chastity, poverty, and obedience. The first of these will be practiced "in accordance with their sacerdotal vows." The document carefully does not explicitly say that the members will not take vows. In fact no other mention of the word is made; neither is the controversial term "voluntary principle" used. Next the Programme lists various private and public devotions that members are required to make. A full regimen of prayers, spiritual reading, and penance was stipulated that included two half-hour meditations daily, an examination of conscience, the Litany of the Blessed Virgin, a half-hour spiritual reading, a visit to the Blessed Sacrament, and a chaplet of the Rosary. In addition they were to observe a weekly chapter of faults and a conference on theology. Although the Paulists were attempting to appear conventional, there is no indication that they secretly wished to do away with any of these things that had been part of their religious lives as Redemptorists. They were sensitized by Walworth's dissent to the importance of spelling out the aspects of their life that would mark them as religious. Hecker knew, although he may have wished it were otherwise, that there were only two options for his new Institute: they would be religious or they would be secular priests. The latter would spell the end of their missions.

The second part of the Programme dealt with the "common labors for the salvation of others" that the Paulists would carry out. It said only that these would be done "in the spirit of St. Alphonsus," and then turned quickly to a mild attempt to restrict their work as much as possible to missions. They were to avoid "secular education" and have only "one parish with one church in any locality." But when a parish was taken, the Programme went on to record, all the duties would be carried out "in the most exact and conscientious manner" according to the wishes of the bishops.

The final part of the document briefly indicated that the

Institute would be governed by a superior elected by a Chapter constituted by all the original members, who would serve for a three-year term.

What the Programme did not say was as important as what it did. Some of the ideas that Hecker had expressed prior to the issuance of the Programme in July 1858 were not present. First, there was no mention of a model of a religious institute without vows. The first draft of the Programme had stated that the Paulists would have no vows but would be formed around the voluntary principle "similar to the Congregation founded by St. Philip Neri."[43]

Second, the intention of giving missions specifically to non-Catholics was not mentioned at all. This was a glaring omission—I think it better to say, a major compromise—on Hecker's part. He was clearly not willing to give up this apostolate—in fact he was interested in a community specifically dedicated to it, but here again he was constrained by the realities of nineteenth-century church life to downplay his novel desires. With hordes of unchurched Catholic immigrants flooding America's cities, and "godless infidels" battering the *ancien régime* of Catholic Europe in the name of liberty and democracy even the powerful enthusiasm of Hecker was forced to cool.

Third, the Programme did not restrict the work of the Paulists to missions but instead laid the groundwork for the perilous double work of missions and parishes. This and the other losses mentioned, however, came in the context of some major gains—gains that, when weighed in the balance, offset the losses, especially for the moment. Recall that less than a year before the Programme, Hecker was watching his plans for American missions suffer at the hands of insensitive Redemptorist superiors. Shortly after, he found himself in a foreign land as an expelled religious. Certainly the thought of a community founded with the blessing of the Pope himself and the good will of the American bishops—even if it embodied only part of his hopes—was a most blessed one. So Hecker settled for the compromise, judging that he had gotten as much of his dream as could be expected for the time. That was in all probability true, and one should not regard lightly their truly remarkable achievement. But the amalgam of dream and reality that in July 1858 became known as the Missionary Society of St. Paul the Apostle would not please an idealist like Hecker forever.

THE 1870s

Vatican I

The 1860s had been an active time for Hecker and the Paulists. They had continued their missions to Catholics successfully covering the East, South, and Mid-West. In 1865 they had begun publishing the *Catholic World* and shortly thereafter founded the Catholic Publication Society. Hecker was busy lecturing to non-Catholics in special Lyceum lectures. In addition he took part in pastoral duties at St. Paul's and edited the *Catholic World*. Active, confident, and contented, he became a leading light in the American Catholic church. His prominence won him a place at the First Vatican Council as the procurator for Bishop Sylvester Rosecrans of Columbus, and later the *peritus* theologian for Bishop James Gibbons. Hecker's attendance at the Council issued in a decade of far-reaching intellectual and spiritual change for the Paulist founder, which resulted in new ideas on the Community and his relation to it.

One of his greatest gifts had always been his ability to win the friendship and the endorsement of prominent persons. To this was added his skill in languages. He could speak German as well as French and could thus function as an important liaison between the American and European bishops at the Council. He quickly gained the confidence of the American bishops and found himself moving in influential circles. Frequent receptions and dinner parties with the powerful studded his calendar. He told his sister-in-law that one could learn more in one day through contact with these knowledgeable and powerful persons than one could in a year at other times. The best minds of the church were gathered together and he found himself in their midst, eager to learn.[44]

The exposure to the larger questions of nineteenth-century Catholic church life worked in him an increased appreciation for American Catholicism. The ultramontane movement that became the dominant force of the Council was in his eyes like the "flickering of an expiring candle." Revolutions in Italy, France, Belgium, and Austria were to him clear signs that the *ancien régime* had seen its day. The implications of the growth of the new republics for religion were that the Church must give a greater place to individual freedom and responsibility; it must see itself as an answer to the valid needs of human nature for freedom and fulfillment rather than as an impediment to the progress of modern ideas. American Catholicism would, he believed, be a model of this type of religion to the Old World in the same way that American politics had inspired the new European democracies. America had demonstrated in both the secular and the sacred realms that what Europe sought for in theory was in fact practicable.[45]

Hecker's optimism, his intuitive perception of the spirit of the times, his mystical sensitivities, and his belief in the providential course of modern history combined to give him an unflappable confidence that God's will would be done through the Council. Before he left for Europe he expressed it plainly to his parishioners. While at the Council, he was in the midst of the infallibility debate working hard for the inopportunists. Thomas Connally, Bishop of Halifax, one of the more vocal opponents of the definition, called him his right hand man. He was obviously aware of the atrocious tactics of the ultramontanes, and like most of the Americans, left before the final vote was taken. Yet he was amazingly unperturbed by this. He looked doggedly for a twofold renewal:

> My hope has been and is that the divine element for the renewal of the world would spring from the light of the Holy Ghost in the Council; but that the human element on which it can alone work, will be furnished by the civilization of our Republic.

His perceptions of the needs of the Church and the society combined with his hopes for renewal to produce a new vision for the Paulists. Since the Paulists reflected the "human element" for renewal—democratic American principles—and since they were men in tune with the Spirit's work—the "divine element"—they could function to bring about renewal in Europe. Paulists preaching and teaching in England, France, Italy, and Germany would "effect a change no one even dreams of. They would be an element of reconciliation, renewal, and regeneration." The American flare for reconciling diversity and unity through democracy was just what the warring European factions needed. From the many, one new organic synthesis could emerge as it had in the New World. Such an expanded role for the Community would require changes. Hecker expressed to George his belief that they had thus far taken the right direction, but that new steps would be needed. What exactly they would be time would tell.[46]

Thus when Hecker returned from the Council in the spring of 1870, he was thoroughly engrossed in the prospects for the Community and filled with more confidence, more zeal, and more energy than ever. His departure from Rome prior to the vote on infallibility was inspired as much by a desire to get home to his work as it was by any political considerations.[47] Upon his return he threw himself into his work. His time at the Council had shown him the importance of the Community's more novel apostolates—publishing and convert work. Talk of any expansion of the Community's efforts overseas gradually was lost in the business of the next two years. Plans were made to resume the missions, which had been halted for six years during the 1860s due to lack of manpower. The publishing business was increased and a project was launched to develop a Catholic daily paper in New York. The scheme was an adventuresome one, even for the likes of Isaac and his entrepreneurial brother George, John Hughes, and the influential laypeople of the newly-founded Catholic Union. In addition Hecker redoubled his efforts as a preacher and lecturer. His time at Rome had won him new friends among the American bishops, and their new admiration for him was shown by numerous invitations to preach at church dedications and to give missions.[48]

The definition of papal infallibility caused Hecker and the Paulists no serious trouble. In fact, he soon came to the conviction that this was a providential act of the Spirit. The external authority of the church, which had been under attack from the time of the Reformation, had been given its most definitive expression. The loss of the papal states and the occupation of Rome by Garibaldi's troops caused Hecker and some of his inopportunist friends like the dean of Rochester Seminary, Alexander Sherwood Healy, to be glad that the pope's spiritual power had been established so clearly. The Paulists wrote a special letter of filial admiration to Pius IX in November 1871 supporting him during the political crisis. As Hecker told his Roman friend S.M. Chatard, "We all feel a deep and lively sympathy with the Holy Father."[49]

The Long Illness

The Paulist superior's desire to move full steam ahead with his projects was thwarted by the onset of a serious illness. Sickness was very much a part of life for nineteenth-century missionaries. Francis Baker had died in 1864 at the age of 45 from the strain of their rigorous life. Hewit had long complained of debilitation that prevented him from pursuing studies the way that he wished to, and frequently one of the fathers would be laid up in bed for a week or two with a malaise of some sort. Though Hecker was used to being waylaid for relatively short periods by bouts of illness, he was not ready for what began to overtake him in December 1871, shortly after his return from Rome. He began to feel exhausted, suffer from headaches, sleeplessness, and later, loss of appetite and pectoral angina. At first he thought it was a touch of "malaria poisoning" that he had contracted in Rome.[50] He took time off to rest at George's country estate on Orange Mountain in nearby New Jersey. This produced enough relief to enable him to continue work, though at a slower pace, through the fall and winter. Still his recovery was unsatisfactory, and he decided to spend the entire summer of 1872 at Lake George in the home of Judge Edmonds near to the Paulist house on the Lake. Removed from the everyday cares of community administration and editorial duties, his mind and soul were free to focus on more fundamental issues. He began thinking almost constantly of the needs of the Church in the age, the destiny of America, and the role of the Community. Ideas that had begun to surface during his time at the Council now emerged from beneath the mental clutter of his countless duties and tasks. What became most clear was that Vatican I had signaled the moment when the church could, and indeed must, turn its attention from the exterior concerns of church polity to the "divine and interior authority of the Holy Ghost," for this was the way to the renewal that both church and society needed.[51]

During the winter of 1872–73, he began following that curious preoccupation of the Gilded Age: traveling for one's health. He journeyed to St. Augustine, Florida, accompanied by George and his wife Josephine, and the Archbishop of Baltimore who was, of course, also traveling for his health. His doctors seemed unable to find a cure for Hecker's "nervous prostration" other than traveling about to free his mind from the cares of the past, which, it was supposed, had worn him to exhaustion. (The most accurate diagnosis he was to get was from a doctor who described his sickness as a "blood disorder." His illness had all the characteristics of what today would be called chronic leukemia.) The first suggestion made by the physicians was that he journey to Europe, a thought that repulsed him because of his disgust with contentious Europeans whose preoccupation with past rivalries made them people whose faces were fixed on the setting sun. But as the weeks of illness stretched into months he became inwardly discouraged, and at the constant advice of George and Hewit consented to spend the summer of 1873 in Europe.[52]

Hewit was acting superior during Hecker's absences from the Community. He was Hecker's friend and confrere of twenty years and also his spiritual director, which meant that Hecker would discuss with him his "interior states," something that he was not inclined to do with any but close friends. Hewit's attitude about Hecker's illness is illuminating. "All the founders of good works get sick and frighten everybody for fear they are going to die, and then get well and are more submissive to the will of God than they were before," he told Hecker in January 1873. But just three months later, Hewit became much less sanguine about his friend's recovery, having received a gloomy prognosis from the medical men. He confided to S.M. Chatard: "There is very little hope of his recovery except through supernatural means." When it later became apparent that Hecker was in no immediate danger of dying, he resigned himself to the idea that Hecker would never fully resume his active ministry. He came to this conclusion by the end of the summer of 1873.

Writing to Hecker, he tried to get him to accept that he was now an old man who must make up his mind to "go down the declivity" and be satisfied if he had another ten or fifteen years to finish up his life's work, by which Hewit meant the work of founding and establishing the Community. All other pursuits should be abandoned.[53]

Hewit was well aware of all that remained to be done with the Community; clearly he had a better grasp of this than Hecker or the other senior Paulist George Deshon. A key matter that had yet to be resolved was the Community Rule. The Programme of Rule of 1858 had been designed as a temporary measure until such time as a permanent Rule could be written. Hewit, who was in his fifties and aware of the fragileness of life, wished to do this directly, so that the Rule could receive approval from Rome. Both he and Hecker were under the mistaken impression that the Community had been given the *Decretum Laudis* ("Letter of Praise") from the Pope, which according to Canon Law had to precede a petition to Rome by the Institute for approval. The letter from Pius IX that Hecker had received in 1868 was indeed a letter of praise but praise of Hecker and his various apostolates and not the official *Decretum Laudis.* Unaware of this, Hewit composed a new Rule, completed it, and had it approved by the April 1874 Chapter meeting of the Institute. Hecker approved the Rule from Europe and petitioned the Holy See for approval during the winter of 1874–75 when he visited Rome. He learned quickly of his error regarding the *Decretum Laudis,* and it became apparent that the process of obtaining approval would require more time and care than the Paulists had thought.[54]

Another important issue that Hewit wished to resolve was the matter of seminary education for Paulist postulates. The burden of educating the young men who sought their vocations with the Institute had fallen on Hewit. He designed the curriculum and taught most of the courses, always well aware of the inadequacy of such a system. By 1872, the Community had ten men in studies, with more applications being submitted each year. His solution was that the Paulists establish a house of studies at a theologate, and his first choice was Rome. Hecker agreed with this idea, and the Community sent Andrew Byrne to

Rome to study; but the formation of a house of studies was still a long way off. Hewit hoped that the Paulists might attract some scholarly priests to serve as professors, which they worked toward by giving some of the young postulates like George Searle and Adrian Rosecrans the academic training to become teachers.[55]

To these concerns was added the building of a new church and convent at Fifty-Ninth Street. The present wooden structure was a bit small for the parish that had grown considerably since 1858. Hecker during his time at the Council had been quite enthused with the project to build "St. Paul's Basilica" and had toured the great European cathedrals to get ideas for their own structure. He visited with famous architects and sent home preliminary plans for the church. At length, the New Jersey architect Jeremiah O'Rourke was chosen and the construction of the $500,000 structure commenced. Also, as the Community grew, the question of establishing new foundations arose and with it debates on the nature and function of such new houses. All of these issues worked on the mind of Hewit, who felt increasingly burdened—a burden intensified by his editorial responsibilities at the *Catholic World* and of course by his superior's absence.

Hecker's attitude during his protracted illness underwent significant changes. From the time that he realized he had a serious disability in 1872 until the summer of 1875, his battle with death removed his attachment to his many temporal activities and rivetted his attention on his interior communion with God. He felt that apart from his will his past was being crushed out. It appeared to him "like a perfect stranger." This movement was accompanied initially by a resignation that enabled him to wait rather patiently for the future, and, as seen, by a new perception of the importance of the Paulists' work in the grand scheme of renewal.[56] With the European trip, which lasted from the summer of 1873 until the fall of 1875, things began to change. The itinerary that the senior Paulist pursued "for his health" would have been enough to try the strength of the fittest. Ireland, Scotland, England, France, Switzerland, Alexandria, Cairo, Nubia, Jerusalem, Rome, Genoa, and back to the Lake Geneva region! Financed by his millionaire brother, Fr. Hecker traveled in comfortable style, always managing to find old and new friends among Catholic intellectuals and litterateurs. The attractions of Europe, and especially those of the East, provided some relief from the most perplexing mental torments: When could he recover? What was God's purpose in all this? Elsewhere I have described the details of Hecker's inner struggles during this time. Here it must suffice to focus on the dynamic that resulted in his changing attitudes toward the Community.[57]

While in Europe, he wished to be completely free from Community business. Although he did consent to negotiating at Rome for the approval of the Rule, his regular disposition was to put out of mind all Paulist business. This was what doctors and friends wished him to do and why they had recommended the European tour. He, however, did this rather more thoroughly than they expected, especially more than Hewit expected or liked. Writing in October 1873 from the Hotel St. James in Paris, Hecker told Hewit to go ahead and govern the Community as he saw fit. "Your judgments are better than mine, trust in God and act. . . ." Hewit should endeavor to have the Community act in unison and should consider that Hecker would give them his carte blanche approval seeing in their decisions "nothing but the will of God."[58]

Hewit was not at all willing to assume such a responsibility. Soon after receiving Hecker's letter he wrote to him urging him to return home at the conclusion of his Nile River trip in Spring 1874. His health had obtained all the benefit from travel that could be expected, and the Community would be subjected to danger were he to remain away, so Hewit felt. Hewit had written this letter, however, without consulting the other fathers. When it became known to the others through George and Josephine that Hecker had been disturbed by Hewit's letter, the others responded with the greatest sympathy for their founder and words of reproof for Fr. Hewit.[59] Hecker himself responded to Hewit, assuring him of his awareness of the difficulties of his position, but telling him again of how he had had his whole past "crushed out . . . by the hand of God." Hewit, with the help of his confreres, became willing to accept the idea that it was indeed best if Hecker remain away a while longer, and that he would return without persuasion when the time was right. Hewit, himself an avid student of ascetical theology, told his superior that his internal state appeared to be clearly what St. John of the Cross called the night of the spirit. He continued: "You will probably never again go back to your former natural activity, but will remain always disposed to solitude, silence, quiet, and the interior state with an aversion for active and external employments." He, nevertheless, could resume the most crucial of his Community duties, with his left hand, as it were.[60]

But around the same time Hewit was writing his scenario for the future, Hecker was composing a very different one of his own. Hecker never had been able to accept the idea that he was an old man who would simply have to sit on the shelf for the remainder of his days. His faith in providence would not allow him to believe that his illness was without purpose, nor would his habit of seeing his own experience as paradigmatic let him see that purpose as a merely personal affair between himself and God. During his European tour, Hecker had been meeting with influential intellectuals and old friends who shared his progressive views, like Msgr. Gaspard Mermillod of Geneva, Cardinal Victor Deschamps, W.L. Lockhard, and Augustine and Pauline Craven. The theme that ran throughout his discussions was the renewal of church and society through a greater awareness of the Holy Spirit's action in the soul, the Church, and the world. His remarks were warmly received and he was encouraged to publish them. He came to believe that God was calling him to remain in Europe and function as an agent for renewal through the establishment of Paulist-like movements throughout Europe and indeed throughout the world. He had changed his mind about sending Paulists to work in other countries. Now he wished to be free of his activities in New York, to let the Community take its course, and to devote himself to new things.[61]

This of course was based on the assumption that his health would improve enough to allow this. His health did improve enough during the last two months of 1874 when as a guest of Count Pisani and his wife at their estate in Viscovano, Italy he wrote and had published the *Exposition on the Needs of the Church and the Age,* which was his programme for renewal. As positive responses to the *Exposition* encouraged him, he came to believe that his ill health was linked to his resisting God's leading to move ahead with his new plans. Occupying himself with past activities would only assure his decline, he thought.[62]

By the summer of 1875, however, Hewit had come to the end of his patience. Alarmed by Hecker's plans to permanently leave the Community, he easily was able to convince the others that indeed they should ask Hecker to return. Hecker had since the end of 1874 expressed his willingness to abide by the Community's decision regarding his return. Now, however, when he wished really to remain it was a difficult and heart-rending decision to return, but return he did. After his return in the fall of 1875 he resumed activities in the Community much in the way Hewit had projected—with his left hand and not without a certain disdain for outward acts. There was no disdain for his brethren, but rather a realization that the Community had taken on as it were a life of its own and gone in a direction that he did not prefer, although he did see its validity.

An established church leader who had won the esteem of bishops and intellectuals in America and Europe, he no longer was constrained by the cautions that had motivated him in 1858 at the founding of the Community. Hence he was free to focus on the novel aspects of the Paulist ideal and to interpret the history of the Community as a move away from these. Writing from Southern France shortly before his return, he had put it plainly:

> The conception of a movement of the Paulists was one which had preoccupied my mind a long while. It was one in which the elements of self-control, conscience, and internal guidance of the Holy Spirit should take lead over the control of discipline, Rule, and external authority. . . .
>
> During the years of the formation of the Paulists, all my companions were more and more inclined to increase the discipline, fixed rules, and external authority than I was. . . .
>
> As soon as my health required my leaving the entire direction of the Community in their hands, which I did, the increase and expansion in the direction they desired became at once manifest.[63]

Vatican I, his illness, and the positive response to his *Exposition* had worked to clarify his perception of the problems of the day and the solutions. He had become convinced that the Church had indeed entered a new era and that new religious institutions were called for. These ideas he delineated in "General Considerations Preliminary to the Subject of New Religious Institutions," an unpublished manuscript written late in 1876. In this document he insisted on religious communities confining themselves to the main activity for which they were constituted. Anything less would "grieve the Holy Spirit" and deprive the Church and society of good.[64] These new institutions should be staffed by persons who knew how to attend to the Spirit's guidance and who could rejoice in the freedom from a preoccupation with externals.

Yet even as Hecker wrote these words, he knew that some in the Community had a very different conception of the importance of external disciplines and supports for the spiritual life. Walter Elliott, the most zealous missionary among the younger generation of Paulists and a faithful admirer of Hecker, wrote a long letter to his superior in August 1876 complaining bitterly about the neglect of the Rule in Paulist houses. He was offended by the laxity he saw among his fellows. Absence at morning and evening meditations was tolerated, servants were allowed to wait on the fathers at table and to keep their rooms, the cloister doors were left open, silence was not observed, and the fathers were allowed to wear slippers in the common rooms and even to use perfumery! What clearer expression could be found of the views shared by Walworth, the Redemptorist Thomas Anwander, and the many other nineteenth-century Catholics who sought an explicit, authoritative guide for their spiritual lives in the formal doctrines and practices of the Church? For them the *vox Dei* was the magisterial teaching of the Church. At the time when Hecker was concerned with a new era of the Holy Spirit in which devotion to the Spirit's internal guidance would create a new breed of Catholic, inner directed, confident to undertake, and able to deal with the challenges of the age, Elliott was proclaiming a new era in the Community inaugurated by Hecker's election as superior under the new expanded version of the Rule.[65]

Yet a third vision of a new era was put forth in 1884, which shows how accurate were Hecker's perceptions about the discontinuity between his new ideas and those of some other Paulists. In 1884 the Paulist General Chapter met to elect a new superior.[66] The meeting became deadlocked due to the efforts of a substantial minority to replace Fr. Hecker as superior. The opposition argued that the Paulists needed demonstrative clear-cut leadership, which the enfeebled, though much beloved and honored, Hecker could not give. They favored Hewit but were turned back by the majority led by Hewit himself. The minority's symbol of a new era was the newly completed St. Paul's Church. The parish ministry with its conventional forms and predictable patterns was their focus; and, in fact, since the late '70s more Paulists had been working full-time in the parish than on the missions.[67] The Rule and the parish—the two symbols that expressed the things that Hecker had since 1857 seen as distinct from the Community he wished to found—had raised their heads again over twenty years later.

Given these tensions, Hecker's return to the Community and labors with them for the last thirteen years of his life were, taken as a whole, another compromise—a compromise with a disease that never gave him back the strength he needed and with a Community that had only imperfectly embodied his hopes. He had changed and moved on to new international horizons. The Community had changed and come to demand new administrative efforts and skills. The compromises he had made at the founding of the Institute had had the consequence of taking the Paulists further from the notions that were the most novel, but to his mind the most essential. The openness to present needs and the corresponding flexibility in the design and polity of the Community had been restricted by the commitment to parish work and parochial missions to Catholics. When Hecker needed these freedoms, for example in 1871 when he proposed sending Paulists to Europe, they were not there: the Community simply could not spare the resources. The desire to missionize non-Catholics had been downplayed in the interest of seeming conventional. Now when that desire moved Hecker to wish to interpret Catholicism to European radicals and non-Christians of the East, the Community could not spare the resource of their superior and administrator.

This new compromise was not a compromise with evil, however, and Hecker knew this, despite the disappointment and anxiety it caused him. It was, rather, a compromise with the realities of nineteenth-century Catholic church life. That life promoted a spirituality that emphasized order and external authority and saw in the definition of papal infallibility a call to greater conformity, not to a new era of increased personal freedom and awareness of the Spirit's inner guidance. For religious, this meant a stricter, more devout observance of their rule and a more sure obedience to their superiors. The life of the church in the Gilded Age was a life centered on the parish, a parish which in America was busy trying to provide its people with a body of theological truths that would give them a Catholic identity in the pluralistic land that threatened to swallow up their cultural and religious notoriety. It was a far cry from the schoolhouse for Yankee Catholic intellectuals that Hecker desired.

The current in which Hecker longed to swim was not the dominant one, and a band that in 1879 numbered only fifteen priests could not possibly address their conventional parochial duties, a national campaign of Catholic missions, plus Hecker's new dreams. The fault lay not in their performance—in fact their success as parish priests and missionaries to Catholics was nothing short of sensational. Rather the problem was with a plan, too ambitious even for the Century of Empire, that was formulated in the heady days of their youth in 1858.

The Paulists as a Movement

The tensions that I have described between Hecker's vision for the Paulists and that held by others can be understood in terms of the description of a religious movement which H. Richard Niebuhr found so useful in his famous analysis of American Protestantism written over two decades ago.[68] It is ironic that an essay on one of the greatest American Catholic apologists should end with a reference to Protestantism; but such was the reality of nineteenth-century Catholicism in the United States: it was articulated in the context of a culture stamped by the values of the Reformation. No analysis of his thought on the Paulists—or on any other subject—can neglect this.

Niebuhr characterized Protestantism in America as having consistently displayed a propensity for process, dynamism, and movement as opposed to structure, stability and order. Marked by an emphasis on revival of human confidence, hunger for liberty and a quality existence, and an eschatological emphasis on the Kingdom of God, Protestantism developed its institutions not as ends in themselves but as necessary instruments and pragmatic devices. The fluidity and changeableness of Protestant attempts at order have been expressions of its essential nature as a movement.

That Niebuhr's analysis of a religious movement is indeed applicable to phenomena other than American Protestantism should be obvious to anyone having the slightest familiarity with religious reform movements in Catholicism such as Franciscanism and Dominicanism, or the efforts of St. Teresa to reform the Carmelites; Niebuhr's attempt to characterize Catholicism en masse as orienting itself constantly toward order and away from movement clearly is simplistic. Nevertheless, it certainly would be true of the ultramontane thrust that dominated the second half of the nineteenth century—a thrust that Hecker collided with.

While Hecker embraced a doctrine of the Church that valued its oneness and its apostolicity, he clearly did not see the Church in static terms. The categories of change, development, life, and spirit, which he imbibed through his immersion in the Romantic mood that swept New England in the 1840s, were crucial to him; yet he was able to reconcile these with a faith in the visible, institutional Roman Catholic church. This reconciliation was the foundation of his conversion.

When it came to formulating the idea for the Paulists, however, Hecker emphasized the dynamic, eschatological dimensions of his thought. The Paulists were a missionary movement founded to foster renewal. Like American Protestantism as seen by Niebuhr, the Paulists were to focus on the individual and to labor with a lively hope for the coming of God's Kingdom.

As such, the Paulists' forms of order, as Hecker viewed them, had to have a changeable, experimental character. This was, to use Niebuhr's language, because they, by their very nature, could contain only imperfectly the dynamic inspiration that constituted them—an inspiration that could not come to rest in any structure.

The second generation of Paulists who opposed Hecker's

reelection as Superior in 1884 viewed the Paulists more as an order than as a movement. For them the Institute had to follow out an existing agenda already set in place by the Rule. For Hecker that agenda was ever new, ever inchoate, always awaiting them.

Yet he was not a Protestant, and his movement was not simply a "Congregation of Semi-Protestants," as the old chestnut goes. It would be easy to characterize it as such, as did Charles Maignen and others after Hecker's death, because it shared with Protestantism all the aspects of a religious movement that Niebuhr so aptly described. But there was more to the Paulists and to their founder than that. That "more" we have seen illustrated in Hecker's consistent attempts to mediate his charismatic personality with the community, his progressive ideas with the realities of nineteenth-century church life, and the future with the past. That he was not able to achieve a perfect synthesis does not negate the fact that he tried sincerely and constantly. In that effort, as fraught with difficulty as it often is, lies the essence of the Catholic soul.

NOTES

1. For secondary literature dealing specifically with the development of the Paulist Community during Hecker's lifetime see Joseph McSorley, *Father Hecker and His Friends* (New York: B. Herder, 1952); John Farina, *An American Experience of God: The Spirituality of Isaac Hecker* (New York: Paulist, 1981); Thomas Jonas, "The Divided Mind: American Catholic Evangelists in the 1890s" (Ph.D. dissertation, U. of Chicago, 1980); and James McVann, "The Paulists, 1858–1970" (Ms., PFA).

McSorley deals with the conflicts between Walworth and Hecker in 1858, but does not address the tensions that arose in Hecker's vision for the Paulists during his later years. Farina deals with the conflict briefly in the context of explaining Hecker's later spiritual development. Jonas treats the conflict between Hecker's later ideas as interpreted by Walter Elliott and the dominant direction of the Community in the 1890s. McVann deals in passing with the tensions mentioned above, but in general is concerned instead with chronicling the overall history of the Community.

On Jan. 26, 1979, Jay P. Dolan gave a talk at St. Paul's College,

Washington, D.C., entitled "The Vision of the Early Paulists." This was a brief semi-popular treatment of the highlights of early Paulist history, which gave excellent descriptions of the first apostolates of the Community but did not deal directly with the conflicts that are the focus of my paper. This study, then, is the first to carefully examine the development of Hecker's ideas on the Paulists during his whole life.

2. See Vincent F. Holden, *Yankee Paul* (Milwaukee: Bruce, 1958), pp. 149ff. for a detailed account of this period.

3. See Nicholas Mauron to Alessandro Barnabò, Sept. 30, 1857; George Ruland to Nicholas Mauron, July 11, 1857; Joseph Helmpraecht to Nicholas Mauron, Aug. 17, 1857. Transcripts in PFA.

4. George Ruland to Nicholas Mauron, April 29, 1858. Transcript in PFA.

5. Augustine Hewit to Alessandro Barnabò [Nov. 1857], copy in PFA.

6. E.g., Clarence Walworth to ITH, Dec. 11, 1857; Augustine Hewit to ITH, July 31, 1857, PFA. Cf. C.SS.R. Consultation 19, Aug. 30, 1857, transcript in PFA.

7. See Nicholas Mauron to George Ruland, Sept. 3, 1857, transcript in PFA, in which Mauron states that the intent of his circular was not to preclude extraordinary visits to the Rector General, but to require his consent for such visits.

8. ITH to George Hecker, Aug. 18, 1857, and Sept. 1, 1857, PFA.

9. Nicholas Mauron to John B. Purcell, March 1, 1858. See also Mauron to Alessandro Barnabò, Sept. 30, 1857, transcripts in PFA.

10. ITH to George Hecker, March 2, 1858, PFA. See also ITH to American fathers, Feb. 26, 1858, PFA.

11. George H. Miles to ITH, Aug. 13, 1858, PFA.

12. See Bernard Smith's response to John Hughes's recommendation of the American fathers, March 4, 1858, transcript in PFA. Smith, an Irish monk who was an influential secretary at Propaganda, anticipated Rome's support of ITH.

13. ITH to American fathers, March 11, 1858, and March 5, 1858, PFA.

14. Nicholas Mauron to Alessandro Barnabò, March 9, 1858; Mauron to George Ruland, March 9, 1858, transcripts in PFA. ITH to George Hecker, March 13, 1858; ITH to American fathers, March 18, 1858, PFA.

15. Cf. ITH to George Hecker, March 9, 1858, and George Ruland to Francis Baker, April 17, 1858, PFA.

16. ITH to American fathers, March 18, 1858, PFA.

17. See Nicholas Mauron to George Ruland, March 11, 1858, transcript in PFA.

18. ITH to Orestes Brownson, Sept. 1, 1857 and ITH to George Hecker, Sept. 8, 1857, PFA.

19. ITH to George Hecker, Jan. 2, 1858, PFA.

20. ITH to Spiritual Director, Jan. 6, 1858, copy in PFA.

21. ITH to George Hecker, Jan. 30, 1858, PFA.

22. ITH to Spiritual Director, Jan. 6, 1858, PFA.

23. George Deshon to ITH, Dec. 14, 1857; Clarence Walworth to ITH, Jan. 3, 1858, PFA.

24. Clarence Walworth to ITH, Jan. 11, 1858, PFA.

25. ITH to American fathers, Jan. 23, 1858, PFA.

26. ITH to American fathers, March 27, 1858. See also ITH to George Hecker, March 27, 1858, PFA.

27. ITH to American fathers, March 18, 1858, PFA.

28. ITH to George Hecker, April 22, 1858, PFA.

29. Augustine Hewit to John McCloskey, June 22, 1858, transcript in PFA.

30. ITH to George Hecker, Jan. 23, 1858, PFA.

31. ITH to Alessandro Barnabò, Feb. 15, 1859, copy in PFA.

32. E.g., George Deshon to Augustine Hewit, Feb. 23, 1859; ITH to Augustine Hewit, March 1, 1859, PFA.

33. George Deshon to Clarence Walworth, July 17, 1858; Augustine Hewit to Walworth, June 20, 1858, PFA.

34. Clarence Walworth to American fathers, June 20, 1858; Walworth to Augustine Hewit, June 26, 1858, PFA; Walworth to Orestes Brownson, July 6, 1858, copy in PFA; Walworth to Francis P. Kenrick, July 13, 1858, transcript in PFA.

35. Clarence Walworth to George Deshon, June 28, 1858, PFA.

36. McSorley in *Fr. Hecker and His Friends* seeks to interpret the conflict largely as a personality conflict. See Chap. VII.

37. Thomas Anwander to Nicholas Mauron, May 1, 1858, transcript in PFA. For a discussion of the trend in nineteenth-century American Catholic piety toward organization and regularity see Joseph P. Chinnici, "Organization of the Spiritual Life: American Catholic Devotional Works 1791–1866," *Theological Studies* 40 (June 1979): 229–255.

38. ITH to American fathers, March 5, 1858, PFA.

39. ITH to American fathers, March 27, 1858; ITH to C.B. Fairbanks, March 2, 1859, PFA.

40. John Hughes to Bernard Smith, June 11, 1858, transcript in PFA; Alessandro Barnabò to ITH, Oct. 6, 1858, PFA.

41. ITH to George Hecker, March 13, 1858; see also Bernard Smith to ITH, Oct. 11, 1858, PFA.

42. All quotations from the Programme are from "The Programme of Rule of the Missionary Priests of St. Paul the Apostle," July 7, 1858, PFA.

43. Rough Draft of Programme of Rule, PFA.

44. ITH to Josephine Hecker, Jan. 13, 1870; ITH to Augustine Hewit, Jan. 22, 1870, PFA.

45. "Notes in Italy," Jan. 5, 20, 1870, PFA.

46. ITH to George Hecker, Jan. 27, 1870; Thomas L. Connally to ITH May 5, 1870 and July 12, 1870; ITH to George Hecker, Jan. 26, 1870. See also ITH to Augustine Hewit, Jan. 13, 1870; ITH to George Hecker, Feb. 24, 1870 and May 8, 1870, PFA. For more on ITH's role at Vatican I see William Portier's essay in this volume.

47. See ITH to George Hecker, May 8, 1870, PFA.

48. ITH preached at the dedications of St. Patrick's Cathedral in New York, St. Rose of Lima, New York, and St. Elizabeth's in Fort Washington during 1870–71.

49. Alexander Sherwood Healy to ITH, Nov. 7, 1870; Paulists' letter to Pius IX, Nov. 30, 1870; ITH to S.M. Chatard, Nov. 30, 1870, PFA.

50. E.g., ITH to Orestes Brownson, Jan. 8, 1872; ITH to Mrs. Cullen, Jan. 19, 1872, and ITH to Mrs. Tucker, March 12, 1872, PFA.

51. ITH to Mrs. Cullen, July 24, 1872, PFA.

This brief account of ITH's time at Vatican I and the period immediately following his return to New York brings to light enough of the historical record to make clear that his illness was not merely a psychologically-induced reaction to the events at the Council. Two points in particular are obvious. In the first place, though he was perturbed, he was not devastated by the outcome of the Council. His decision to return early was motivated by a desire to get on with his work at home, not only by dissatisfaction with the Council. The disappointment intensified his commitment to the Paulist apostolate and his hope in American Catholicism. (See ITH to George Hecker, Jan. 26, 27, 1870; ITH to Augustine Hewit, Jan. 13, 1870, PFA.)

Secondly, the illness, which was diagnosed as a blood disorder and had all the symptoms of chronic leukemia, did not manifest itself until late 1871, and not intensely until 1872. When Hecker returned from the Council in the spring of 1871 he described himself as having "more confidence, more zeal, more energy" than ever. (ITH to George Hecker, May 8, 1870, PFA.) Moreover, this statement about his own condition was borne out by his actions for the second half of 1871. During that time he gave more lectures to non-Catholics than in the year before leaving for the Council. He preached at numerous church dedications, continued working to establish the children's magazine, the *Young Catholic*, and made plans to start a Catholic daily newspaper, which involved a scheme to buy the *New York Herald Tribune*. These are hardly the words and actions of a crestfallen man whose depression is about to manifest itself in psychosomatic disorders!

It is true that his disappointment at the Council did affect his theological thinking, as Portier has suggested. But this dynamic is entirely separate from the alleged connection, which Baer states in his essay in this book, between ITH's psychological state in the spring of 1871 in Rome and his physical condition nearly a year later in America. To link psychological states to physiological manifestations is precarious even with the living. To do so with persons of the past, when the historical record suggests the contrary, is dubious.

52. Ibid.; Augustine Hewit to ITH, Jan. 9, 1873, PFA.

53. Augustine Hewit to ITH, Jan. 27, 1873; Hewit to S.M. Chatard, April 16, 1873; Hewit to ITH, Sept. 16, 1873, PFA.

54. See ITH to George Hecker, Feb. 23, 1875, PFA.

55. See ITH to Augustine Hewit, Jan. 2, 1875; and Hewit to ITH, Feb. 8, 1875, PFA.

56. See ITH to Augustine Hewit, April 26, 1873, PFA.

57. Farina, Chaps. X–XII.

58. ITH to Augustine Hewit, Oct. 7, 1873, PFA.

59. Augustine Hewit to ITH, Jan. 15, 1874; George Hecker to ITH, Jan. 31, 1874; and George Deshon to ITH, July 28, 1874, PFA.

60. ITH to Hewit, April 7, 1874; Hewit to ITH, May 3, 1874; Hewit to ITH, Nov. 14, 1874, PFA.

61. "Notes on Interior States, 1874–76," Nov. 17, 1874. See also, April 5, 1875.

62. Ibid., Feb. 27, 1875.

63. Ibid., Sept. 17, 1875.

64. "General Considerations Preliminary to the Subject of New Religious Institutions," PFA.

65. Walter Elliott to ITH, Aug. 21, 1876, PFA.

66. See Farina, p. 173f.

67. "Summary of Report of the Condition of the Works of the Institute of Missionary Priests of Saint Paul the Apostle of New York

to the Congregation of the Propagation of the Faith," Feb. 24, 1879, PFA.

68. H. Richard Niebuhr, "The Protestant Movement and Democracy in the United States." In James W. Smith and A. Leland Jamison, eds., *The Shaping of American Religion, Vol. I* (Princeton: Princeton University Press, 1961), pp. 20–71.

Annotated Bibliography

Since 1977 secondary sources on ITH have increased significantly, as can be seen in the section dealing with them below. It, however, is as true today as it was in 1958 at the publication of Vincent Holden's *Yankee Paul* that the most significant source of information on ITH is unpublished archival material. In this regard credit must be given to the archivists for the Paulist Fathers who have collected, ordered, and preserved the Hecker legacy. Walter Elliott, Theodore C. Peterson, Thomas Malloy, James McVann, Vincent Holden, and Lawrence McDonnell have laid a foundation by their labors upon which all recent research stands. The meticulous care and accuracy with which the work has been done is a testimony to their esteem for their patron and their commitment to historical truth.

In compiling this bibliography I have chiefly relied upon their work and my own research in the PFA. I also have consulted John J. Kirvan's "A Bibliography of Paulist Writings to 1895" (M.S. dissertation, Catholic University, 1959) and the bibliographies in the Ph.D. dissertations listed below. The bibliography that follows is confined to primary sources and those secondary sources that deal specifically with ITH. For a list of background materials the student may refer to the bibliographies in the books and dissertations cited as secondary sources below.

PRIMARY SOURCES

Archives
Archdiocese of Baltimore Archives. Baltimore, MD.
> ITH correspondence and related materials may be found in the papers of James R. Bayley, James Gibbons, Francis P. Kenrick, and Martin J. Spalding.

Archdiocese of New York Archives. Yonkers, NY.
>   ITH correspondence and related materials may be found in the papers of Michael A. Corrigan, John Hughes, and John McCloskey.

Diocese of Charleston Archives. Charleston, SC.
>   The papers of Patrick N. Lynch contain correspondence with ITH.

English College Archives. Rome, Italy.
>   Letter from Edward Douglas, C.SS.R. to Msgr. George Talbot on ITH case, in Talbot Papers.

Irish College Archives. Rome, Italy.
>   Letter from John McCloskey to Tobias Kirby regarding ITH case, in Kirby Papers.

New York Public Library. Methodist Church Records, Forsyth Street Church Records. New York, NY.
>   Information on Caroline Hecker's church.

Paulist Fathers Archives. New York, NY.
>   ITH's diaries, letters, sermons, manuscripts, and notes dating from 1841 to 1888 are contained in the Hecker Papers collection, plus pertinent photostats of material from all other archives listed in this bibliography, with the exception of New York Public Library, Methodist Church Records, and New York City, Hall of Records. ITH-related materials are also in Hewit, Baker, Walworth, Deshon, Young, Rosecrans, and Elliott papers.

Congregation de Propaganda Fidei Archives. Rome, Italy.
>   ITH-related materials are in *Lettere e Decreti della S.C. e Biglietti di Mms. Segretario* (Vols. 348–49), and *Scritture referite rei Congressi, America Centrale* (Vols. 17–18).

Redemptorist Fathers Archives. Brooklyn, NY, Clapham (London), England, and Rome, Italy.
>   ITH-related materials are in the Baltimore Provincial Archives, George Ruland papers, Edward Douglas papers, and Provincial Personnel File in Brooklyn; the *Archivium Generale* in Rome; and the *Chronica Studentatus* from Wittem and Clapham (London).

Diocese of Rochester Archives. Rochester, NY.
>   ITH correspondence with Bernard J. McQuaid is in the McQuaid papers.

University of Notre Dame Archives. South Bend, IN.

> ITH correspondence with John B. Purcell is in the Cincinnati papers, with Francis P. McFarland in the Hartford papers, with O.A. Brownson in the Brownson papers, with James A. McMaster in the McMaster papers; related materials in the Kehoe-Hammond papers, the William J. Orahan papers, the William Sadlier papers, the Detroit papers, and the New Orleans papers.

St. John's Abbey Archives. Collegeville, MN.

> Copies of Bernard Smith, O.S.B. papers, which contain correspondence with ITH and material on ITH case.

Hall of Records. New York City. New York, NY.

> The Books of Conveyances, Registry of Wills give information on the Hecker family.

Published Materials

Articles that appeared in CW are unsigned, making the identification of the author difficult, and hence the list may be incomplete. Entries are chronological by year of publication.

Hecker, Isaac Thomas. *Questions of the Soul.* New York: D. Appleton & Company, 1855.

———. *Aspirations of Nature.* New York: James B. Kirker, 1857.

———. "The Present and Future Prospects of the Catholic Faith in the United States of North America." *Freeman's Journal* (Dec. 12, 19, 26, and Jan. 2, 1857–58).

———. "Reflexions sur l'état présent et sur l'avenir du Catholicisme aux Etats-Unis d'Amerique." *Revue Catholique* (Louvain, 1858 t. 16): 37–54, 99–163.

———. "Riflessioni Sopra il Presente e l'Avvenire del Cattolicismo negli Stati Uniti d'America." *La Civiltà Cattolica* 3rd Series 8 (Nov. 6, 19, 1857): 385–402, 513–29.

———, ed., Julia C. Smalley, compiler. *The Young Converts.* New York: Peter O'Shea, 1861.

———. "Giving Testimony." in *Paulist Sermons, 1861.* New York: Van Parys, Hugot & Howell, 1861, pp. 63–75.

————. "Renunciation," Ibid., pp. 158–75.

————. "Self-Denial," Ibid., pp. 330–45.

————. "The Ruling Passion," in *Paulist Sermons, 1862.* New York: D & J. Sadlier, 1862, pp. 97–109.

————. "Death," in *Paulist Sermons, 1863.* New York: D. & J. Sadlier, 1864, pp. 277–92. Rpt. New York: Arno, 1979.

————. "How to be Happy," Ibid., pp. 58–70.

————. "The Saint of Our Day," Ibid., pp. 90–102.

————. Preface to Juliana Anchoret, *Sixteen Revelations of Divine Love.* Boston: Ticknor & Fields, 1864, pp. v–vi.

————. "Christ's Human Side," in *Paulist Sermons, 1864.* New York: Appleton, 1865, pp. 296–309.

————. "Fidelity to Conscience," Ibid., pp. 9–19.

————. "Filial Freedom," Ibid., pp. 217–28.

————. "The Future Triumph of the Church," in *Sermons Delivered During the Second Plenary Council of Baltimore.* Baltimore: Kelly & Piet, 1866, pp. 66–86.

————. "La Situation Religieuse des Etats Unis." *Revue Général* 6 (Oct. 1867): 348–58.

————. "Father Hecker's Farewell Sermon," (Preached at St. Paul's Church, New York, Sunday, Oct. 17, 1869, previous to his departure for Europe to attend the Oecumenical Council) CW 10 (Dec. 1869): 289–93.

————. *Life and Doctrine of St. Catherine of Genoa.* (Translated from the Italian.) Edited and with an introduction by ITH. New York: The Catholic Publication Society, 1874.

————. *Die Kirche betrachtet mit Rucksicht auf die gegenwartinen Streitfragen und die Bedurfnisse unserer Zeit von einem Amerikaner.* Autoriserte Obersetzung aus dem Englischen. Freiburg im Breisgau, Herder'sche Verlagshandlung, 1875.

————. *L'Eglise en presence des controverses actuelles et des besoins de notre siècle.* Traduit de l'anglais (par Pauline Craven). Paris: Imprimerie Racon et Compagnie, 1875.

————. *An Exposition of the Church in View of Recent Difficulties and Controversies, and the Present Needs of the Age.* London: Basil Montagu, 1875. CW 21 (April 1875): 117–38.

————. "The Transcendental Movement in New England." CW 23 (July 1876): 528–37.

————. "The Unitarian Conference at Saratoga." CW 24 (Dec. 1876): 289–99.

————. "What Is Dr. Nevin's Position?" CW 24 (Jan. 1877): 459–68.

————. "Dr. Knox on the Unity of the Church." CW 24 (Feb. 1877): 657–67.

————. "The Political Crisis in France & Its Bearings," CW 25 (Aug. 1877): 577–90.

————. "The Outlook in Italy." CW 26 (Oct. 1877): 1–21.

————. "The Free-Religionists." CW 26 (Nov. 1877): 145–61.

————. *The Catholic Church in the United States: Its Rise, Relations with the Republic, Growth and Future Prospects.* 2nd ed. New York: Catholic Publication Society, 1879.

————. "The Catholic Church in the United States." CW 29 (July 1879): 433–56.

————. "A Reply to C.C. Tiffany's Attack on the Catholic Church in *Scribner's Monthly.*" CW 29 (May 1879): 249–54.

————. "Science and Sentiment." CW 29 (June 1879): 403–12.

————. "The Crisis in Italy." CW 29 (Aug. 1879): 679–85.

————. *Catholics and Protestants Agreeing on the School Question.* New York: The Catholic Publication Society, n.d.

————. "Catholics and Protestants Agreeing on the School Question." CW 32 (Feb. 1881): 699–713.

————. "The True and False Friends of Reason." CW 33 (June 1881): 289–98.

————. "What Does the Public-School Question Mean?" CW 34 (Oct. 1881): 84–90.

————. "Catholic Musings on Tennyson's 'In Memoriam.' " CW 34 (Nov. 1881): 205–11.

_____. "The German Problem." CW 34 (Dec. 1881): 289–97.

_____. "The Liberty and Independence of the Pope." CW 35 (April 1882): 1–10.

_____. "A New But False Plea for Public Schools." CW 36 (Dec. 1882): 412–22.

_____. *Martin Luther, Protestantism vs. the Church. Luther and the Diet of Worms.* New York: Catholic Publication Society, 1883. Also New York and San Francisco: Christian Publication Association, n.d.

_____. "The Impending Issue of the School Question." CW 36 (March 1883): 849–54.

_____. "Protestantism vs. the Church." CW 38 (Oct. 1883): 1–13.

_____. "Luther and the Diet of Worms." CW 38 (Nov. 1883): 145–61.

_____. "Thomistic-Rosminian Emersonianism, or 'A Religion for Italy.'" CW 38 (March 1884): 799–810.

_____. "The Churchman." CW 42 (March 1886): 831–36.

_____. "The Broad Church." CW 43 (April 1886): 101–11.

_____. *The Church and the Age, An Exposition of the Catholic Church in View of the Needs and Aspirations of the Present Age.* New York: Catholic Publication Society, 1887.

_____. "Dr. Brownson and Bishop Fitzpatrick." CW 45 (April 1887): 1–7.

_____. "Dr. Brownson and the Workingman's Party Fifty Years Ago." CW 45 (May 1887): 200–208.

_____. "Cardinal Gibbons and American Institutions." CW 45 (June 1887): 330–37.

_____. "Dr. Brownson in Boston." CW 45 (July 1887): 466–72.

_____. "The Guidance of the Holy Spirit." CW 45 (Aug. 1887): 710–12.

_____. "The Guidance of the Holy Spirit." CW 45 (Sept. 1887): 846–47.

_____. "Life Is Real." CW 46 (Oct. 1887): 136–38.

_____. "Dr. Brownson's Road to the Church." CW 46 (Oct. 1887): 1–11.

_____. "Dr. Brownson and Catholicity." CW 46 (Nov. 1887): 222–35.

_____. "Leo XIII." CW 46 (Dec. 1887): 291–98.

_____. "Spiritual Guidance." CW 46 (Feb. 1888): 715–16.

_____. "Race Divisions and the School Question." CW 46 (March 1888): 736–42.

_____. "Silver and Gold." CW 46 (March 1888): 847.

_____. "The Things that Make for Unity." CW 47 (April 1888): 102–09.

_____. "John R. G. Hassard." CW 47 (June 1888): 397–400.

_____. "Two Prophets of the Age." CW 47 (Aug. 1888): 684–93.

_____. "The Mission of Leo XIII." CW 48 (Oct. 1888): 1–7.

SECONDARY SOURCES

Books

Barry, William. *Father Hecker, Founder of the Paulists.* New York, n.d.
Seventy-five page reprint of review of Elliott's *Life of Father Hecker,* which appeared in *Dublin Review* (July 1892).

Burton, Katherine. *Celestial Homespun.* New York: Longmans, Green, 1943.
Fictionalized biography that takes liberty with the historical record.

Elliott, Walter, C.S.P. *The Life of Father Hecker.* New York: Columbus Press, 1891. Reprint. New York: Arno, 1972.
The first biography of ITH, written by his devoted protégé. The book may be criticized for the lack of balance and care that are characteristic of hastily-written works. Holden criticized Elliott for producing "Elliott's Hecker," not "Hecker's Hecker." He was overly concerned about Elliott's treatment of ITH's theology given the stir that the French edition of the work created. No doubt Elliott at times uncritically leaves his avowed role as chronicler and becomes the preacher of the virtues of a man he believed saintly. But the fact remains that "Hecker's Hecker" was known to one

person: Hecker; and we must each now see him through our own eyes. Elliott saw him in the flesh and blood, and his picture of him contains insights that are still valuable.

————. *La Vie du Père Hecker.* Trans. Countess de Revilliary. Paris, 1897.

The famous French edition of Elliott's *Life* that became part of the Americanist controversy.

Farina, John. *An American Experience of God: The Spirituality of Isaac Hecker.* New York: Paulist, 1981.

This is the first book since the turn of the century to deal with ITH's whole life. It attempts to analyze the spirituality of the Paulist founder in the context of his life story and argues that an understanding of the dynamics of his spirituality is essential in understanding the man.

Gower, Joseph F. and Leliaret, Richard M. eds. *The Brownson-Hecker Correspondence.* Notre Dame: University of Notre Dame Press, 1979.

This is a collection of the complete Brownson-Hecker correspondence, which extended more than thirty years. It contains valuable introductions and notes. Its style of transcription, unfortunately, follows the outmoded practice of supplying silent corrections in the text, thus making the reconstruction of the original text impossible.

Goy, Andreas, C.SS.R. *Semblanza del P. Hecker, fundador de las Padres Paulistas.* Mexico, 1955.

A popular picture of ITH written by a Redemptorist, but marred by inaccuracies.

Holden, Vincent F., C.S.P. *The Early Years of Isaac Thomas Hecker, 1819–1844.* Washington, D.C.: Catholic University of America. 1939.

This Ph.D. dissertation, which Holden himself criticized as at times "scarcely more than a stringing together of documents and letters" was, nevertheless, the beginning of a critical attempt to reconstruct ITH's life. It paved the way for Holden's later work with its careful style that students may still find helpful.

————. *The Yankee Paul: Isaac Thomas Hecker.* Milwaukee: Bruce, 1958.

Despite Holden's at times debilitating preoccupation with defending ITH against charges of being a rebellious religious, or worse, a heretic, this book stands as a fine work of historical scholarship. Its quality lies in its scrupulous reconstruction of the past on the basis of careful research in a vast topic upon which relatively little scholarship had been done. It, however, deals only with ITH's life until 1858; a second volume was begun but never finished.

McSorley, Joseph, C.S.P. *Father Hecker and His Friends.* New York: B. Herder, 1952.
    A series of essays on ITH and the early Paulists. Informative and accurate, these essays are valuable general treatments of early Paulist history.

McVann, James A. "The Paulists, 1858–1970." PFA.
    This is a long chronicle of Paulist history, carefully done and based on research in the PFA. It lacks analysis, but, nevertheless, reconstructs numerous important pieces of the past that receive treatment nowhere else.

Maignen, Charles. *Etudes sur l'Américanisme: Le Père Hecker, est-il un Saint?* Paris: V. Retaux; Rome: Desclée, 1899. English trans. *Father Hecker, Is He a Saint?* London: Burns and Oates, 1898. (No translator given.)
    This is the vitriolic attack on ITH and his ideas written by a French priest of the Brothers of St. Vincent de Paul during the peak of the Americanist controversy. As an *ad hominem* attack on a man whose character from all that I have learned from the historical record was indeed saintly, this book is, as Holden judged, slanderous. But as a representation of the French conservative critique of his ideas, it merits attention—attention which some of the more recent studies of Americanism such as those by Reher and Portier listed below give it.

Sedgwick, Henry P., Jr. *Father Hecker.* Boston: Beacon, 1900.
    A brief, popular account of ITH's life, based on Elliott, that adds a concluding chapter on the issues of the Americanist controversy thus beginning a lamentable, though understandable, habit of forcing the story of ITH's life into the mold of the Americanist controversy. There are many aspects of his thought and personality that cannot be understood from the narrow theological framework of that controversy.

Dissertations

The point made earlier that the boom in Hecker studies did not begin until the late seventies is well illustrated by Gerald W.

McCulloh's "Bibliography of Dissertations in Nineteenth-Century Theology, 1960–76 [in North America]," which lists zero dissertations on ITH. (By way of contrast, John Henry Newman, who once described himself as ITH's English counterpart, was the subject of ten dissertations.)

Baer, Robert W., C.S.P. "Isaac Thomas Hecker: A Study in Individuation and the Collective." Diploma thesis, C.G. Jung Institute, Zurich, 1982.

This is a one-hundred-page Jungian analysis of the process of individuation in the life of ITH. The piece addresses the whole of ITH's life but focuses on the years 1842–44 as reflected in the early diary. Done with care for the historical record, the analysis is nontechnical enough to appeal to one uninitiated in Jung's theories.

Farina, John. "Isaac Hecker and the Holy Spirit." Ph.D. dissertation, Columbia University, 1979.

A study of ITH's spirituality with special attention to his understanding of the Holy Spirit.

Ghering, Harold A. III. "The Theology of Isaac Thomas Hecker and *Testem Benevolentiae*." M.A. thesis, Christ the King Seminary, East Aurora, NY, 1979.

This brief study concludes that ITH's theology was characterized by a certain lack of definition and precision that opened it to the attacks of critics like Maignen.

Gower, Joseph F. "The New Apologetics of Isaac Thomas Hecker (1819–1888)." Ph.D. dissertation, University of Notre Dame, 1978.

An exercise in historical theology that traces the development of Hecker's apologetic and argues for its uniqueness and importance in nineteenth-century Catholic theology.

Kirk, Martin J. "The Spirituality of Isaac Thomas Hecker: Reconciling the American Character and the Catholic Faith." Ph.D. dissertation, St. Louis University, 1980.

This study traces the development of ITH's spirituality with special emphasis on his ideas about spiritual formation and guidance.

Langlois, Edward J., C.S.P. "The Formation of American Catholic Political Thought: Isaac Hecker's Political Theory." Ph.D. dissertation, Cornell University, 1977.

This dissertation was the first of the new wave of Hecker studies, and is summarized in an essay by Dr. Langlois in this book. It maintains that ITH had a crucial role in the development of American Catholic political thought.

Perschbacher, Susan J. "Journey of Faith: The Conversion and Reconversions of Isaac Hecker," Ph.D. dissertation, University of Chicago, 1981.
Written by a sociologist, this work uses ITH's life plus current sociological and psychological theories to construct a model of conversion as an ongoing process involving consolidation through reconversion experiences.

Portier, William L. "Providential Nation: An Historical-Theological Study of Isaac Hecker's Americanism." Ph.D. dissertation, University of St. Michael's College, 1980.
This study is the basis for Dr. Portier's essay in this book. It examines the question of whether *Testem Benevolentiae* censured ideas that indeed were held by ITH, and argues for the importance of ITH's doctrine of providence in his theology.

Articles

Barry, Canon William. "Father Hecker, Founder of the Paulists." *Dublin Review* 2 (July 1892): 63–95. (A review of Elliott's *Life*.)

Brownson, Orestes A. "Transcendental Road to Rome." *Brownson's Quarterly Review*. New York Series 2 (Oct. 1857): 459–503.

Burke, John J. "Father Hecker and Present Problems." CW (Jan. 1920): 564–75.

Cross, Robert D. "Isaac Hecker's *The Church and the Age,* or, Was Hecker a Heretic?" Paper delivered at Hecker Symposium, St. Paul College, Washington, D.C., 1974.

Dolan, Jay P. "The Vision of the Early Paulists." Talk given at St. Paul's College, Washington, D.C., Jan. 26, 1976.

Dufresne, L'Abbé Xavier. "Personal Recollections of Father Hecker." CW 68 (June 1898): 324–40. From *Revue de Clergé Francais,* March 1898, trans. Elizabeth Gilbert Martin.

Farina, John. "Hecker's Appeal for Today." *Paulist '82,* pp. 40–41.

————. "Isaac T. Hecker's American Spirituality." *New Catholic World* 225 (July/Aug. 1982): 166–69.

————. "Nineteenth-Century United States Interest in Catherine of Genoa." *Catholic Historical Review,* in press.

————. "Isaac Hecker: Spiritual Director." *Journal of Formative Spirituality,* 4 (Feb. 1983): 109–116.

"Father Isaac Thomas Hecker." *Freeman's Journal* (Dec. 1888).

Gasquet, Abbot Francis A., ed. "Some Letters of Father Hecker." CW 83 (May 1906): 233–45, 356–65, 456–65. These are letters of Hecker to Richard Simpson.

Gillis, James M., C.S.P. "Father Hecker and His Friends." *American Benedictine Review* 4 (1953): 47–64.

Gower, Joseph F. "A 'Test Question' for Religious Liberty: Isaac Hecker on Education." *Notre Dame Journal of Education* (Spring 1976): 28–43.

————. "Democracy as a Theological Problem in Isaac Hecker's Apologetics." In *America in Theological Perspective,* Thomas M. McFadden, ed. New York: Seabury Press, 1976.

Handy, Robert T. "Father Hecker, A Bridge Between Catholic and Protestant Thought." CW 202 (Dec. 1965): 158–59.

"Hecker, Isaac Thomas." *Appleton's Cyclopedia of American History* by Wilson and Fiske. New York: D. Appleton, 1889.

Hess, M. Whitcomb. "Thoreau and Hecker, Freemen, Friends, Mystics." CW 209 (1969): 265–67.

Hewit, Augustine F. "Tribute of *The Catholic World* to Its Founder, Father Hecker." CW 68 (Jan. 1889): 571a–576a.

Holden, Vincent F. "An American Ahead of His Time." *Ave Maria* 97 (June 8, 1963): 5–8.

————. "Myth in L'Américanisme." *Catholic Historical Review* 31 (1945): 154–70.

————. "Father Hecker's Vision Vindicated." *Historical Records and Studies* 50 (1964): 40–52.

Keane, Archbishop John J. "Father Hecker," CW 49 (1889): 2–9.

Marschall, John P. "Kenrick and the Paulists; a Conflict of Structures and Personalities," *Church History* 38 (1969): 88–105.

McDonnell, Lawrence V., C.S.P. "Father Hecker—A Man of Letters." Paper delivered at Hecker Symposium, St. Paul's College, Washington, D.C., 1974.

O'Connell, Bishop Denis J. "A New Idea in the *Life of Father Hecker.*" Address given at the Fribourg Congress of 1897. The text appears in Fogarty, Gerald P., *The Vatican and the Americanist Crisis.* Rome: Gregorian University Press, 1974.

Ong, Walter F. "Man Between Two Worlds; St. Paul, the Paulists, and American Catholicism." CW 186 (May 1958): 86–94.

Parsons, Wilfrid. "Brownson, Hecker, and Hewit." CW 153 (1941): 396–408.

Parton, James. "Our Roman Catholic Brethren." *Atlantic Monthly* 21 (April/May 1868): 432–51; 556–74.

Portier, William L. "Isaac Hecker and Americanism." *Ecumenist* 19 (Nov./Dec. 1980): 9–12.

————. "Isaac Hecker and the First Vatican Council." *Catholic Historical Review,* in press.

Powers, Charles J. "Father Hecker's Centenary." *America* 22 (Dec. 20, 1919): 184–85.

Reher, Margaret Mary. "Americanizing the Catholic Church." *Dialog* 14 (Fall 1975): 289–96.

Russell, E.H. "A Bit of Unpublished Correspondence Between Henry Thoreau and Isaac Hecker." *Atlantic Monthly* 90 (1902): 370–76.

Ryan, Gerry. "Father Isaac Hecker, Pioneer of Catholic Press." *Tablet* (New York), Feb. 24, 1962.

Simpson, Richard, "The Church and Young America." *Rambler* Second Series 9 (Jan. 1858): 35–49.

"Up the Nile." CW 24 (Feb. 1877): 633–42.
  This article was written by ITH or one of the three Americans accompanying him on his trip up the Nile during the winter of 1874–75. It resembles in style and content ITH's own notes written during the trip and is a fascinating travelogue.

Reviews of ITH's Writings

Brownson, Orestes A. *"Questions of the Soul." Brownson's Quarterly Review* Third Series 3 (April 1885): 209–27.

————. *"Aspirations of Nature." Brownson's Quarterly Review* New York Series 2 (Oct. 1857): 459–503.

"The Church and the Age." The Month 289 (July 1888): 433–38.

Norsa, Davide. "Stato Presente e Futuro della Chiesa." *Rivista Universale* 22 (1875): 457–73. A review of ITH's *Exposition.*

"Questions of the Soul." Catholic Institute Magazine (Oct. 1855): 21–24.

"Questions of the Soul." The Leader (St. Louis). March 31, 1855.

"Questions of the Soul." Pilot (Boston). N.d.

Simpson, Richard. "Short Notices, *Questions of the Soul." Rambler* New Series 6 (Aug. 1856): 152–53.

Newspaper Reports on ITH Lectures

During 1859–1871 ITH travelled about the country giving public lectures directed toward non-Catholic audiences. Below is a list of newspaper reports of some of his lectures, arranged alphabetically by the name of the newspaper.

Advertiser and Tribune (Detroit). May 15, 1868, Oct. 26, 1869, March 9, 1871.
Brooklyn Times (Brooklyn, NY). May 31, 1868.
Chicago Republican (Chicago). May 13, 1868, Jan. 19, 1869.
Chicago Times (Chicago). Jan. 10 and 18, 1869.
Chicago Tribune (Chicago). May 14, 1868, Jan. 9, 1869.
Constitutional Union (Washington, DC). Nov. 16, 1868.
Daily Citizen (Jackson, MI). Dec. 17, 18, 19, 23, 28, 30, 1868.
Daily Milwaukee News (Milwaukee). April 21, 22, 23, May 5, 6, 10, 20, 24, June 2, 7, 17, 1868.
Davenport Daily (Davenport, IA). Dec. 23, 1868.
Detroit Daily Post (Detroit). Feb. 18, 1871.
Evening Post (Chicago). Jan. 9, 1869.
Evening Express (Washington, DC). Nov. 16, 1868.
Freeman's Journal (New York). Feb. 12, 1859, Dec. 30, 1866, Feb. 23, 1867, Sept. 18, 1869, Jan. 14, 1871.
Manchester Daily Union (Manchester, NH). Oct. 17, 1865.

Meriden Republican (Meriden, CT). March 9, 1871.

Monday Evening Herald (Cleveland, OH). Jan. 11, 14, 1869.

Peninsular Courier (Ann Arbor, MI). Dec. 24, 1868.

Pilot (Boston). Feb. 9, 1867, April 9, 1869, March 11, 1871.

Tablet (New York). Dec. 9, 1865, Jan. 13, Nov. 3, 1866, Feb. 27, 1869, Dec. 19, 1870, Nov. 25, 1871.

Notes on the Contributors

ROBERT W. BAER, C.S.P. has recently finished a training program as an analyst at the C.G. Jung Institute in Zurich and is establishing a private practice in Boston.

EDWARD J. LANGLOIS, C.S.P. is chaplain for the Catholic students at McGill University, Montreal.

WILLIAM L. PORTIER is assistant professor of theology at Mount Saint Mary's College, Emmitsburg, MD.

DAVID J. O'BRIEN is professor of history at the College of the Holy Cross, Worcester, MA.

JOHN FARINA is archivist for the Paulist Fathers and an associate editor for Paulist Press.

Index

Abell, Aaron, 52
Abraham, 188
Aggiornamento, 4, 83
Ahlstrom, Sydney, 83
Alchemy, 152
Alcott, Bronson, 3, 8, 133, 151
Alphonsus, St., 3, 189, 195, 197, 199
America: the American Catholic Church, 2, 87–130; evangelization of, 178; as the new world, 2; political thought in, 49–89; as the Redeemer nation, 51–52, 55, 56, 59, 65, 81
American Experience of God: The Spirituality of Isaac Hecker (Farina), 5
Americanist Controversy, the, 4, 6, 11–48, 126, 187
American Revolution, the, 89
Anima, the, 140, 152, 157–164
Anwander, Thomas, 196, 211
Aspirations of Nature (Hecker), 5, 8, 24, 62, 116

Baer, Robert W., 6–7
Baker, Francis, 125, 183, 188, 191, 194–195, 197, 204
Bangs, Nathan, 3
Barlow, Almira, 158–159, 160
Barnabò, Cardinal Alessandro, 188–189, 190, 192–194, 198
Barry, Bishop John, 187–188

Bayley, Bishop James, 108, 193, 198
Bedini, Archbishop Cajetan, 190, 192
Beers, Julia D., 4
Bill of Rights, the, 55, 65, 88
Blessed Sacrament, the, 199
Blondel, Maurice, 21
Bradford, George, 155
Brook Farm: Hecker at, 57–59, 96–98, 104, 142–143, 150, 172; mentioned, 8, 54, 56, 62, 167, 177; the women of, 158–160
Brownson, Orestes: and American Catholicism, 26; as Hecker's critic, 39, 108, 110–111, 126, 156–157; his influence on Hecker, 137, 141–142, 176; mentioned, 3, 8, 99, 104, 133, 162–163, 188; and New England theology, 24, 25, 30; and politics, 50, 54, 56–57, 58–59, 66, 95
Brownson's Quarterly Review, 188
Burke, Monsignor John J., 51
Byrne, Andrew, 206–207

Calvinism, 25, 35, 37, 56, 107
Catechism of the Council of Trent, the, 96
Catherine of Genoa, St., 3
Catholic Publication Society, 9, 201